Remembering the
Germans in Ghana

AMERICAN
UNIVERSITY
STUDIES

SERIES IX

HISTORY

VOL. 209

This book is a volume in a Peter Lang monograph series.
Every volume is peer reviewed and meets
the highest quality standards for content and production.

PETER LANG
New York • Bern • Frankfurt • Berlin
Brussels • Vienna • Oxford • Warsaw

Dennis Laumann

Remembering the Germans in Ghana

PETER LANG
New York • Bern • Frankfurt • Berlin
Brussels • Vienna • Oxford • Warsaw

Library of Congress Cataloging-in-Publication Data

Names: Laumann, Dennis, author.
Title: Remembering the Germans in Ghana / Dennis Laumann.
Description: New York: Peter Lang.
Series: American university studies. IX, History; vol. 209 | ISSN 0740-0462
Includes bibliographical references and index.
Identifiers: LCCN 2007000752 | ISBN 978-0-8204-8621-5 (cb: alk. paper)
ISBN 978-1-4331-4403-5 (ebook pdf) | ISBN 978-1-4331-4404-2 (epub)
ISBN 978-1-4331-4405-9 (mobi)
Subjects: LCSH: Germans—Ghana—History.
Classification: LCC DT510.43.G47 L38 | DDC 966.7/00431—dc22
LC record available at https://lccn.loc.gov/2017013132
DOI 10.3726/b11203

Bibliographic information published by **Die Deutsche Nationalbibliothek.**
Die Deutsche Nationalbibliothek lists this publication in the "Deutsche
Nationalbibliografie"; detailed bibliographic data are available
on the Internet at http://dnb.d-nb.de/.

Cover image: Kente cloth from Kpetoe in the Volta Region of Ghana,
from the personal collection of the author. Photo by Keith Bratton.

© 2018 Peter Lang Publishing, Inc., New York
29 Broadway, 18th floor, New York, NY 10006
www.peterlang.com

Printed in Germany

In memory of my father, Heinz Laumann,
and my father-in-law, David Kwesi Van-Dyck

My only explanation is that just as real events are forgotten, some that never were can be in our memories as if they happened.

—Gabriel García Márquez, *Memories of My Melancholy Whores*

Table of Contents

Illustrations

Tables

Acknowledgments

Many individuals, in different ways, and over the years, contributed to making this book possible, and I apologize if I neglect to acknowledge anyone who somehow influenced this work. First and foremost, I am profoundly thankful to the oral historians in the central Volta Region who allowed my co-researchers and me to interview them.

As an undergraduate student at Binghamton University, I benefited from the wisdom and kindness of my advisors Akbar Muhammad and the late Ali A. Mazrui. At the University of California, Los Angeles (UCLA), I was fortunate to be advised by the great historians Christopher Ehret, the late Boniface I. Obichere, and above all my mentor Merrick Posnansky, as well as the anthropologist Anna Simons, as I carried out my research and wrote my dissertation. Many graduate school friends helped shape the ways I think and write about African history, especially Nwando Achebe, Agbenyega Adedze, Gibril R. Cole, T.J. Desch-Obi, Mary Dillard, Catherine Cymone Fourshey, Rhonda Gonzales, L. Lloys Frates, Michael R. Mahoney, Kendahl Radcliffe, Jasamin Rotsam-Kolanyi, Bridget A. Teboh, and Susanna Wing.

My research in Ghana would not have been possible without the guidance and companionship of my very good friend Kofi Baku, a historian at the University of Ghana. I am particularly thankful to my coresearchers, Cornelius Adedze, Joseph "Montana" Asamoah, Divine Dzokoto, and Gavivina Tamakloe, who helped arrange and conduct the interviews that generated the oral history examined in this book. I also thank Vivian Asempa and Olivia Baku who transcribed many of these interviews.

In Germany and Togo, on innumerable occasions, Peter Sebald generously shared his time, knowledge, and materials with me as well as guided my research and writing. I am grateful to him and Sybille Senger for welcoming me into their home after long days at the archives in Berlin.

At The University of Memphis, my former chair, Janann Sherman, was very supportive of my research and Anne Reef, then a graduate student, expertly edited a draft of the introduction.

I am thankful to the scholars who offered valuable feedback on previous versions of this monograph and related publications and conference presentations, including: Emmanuel K. Akyeampong, Lynne Brydon, Sandra E. Greene, Stephan F. Miescher, David Owusu-Ansah, Paul Nugent, Richard Rathbone, Larry Yarak, and Andrew Zimmerman.

I appreciate the encouragement and guidance of several editors at Peter Lang, especially Meagan Simpson, Jackie Pavlovic, and Phyllis Korper. Petra Gebeschus at the Staatsbibliothek zu Berlin kindly granted permission for reproduction of archival photos and Onno Brouwer, Director of the University of Wisconsin-Madison Cartographic Lab, created the precise maps featured in this book.

My wife, Rebecca, has been with me during every stage of this project, providing love, encouragement, and advice. I am eternally grateful to her and to our awesome son, Max, whose affection and enthusiasm inspire me.

The research for this book was possible thanks to funding from, in chronological order: the University of California, Berkeley Center for German and European Studies; the UCLA Department of History; the James S. Coleman African Studies Center at UCLA; the International Institute of Education, which awarded me a United States Fulbright Grant; the Department of History at The University of Memphis; and the College of Arts and Sciences at The University of Memphis, which awarded me a Faculty Research Grant.

Preface

This book originated in research I began over two decades ago as an undergraduate student. During my senior year, I wrote an honors thesis on German administration and African resistance in Germany's colonies of Togoland in West Africa and Tanganyika in East Africa. As I worked my way through the secondary sources, mostly written by non-Africans and often sympathetic to German rule, I thought it would be important and fascinating to solicit African perspectives on German colonial rule through oral history work. As a student, I embraced Marxist theory and practice—and I still do—so I considered it a duty to "set the record straight" (in response to the colonial apologists of the Hoover Institution, for example) and present African voices (to balance the Eurocentrism of most of the existing literature) as a small contribution to the seemingly never-ending struggle against imperialism and racism. In my first years of graduate school, I decided to focus on German Togoland so I began the task of more extensively reading the literature on the colony; familiarizing myself with archives in Ghana, Togo, and Germany; and spending time in the Central Volta Region of Ghana—selected as the site of my research for a variety of scholarly and practical reasons—to meet people, learn about its history and cultures, and generally get a feel for the place.

It was during my predissertation research that I realized my broad assumptions about what the oral history would tell us was contradicted by reality: many Ghanaians in the Central Volta Region spoke about the German colonial period in mostly positive ways. *Remembering the Germans in Ghana* attempts to explain that reality. It addresses the following questions: What is the oral history of the German occupation of the central Volta Region of Ghana? How did it develop in the decades after the Germans left? What factors shape the way it is maintained? And, what larger lessons can we draw from examining this oral history?

Objectivity demands that historians respect the voices and opinions of the people about whose history we write. Clearly, as a Marxist, it was not my intention nor my desire to produce a book about what might be perceived as colonial nostalgia but, as a historian of Africa, particularly one of European origin, it is my responsibility not to denigrate or dismiss the interpretations of the oral historians who kindly shared their time and expertise with me. Although I may not agree with their perspectives on the past, my primary duty is to present their oral history and, secondarily, contextualize it based on my understanding of the larger history.

The book tackles the aforementioned questions and fulfills these duties in a mostly chronological narrative: in the first chapter, I explain my research methodology and I discuss related theoretical issues; in the second chapter, I offer an overview of the early history and cultures of the central Volta Region; a history of German colonial rule in the central Volta Region, based on written accounts, is presented in the third chapter while the oral history on the same subject constitutes chapter four; in the fifth chapter, the post-German colonial period is examined, with a focus on the Ewe unification and Togoland reunification movements; the sixth and final chapter analyzes how and why memories of the Germans are maintained today by highlighting the role of German Scholars, the dynamics of public performance, the influence of physical remains and reminders of the Germans, and the research process itself. The conclusion sums up the book's arguments and its wider implications.

In addition to presenting the case for more deliberate and extensive use of oral history in reconstructing the African colonial past, and providing a methodology for its collection and analysis, this book is intended to make important contributions to the existing literature on the history of the Ewe and neighboring peoples, the German Togoland colony, and German colonialism in general.

CHAPTER ONE

Theoretical and Methodological Contexts

The first extensive, scholarly, historical studies of European colonial rule in Africa were published in the 1960s, the decade when many African nations won back their independence. Based almost exclusively on archival materials produced by Europeans, many of these works seemed to depict colonialism as a political contest between European colonial officials and the Africans they colonized. The focus was often on administrative policies implemented by the European regimes and the methods employed by Africans to oppose them. Apologists for colonialism emphasized what they argued were positive aspects of European colonial rule while radical scholars highlighted African resistance and the negative economic consequences of alien occupation. Yet, for practical and sometimes ideological reasons, seldom were African sources—and then usually only newspapers written by elites who were granted some access to western education during the colonial era—incorporated into the analysis.

In the decades that followed, historians of Africa developed more nuanced theoretical approaches to understanding colonialism, collected and analyzed non-traditional sources, and explored innovative—albeit at times narrow—subjects. Beginning with studies of women and gender, this body of literature considered wide-ranging and illuminating topics in the colonial epoch such as labor, medicine and disease, law, ecology, and boundaries, among others. Scholars utilized oral histories, life stories, popular arts, and material culture in attempts to let African voices speak. Notable examples of these original approaches include works by historians of Ghana, such as Emmanuel K. Akyeampong, Jean Allman and Victoria Tashjian, Sandra E. Greene, Stephan F. Miescher, and, especially germane to my work, Paul Nugent.[1]

A particularly intriguing issue to scholars across geographic fields and historical epochs has been memory. Theories and methodologies articulated by psychologists, anthropologists, and historians have been elaborated upon by scholars investigating slavery,[2] for example, but little work has been produced by specialists on colonial Africa. One significant exception is Jennifer Cole's groundbreaking book on memory in Madagascar, *Forget Colonialism?*[3] An anthropologist, Cole examines why the people of eastern Madagascar, who endured a brutal French settler regime and a failed anticolonial uprising, today largely have forgotten this history. In contrast, memories of the Germans in the central Volta Region of Ghana are deep and vivid and routinely invoked in oral history.

Using open-ended interviewing techniques, I collected oral history in towns across the central Volta Region over various periods between 1995 and 2001 but mainly during several months of fieldwork in 1996–1997 [Figure 1.1]. Generally, Ghanaian oral historians describe the violence, burdens, and inconveniences they associate with German rule, but place greater emphasis on the introductions by German missionaries of Christianity and western education and the prevalence of what they say was the "honesty," "order," and "discipline" of the German colonial period.

This book investigates the foundations and the formulations of these memories. By assessing the oral history, contrasting it to the written history of German Togoland, and interrogating my fieldwork, two points become clear. First, there is a direct correlation between "positive" memories of the Germans and the perceived marginalization of the former Togoland during the British mandate/trusteeship period. It was during that time that Ewe ethnic and Volta regional identities were (re)created. Second, male elders, chiefs, and "German Scholars" are largely responsible for the articulation and sustenance of this oral history. The role of these locally known German Scholars—elderly men (or their sons) who are Christian, German-educated, and in many cases served as cultural brokers or, to use Nancy Rose Hunt's term, "middle figures"[4] between Africans and Europeans—is especially crucial to understanding the oral history.

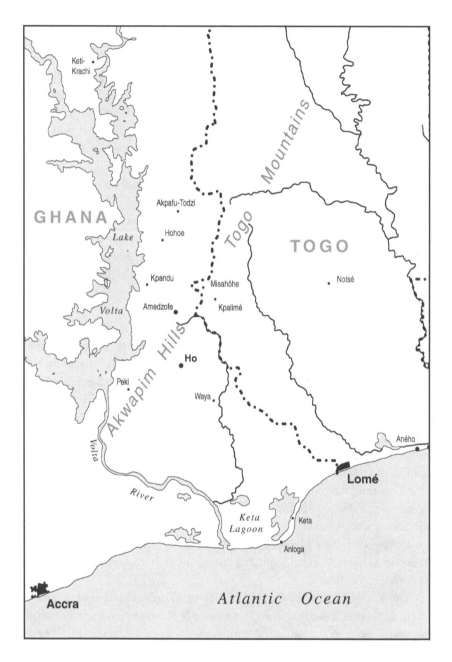

Figure 1.1 Central Volta Region with interview sites highlighted. (Courtesy of University of Madison-Wisconsin Cartography Lab)

Fundamentally, I argue that oral history can be (re)constructed as a written text to understand how the colonial past is remembered in a localized area. This book treats oral history not simply as a methodology—that is, the act of gathering spoken accounts—but as an actual document of the past, solicited orally from individuals and then composed in written form by the researcher. Thus, rather than using oral history as a supplement to written sources—to complement the silences in the archival records, for example—this book privileges this source material to show how a popular narrative has been produced, maintained, and disseminated in Ghana's central Volta Region. In a sense, my approach is similar to Jan Vansina and his students, who record oral traditions of the precolonial period, yet I am focusing on much more recent, colonial history.[5]

Moreover, while other studies trace historical memory in rituals and visual representations, my study examines how it is verbalized in public settings as oral history. I consider the impact of performance, sites of memory, literature, and my role as a researcher, on the creation of this oral history. This book explores how memory is expressed through oral history and, in turn, how oral history influences memory.

Lastly, I examine the ways oral history reflects and shapes ethnic and regional identities in the central Volta Region. Oral historians interpret and use the German experience as a means to sculpt identities, which contrast with those of "other" Ghanaians. Beyond various distinct languages and cultural practices, what distinguishes the central Volta Region from the rest of Ghana is the encounter with German colonialism. The emphasis oral historians place on this historical experience testifies to its significance in the forming of identity. Through an exploration of the earliest manifestation of this tendency, with the formation of the pro-German Togobund in the 1920s, to contemporary German ties through the Evangelical Presbyterian church and German nongovernmental organizations, I dissect the connections between the German presence and Ewe ethnic and Volta regional identities. The essential text for this examination is oral history—a strategy I believe should illuminate similar studies across Africa and beyond as most work on identity draws from archival records, written sources, and material culture.

In short, this book presents an oral history, scrutinizes its sources and presentation, contextualizes it historically, and uses it to make larger arguments about memory and identity. It examines the production of oral history and how oral history shaped, and had been shaped by, memories and identities. Before presenting the methodology used to collect the oral history, it is imperative to define theoretical concepts that inform my analysis as well as key terms employed in this study.

Concepts and Terms

Historical memory is always self-serving—to individuals, to groups, to nations. We reconstruct and recollect our pasts in order to rationalize, delineate, organize, and lend legitimacy to our present. Collective memory is constantly elaborated, challenged, enforced. Memory, Pierre Nora explains,

> … is life, borne by living societies in its name. It remains in permanent evolution, open to the dialectic of remembering and forgetting, unconscious of its successive deformations, vulnerable to manipulation and appropriation, susceptible to being long dormant and periodically revived … Memory is perpetually actual phenomenon, a bond tying us to the eternal present…. Memory, insofar as it is effective and magical, only accommodates those facts that suit it.[6]

The theoretical construct of collective memory was pioneered by Maurice Halbwachs who argued that individuals remember only as part of a group.[7] This idea has since become orthodoxy amongst most historians, who have built upon Halbwachs' thesis by examining a range of historical episodes, such as genocides or presidential administrations, and a variety of expressions of memory, from public commemorations to television documentaries.

Iwona Irwin-Zarecka writes that "A 'collective memory'—as a set of ideas, images, and feelings about the past—is best located not in the minds of individuals, but in the resources they share."[8] These resources may include scholarly texts, popular films, or, in the case of the central Volta Region, oral history. Together, these resources help form the collective memories of societies. By examining the resources, which circulate and inform in any society, we can comprehend not only *how* that society collectively remembers the past, but also *why* they remember it in a particular way.

Recognition of the dynamics of collective memory is not limited to academia. On the contrary, the construction and maintenance of collective memory and the opposition to it in any society is always contested by the actors involved in those dynamics. This is not to suggest that the process of memory construction is rapid or tractable. It is always disputed and is constantly evolving. Nonetheless, it exists, and each and every society forms a collective memory of its past, one which may be challenged, but prevails. It is the dominant class which is responsible for its sustenance and, as importantly, its very formulation.

Repositioning the study of collective memory to include considerations of class dynamics—indeed to propel this strategy to the center of our inquiries—is of primary importance to materialist analysis. Understanding how and why a society collectively remembers the past is insufficient; identifying *who* is responsible for the articulation and maintenance of that collective memory—or, in other words, who controls the resources which shape the collective memory—provides critical insight into intellectual hegemony within that society.

Fredric Jameson pointed out that "'Postmarxisms' regularly emerge at those moments in which capitalism itself undergoes a structural metamorphosis."[9] When I carried out most of this research, we were purported to be living in the era of "postmodernity," in which the "death" of Marxism and the "triumph" of capitalism were celebrated by scholars who embraced "postmodernist" theories they believed challenged "modernist" "metanarratives." Yet, as Jameson correctly argues, "it is incoherent to celebrate the 'death of Marxism' in the same breath with which one announces the definitive triumph of capitalism and the market."[10]

Regardless of academic and political trends, relations at all levels of most societies—local, national, and international—remain shaped by class antagonisms and a materialist analysis is crucial to interrogating these dynamics. In nearly every community, a ruling class has control of the means of production, including material resources, while the majority does not. This control translates not only into economic domination, but into intellectual power, as well. As Marx and Engels argue,

> The ideas of the ruling class are in every epoch the ruling idea, i.e., the class which is the ruling *material* force of society, is at the same time the ruling *intellectual* force. The class which has the means of material production at its disposal, has control at the same time over the means of material production, so that thereby, generally speaking, the ideas of those who lack the means of mental production are subject to it. The ruling ideas are nothing more than the ideal expression of the dominant material relationships, the dominant material relationships grasped as ideas; hence of the relationships which make the one class the ruling one, therefore, the ideas of its dominance.[11]

While the material resources at the disposal of the dominating class of the central Volta Region may be negligible, the German Scholars and other elderly men shape and control intellectual resources, including oral history.

In order to examine collective memory, the researcher must first identify the material resources which will be investigated and then establish the means by which these will be assembled and analyzed. As Kwesi Yankah observes, "loyalty to the spoken word" has not diminished in African societies, despite the expansion of print and online media.[12] Since the communities of the central Volta Region continue to collectively remember the past through mostly oral means, I set about to gather and examine the oral history of the area.

In the words of Renato Rosaldo, "Doing oral history involves telling stories people tell about themselves."[13] Oral history and oral tradition are oral documents, which exist in every African society and represent their collective memories of the past. Vansina offers the following distinction between oral tradition and oral history:

The sources of oral historians are reminiscences, hearsay, or eyewitness accounts about events and situations which are contemporary, that is, which occurred during the lifetime of the informants. This differs from oral traditions in that oral traditions are no longer contemporary. They have passed from mouth to mouth, for a period beyond the lifetime of the informants.[14]

The oral history of the European occupation of most parts of the African continent is thus gradually becoming oral tradition. In the case of the German occupation of the central Volta Region, the line between what is oral tradition and what constitutes oral history is vague, but I have opted to employ the latter term, since a number of "eyewitnesses" from the period contribute to the shaping of the collective memory.[15]

Beyond simply collecting the oral history and accepting it as a static, fully formed document, however, I have sought to examine the forces which helped mold it and, by extension, the collective memory of the German occupation of the central Volta Region. In pursuing this objective, I have considered what David William Cohen coined "the production of history"[16] and laid out the larger historical context and, as importantly, the backgrounds, biases, and agendas of the oral historians, all of which I argue helped form the oral history.

The people whom my coresearchers and I interviewed in the central Volta Region and who provided the oral history that constitutes the primary source material for this book bear the status of oral historians. None of these oral historians received academic training in the discipline of history nor did they hold official positions as historians in their towns. Yet, since they were identified as experts on the German occupation by their communities, their status as oral historians (if only of the German period) was confirmed by their very selection. In a small town such as Akpafu Todzi, one of the sites in which we conducted interviews, people have little or no access to scholarly texts. As a result, many of the residents of Akpafu Todzi acquired their knowledge of the German occupation exclusively from these oral historians. While those interviewed may not self-identify as "oral historians" (as opposed to "farmers" or "pastors"), this term accurately describes not only their role in this project but also as protagonists in the maintenance of the oral history of the German occupation.

The Europeans—mostly Germans—who are invoked in the oral history were imperialists. V. I. Lenin's dictum that imperialism is the highest stage of capitalism has been challenged by subsequent transformations of capitalism, but his definition of imperialism remains apropos:

Imperialism is capitalism in that stage of development in which the dominance of monopolies and finance capital has established itself; in which the export of capital has acquired pronounced importance; in which the division of the world among the international trusts has begun; in which the division of all territories of the globe among the great capitalist powers has been completed.[17]

Imperialism was a violent process implemented and supervised by individuals. Those employed by the imperialist nations of Europe in their colonies—as governors, district officials, soldiers, medical doctors, engineers, and so forth—and those who otherwise worked in the colonies, such as missionaries, assisted the process of imperialism, were crucial to its success, and thus were imperialists. This is a historical fact and not a latter-day judgment of the character and motivations of each of these individuals. Rosaldo has aptly condemned the capacity of imperialist nostalgia "to transform the responsible colonial agent into an innocent bystander."[18] I therefore use the term imperialist to designate these agents of colonialism.

While imperialism is a process, colonialism is the method by which imperialist nations maintain foreign territories for economic exploitation. I prefer to describe what is popularly referred to as the "colonial period" of African history as a period of European occupation in order to accentuate the often violent seizure, always illegitimate administration, and (in some areas) alien settlement of African territories by European imperialists. While the term "colonization" depicts the means of imperialist penetration into the African continent during the late nineteenth and most of the twentieth centuries, the illegitimacy of European colonial "rule" has been an often bypassed issue in historical studies, if only because this fact is assumed. Thus, I often employ the pointed term "occupation," with all its implications.

The central Volta Region was occupied by European imperialists for approximately eighty years. Since the late nineteenth century, this area has been part of several larger entities, namely the German Togoland colony, the British Togoland mandate, the British Togoland trusteeship and, since the return to independence in 1957, Ghana (Table 1.1). Although "Togo" and "Togoland" are both used to identify the former German colony in archival materials and secondary sources,[19] "Togoland" is used here to distinguish the colony from the present-day nation of Togo, which constitutes only approximately two-thirds of Togoland. The area in which I conducted my research is part of Ghana, where the remaining one-third of Togoland is located. "Togoland" will also be employed in reference to the British territory of the same name, which was created after the defeat of the Germans during the First World War and their expulsion from the colony. Additionally, those people who resided in Togoland during the German and British occupations are referred to as "Togolanders" in contrast to the "Togolese" of the present-day nation of Togo.

Table 1.1 Territories in which the central Volta Region has been included

Territory	Administrator	Status	Dates
Togoland	Germany	Colony	c. 1884–1914
British Togoland	United Kingdom	Mandate	1919–c.1939
British Togoland	United Kingdom	Trusteeship	1946–1957
Volta Region	Ghana	Region	1957–present

Methodology

As the primary objective of this book is to analyze the oral history of the German occupation, presenting the methodology I employed in the field is of critical importance to any consideration of my findings. Open-ended interview techniques allowed the oral historians I interviewed to assume (at least) partial to (nearly) total control of the scope of our interviews. This methodology provides historians with the ability to collect spontaneous oral histories, which in turn permit us to comprehend the collective memories of the communities and the historical episodes we study. By following this methodology, I argue, historians of colonial Africa will be better able to access an often ignored but crucial and complex source material that elucidates our understanding of African perspectives on the European occupation.

Since the overall aim of my research was to investigate how people in the central Volta Region remembered the German occupation, I rejected the usual historian's practice of nearly exhausting archival materials before conducting fieldwork. The rationale for this position was twofold. The methodology I applied necessitated that those interviewed guide the content and direction of the interviews. It was therefore crucial that I not enter the field with a preconceived research agenda dictated by the archival materials. I did not utilize a rigid questionnaire, nor did I approach interviews with a set list of topics the oral historians were to address. On the contrary, I asked the oral historians to speak freely on what they knew about the German occupation.

Second, as my goal was to study the nature and content of the oral resources, and since a great deal of the archival materials have been thoroughly analyzed and extensively used by historians in previous studies on Togoland, I deemed it not of the foremost importance, in the context of my project, to revisit in great detail the same sources. I did not shun these materials, of course, but reversed the order of research somewhat, by allowing the oral history to influence what I investigated in the archives. As a result, after acquainting myself with the types of archival sources available in Europe and West Africa, my research plan in the archives was guided by the interviews I conducted in the central Volta Region.[20] After preliminary visits in 1993 and 1995, during which I identified research sites, carried out several interviews, discussed my project with scholars, and briefly surveyed archival materials, I returned to Ghana in 1996 to undertake my doctoral fieldwork. This research was conducted with Ghanaian coresearchers Cornelius Adedze, Joseph "Montana" Asamoah, Divine Dzokoto, and Gavivina Tamakloe.[21] Together, we interviewed 45 oral historians in the central Volta Region between February and July 1997.[22] These interviews were carried out in seven sites across the central Volta Region—namely, Akpafu Todzi, Akpafu Mempeasem, Amedzofe, Ho, Hohoe, Kpandu, and Waya—each of which differs in size and economic basis (Table 1.2). Several subsequent interviews were conducted by Asamoah and me between 2002 and 2005.

Table 1.2 Interview sites during 1996–97

Town	General size	Location in central Volta Region	Primary economic activities of town	Number of oral historians interviewed
Akpafu Mempeasem	Small town	North	Agriculture	4
Akpafu Todzi	Small town	North	Agriculture	7
Amedzofe	Medium-sized town	Central	Agriculture and education	3
Ho	Small city	Central	Administration, commerce, and education	8
Hohoe	Large town	North	Commerce and education	5
Kpandu	Large town	West	Commerce and education	6
Waya	Small town	South	Agriculture	12

Generally speaking, the oral historians represented a cross-section of the population of the central Volta Region, at least in reference to occupation (Table 1.3). The typical oral historian we interviewed was an elderly Christian Ewe man engaged in agriculture. Most described themselves either primarily or secondarily as farmers, especially in the small and medium-sized towns, that is, Akpafu Todzi, Akpafu Mempeasem, Amedzofe, and Waya. An almost equal number of oral historians identified themselves as teachers (including several "educationalists" and one former school headmaster) or religious officials (especially pastors). Most of the oral historians classified themselves as retired from their occupations, but a good number claimed they still farm.

Table 1.3 Occupations of oral historians

Occupation	Number
Farmers	17
Teachers/educators	7
Religious officials[23]	7
Chiefly officials[24]	5
Other[25]	6
Traders/merchants	4
Unknown	6
Total[26]	**52**

We did not ask oral historians to reveal their ethnicity or their religious background, but it was often possible to deduce these from the interviews. Based on their choice of language during the interviews as well as their town of residence, it appears most of the oral historians we interviewed were Ewe. A minority of them lived in towns with majority populations of speakers of Central-Togo languages (i.e., Akpafu Todzi, Akpafu Mempeasem, and Amedzofe), but that does not necessarily imply that each of these oral historians belonged to one of those ethnic groups. For instance, a town like Amedzofe, in which Avatime is the primary language, includes a significant population of Ewe and people of other ethnic groups, since it is an educational center. In terms of religion, most of the oral historians directly stated or implied during the course of their interviews that they were Christian. In fact, no one suggested they were followers of any other religion and Christianity is the dominant religion in the central Volta Region.

Most of the oral historians were introduced to us by the various contacts my coresearchers and I already had in each of the sites. These were generally local bureaucrats, church officials, or educators with whom at least one of my coresearchers or I had previously interacted. When we arrived at a site for the first time, we met with the contact, described our project (if we had not done so previously), and he (never she) then directed us toward potential interviewees. At sites in which we did not have any contacts, such as Waya, we introduced ourselves to the chief(s) and/ or elder(s) to whom we explained our project. They generally recommended people we should interview in the community. This process is in itself revealing, of course, since who we interviewed was almost always predetermined by the knowledge, relationships, and preferences of our first contacts at any given site. Occasionally, the oral historians we interviewed suggested other people to us and at other times we simply happened upon someone who appeared knowledgeable about the German era.

We were quite often deterred by our contacts, various officials (governmental and otherwise) and, frequently, the male oral historians, from interviewing women. While my coresearchers and I stressed our desire to interview female oral historians, our entreaties were dismissed by some and ignored by others. The former group predictably argued that women had little to say since they would not be knowledgeable about the German period. This, of course, was not the case from our perspectives, and despite our objections and repeated attempts, we were unsuccessful in interviewing a significant number of female oral historians (Table 1.4). As suggested above, the selection process, in this case the obstacles we faced interviewing women, is itself significant, and informs my analysis of the oral history.

Table 1.4 Numbers of female oral historians

Site	Number of women	Number of oral historians
Akpafu Mempeasem	0	4
Akpafu Todzi	2	7
Amedzofe	0	3
Ho	2	8
Hohoe	1	5
Kpandu	1	6
Waya	1	12
Total	**7**	**45**

Interview settings ranged from private bedrooms to public gatherings, but most of the interviews took place in the sitting rooms or in front of the homes of the oral historians. The interviews were conducted by myself and, at different times, my four coresearchers. These researchers each brought different strengths to the project. Tamakloe served as an unofficial coleader (with myself) of the group, usually presiding over the formalities at interview sites (e.g., contacting officials, arranging interviews, etc.). Adedze and Dzokoto also interviewed a considerable number of oral historians, although they were involved in the project for only brief periods. Asamoah's numerous contacts in the central Volta Region and unmatched familiarity with the area helped expedite our research, and he, too, participated in the interviews, generally by asking follow-up questions. While I coordinated the project, including conceiving the original research proposal, selecting the sites, and formulating our standard interview procedures, Tamakloe was largely responsible for leading the interviews, especially those conducted in Ewe, since I am not a speaker of that language.

Oral historians were asked to select the language in which they preferred to be interviewed. My primary concern was to allow each oral historian to be interviewed in the language in which they were most comfortable. As a result, the majority opted for Ewe, while a substantial minority selected English (Table 1.5).[27]

Table 1.5 Languages in which interviews were conducted

Language(s)	Oral historians
Ewe	25
English	11
Mostly Ewe and some English	5
Siwu	3
Mostly Ewe and some German	1
Total	**45**

During the interviews in Ewe, simultaneous translations into English (for my benefit) were not performed. In fact, my role during those interviews was relegated to that of a bystander, since the interviews were exchanges in Ewe between one, two, or three of the coresearchers and the oral historian. During these interviews, I mostly observed, although my coresearchers would occasionally ask me a question or direct a comment toward me. This decision to forego immediate translations derived from our determination not to interrupt the delivery of oral history. When oral historians opted to be interviewed in English, I was primarily responsible for the questioning, although my coresearchers were free to contribute at any point. Neither my coresearchers nor I were able to conduct interviews in Siwu, three of which occurred in Akpafu Todzi. As a result, we relied on oral historians fluent in both Ewe and Siwu to translate so that my coresearchers could conduct those interviews.

While we did not circulate a questionnaire or approach the oral historians with a set list of questions, I outlined a general layout for the interviews, which included the phrasing of our initial description of the project to each oral historian and the broad themes which interested us. These included not only the history, particularly of the German period, but also the origins of each town. We expressed our research agenda in general terms, for instance, "We would like you to tell us about the German period." It was hoped that by formulating our sentences in such an open-ended manner, the oral historians themselves would assume responsibility for directing the flow of the interview. At times, we would interview a reluctant oral historian, unwilling to seize the initiative. In these situations, we intervened to a greater extent, guiding the interviews toward certain subjects, for example, agriculture, education, and so forth. When we conducted a second or third interview with those oral historians who appeared especially knowledgeable about the German occupation, we did return with a list of more specific topics which we requested the oral historian to discuss. These included subjects mentioned in prior interviews about which we hoped for further elaboration or issues not addressed previously by some oral historians but discussed by others.

Besides the oral historian, me, and from one to three of my coresearchers, at least one other person from the site was usually present at any interview. More often, there were at least several, and sometimes more, additional people witnessing an interview. They included, at different times in various sites, our local contacts; the oral historian's family members, friends, neighbors; children; and/or officials from the site. These individuals were either already present at the interview site or joined the audience as the interview progressed, thus making nearly every interview a public spectacle.

Each interview was taped on a microcassette recorder, with the permission of the oral historian(s), and minimal (if any) notes were written during the interviews. The latter decision was based on the belief that conspicuous note taking during an interview might influence the information presented by an oral historian, since s/he may discern which comments elicited written recording by the interviewer and which did not. The oral historian might thus respond by shifting the course of the narrative in the belief that s/he was satisfying the perceived interests of the interviewer.

The tape-recorded interviews were later transcribed by either me, Dzokoto, or two other translators.[28] I transcribed most of the English-language interviews while Dzokoto and the others translated the Ewe (and the Siwu-into-Ewe) interviews as they concurrently transcribed the tapes. The translations were verbatim and never paraphrased. Once I began organizing my research material, I created a standard transcription format, into which I copied all the transcriptions and included details about the interviews based on my fieldnotes. These notes were generally written immediately after interviews and listed the following: who was present [i.e., the researchers, oral historian(s), and any other participant(s)]; where the interview was conducted; who translated and/or transcribed the interview; and any other information regarding the setting, such as relevant conversation prior to or after the interview and whether any gifts were exchanged. All oral historians as well as the interview settings were photographed by permission. Those interviewed were not offered any financial compensation for their time, the exception being some particularly elderly oral historians, who on occasion received a small "dash" following the interviews.[29] The tapes and photographs were catalogued during our fieldwork and additional copies of both were made in Ghana and the United States.

When I had initially conceived of this project, I proposed utilizing open-ended interviewing techniques developed by psychocultural anthropologists, in which (1) the interviewer refrains from asking leading questions, (2) the interviewee is allowed to determine the content and direction of the interview, and (3) the researcher elicits detailed biographical information.[30] The first two aspects of this methodology have been discussed above, but the third presented a dilemma. I was attracted to this strategy as it promised to reveal how the oral historians' personal histories (including class and/or ethnic identity, educational background, personal experiences, etc.) might influence the manner in which they portrayed the period as well as the type of stories they recollected. During the first series of interviews, it became apparent we needed to partially reevaluate this methodology.

I had anticipated interviewing a limited number of oral historians with extensive knowledge of the German period. I thought it would be possible to repeatedly interview the same group of oral historians, recording their histories of the German occupation and collecting their individual biographical data. We quickly discovered that each oral historian's limited recollections of the German period did not warrant extensive and/or repeated interviews.[31] We thus interviewed a much larger group of people and abandoned our goal of acquiring detailed personal information from each of those interviewed.

The significantly increased number of oral historians made it impossible to conduct extended biographical interviews,[32] but we collected sufficient biographical data to inform my broad analysis of the backgrounds, agendas, and biases of the oral historians. This information was generally solicited after the formal interview or, in other words, after the oral historian had decided that s/he had absolutely exhausted their knowledge of the German period. At this point, comfortable that our contributions would not impose direction on the flow of the narrative, we would ask more pointed questions, such as the sources for the oral historian's stories or their experiences with German missionaries. We also continued to employ open-ended interviewing techniques in order to assure that our interventions did not guide the interviewees or determine the scope of their recollections. Therefore, while I refrain from labeling our methodology "psychocultural anthropology," as we did not attempt to strictly follow the model formulated by practitioners of this subfield, we adhered to the basic interviewing techniques articulated by these scholars (among others), and their literature certainly influences my understanding of this oral history.

Each of my coresearchers had previously conducted historical field research for various lengths of time, but none had been familiar with these open-ended interviewing techniques. Thus, before we began the interviews, I discussed this methodology with each of the coresearchers, particularly since I not only encouraged them to actively contribute to the interviews, but as already stated one or more of them were responsible for leading the majority of interviews. Prior to each of the first series of interviews, I summarized the technique until I felt confident that my coresearchers were conversant with the methodology and, adhering to it, they increasingly assumed a passive role in the interviews.

Most of the interviews, unguided by the researchers, followed the same overall format (Table 1.6). After a (usually) brief exchange of greetings and introductions,[33] one or more of my co-researchers and/or I would describe our project to the oral historian in generalized terms. For example, we did not inform the oral historians that I was attempting to compare the oral history with the written history of the former Togoland colony nor did we suggest that I was seeking to investigate present-day opinions of the German occupation. We merely explained that we were interested in learning about "the period of the Germans." After this brief elaboration of our project, the tape recorder was started and one of the researchers asked the oral historian(s) to state their name, age, and occupation, and, finally, to share what they knew of the German period.

These open-ended interviewing techniques allowed oral historians to guide the interviews and dictate their content without extensive and persuasive interventions by the researchers. The oral history that emerged is comprehensive and enlightening, as will be evident in the following chapters on the precolonial and colonial history of the Central Volta Region.

Table 1.6 Progression of the typical interview

---

1. Greetings and introductions [by oral historian(s) and researcher(s)]
2. Explanation of project [by researcher(s)]
3. Formal interview in which oral historians provide, generally in this order:
   A. Discussion of town's origins, beginning with migration stories and including details of early trade with Europeans and later invasions and occupation by the Asante
   B. Explanation of her/his knowledge of German period and/or personal interaction with Germans
   C. Series of stories from German period and/or listing of German contributions to region (the former usually emphasizing negative aspects of German occupation, the latter comprised largely of positive impacts)
   D. Comparison of German period with British period (almost always), and/or precolonial era (usually), and/or independence era (occasionally)
   E. Expression of general (almost always, positive) sentiments relating to German period
4. Informal discussion (usually in the form of questions from oral historian(s) directed toward researchers about their backgrounds).

Notes

1. Emmanuel Kwaku Akyeampong, *Between the Sea and the Lagoon: An Eco-Social History of the Anlo of Southeastern Ghana c. 1850 to Recent Times* (Athens: Ohio University Press, 2001); Jean Allman and Victoria Tashjian, *"I Will Not Eat Stone": A Women's History of Colonial Asante* (Portsmouth: Heinemann, 2000); Sandra E. Greene, *Sacred Sites and the Colonial Encounter: A History of Meaning and Memory in Ghana* (Bloomington: Indiana University Press, 2000); Stephan F. Miescher, *Making Men in Ghana* (Bloomington: Indiana University Press, 2005); and Paul Nugent, *Smugglers, Secessionists, and Loyal Citizens on the Ghana-Togo Frontier* (Athens: Ohio University Press, 2002).

2. See Pier M. Larson, *History and Memory in the Age of Enslavement: Becoming Merina in Highland Madagascar, 1770–1822* (Portsmouth: Heinemann, 2000) and Rosalind Shaw, *Memories of the Slave Trade: Ritual and the Historical Imagination in Sierra Leone* (Chicago: University of Chicago Press, 2002).

3. Jennifer Cole, *Forget Colonialism? Sacrifice and the Art of Memory in Madagascar* (Berkeley: University of California Press, 2001).

4. Nancy Rose Hunt, *A Colonial Lexicon of Birth Ritual, Medicalization, and Mobility in the Congo* (Durham: Duke University Press, 1999).

5. Jan Vansina, *Oral Tradition as History* (Madison: University of Wisconsin Press, 1985) is the seminal work on this approach.

6. Pierre Nora, "Between Memory and History: *Les Lieux de Mémoire*," "Memory and Counter-Memory," Special Issue of *Representations*, ed. by Natalie Zemon Davis and Randolph Starn, 26 (Spring, 1989), 8.

7. Maurice Halbwachs, *La mémorie collective* (Paris: Presses Universitaires de France, 1968).

8. Iwona Irwin-Zarecka, *Frames of Remembrance: The Dynamics of Collective Memory* (New Brunswick: Transaction Publishers, 1994).

9. Fredric Jameson, "Five Theses on Actually Existing Marxism" *Monthly Review*, 47:11 (April 1996), 1.

10. *Ibid.*

11. Karl Marx and Frederick Engels, *The German Ideology*, Part One, ed. by C. J. Arthur (New York: International Publishers, 1993), 64.

12. Kwesi Yankah, "African Norms of Communication and the Crisis of the Global Order," The James S. Coleman African Studies Center Winter 1999 Lecture Series, University of California, Los Angeles (March 15, 1999).

13. Renato Rosaldo, "Doing Oral History," *Social Analysis* 4 (September 1990), 89–99.

14. Vansina, 12–13.

15. In contrast, I term "oral tradition" the interview material I incorporate into my overview of the period before the European occupation in Chapter 2.

16. David William Cohen, *The Combing of History* (Chicago: University of Chicago Press, 1994).

17. V. I. Lenin, *Imperialism: The Highest Stage of Capitalism: A Popular Outline* (New York: International Publishers, 1977), 89. For further elaboration, see Dennis Laumann, *Colonial Africa, 1884–1994* (New York: Oxford University Press, 2013).

18. Renato Rosaldo, "Imperialist Nostalgia," "Between Memory and History: *Les Lieux de Mémoire*," "Memory and Counter-Memory," Special Issue of *Representations*, ed. by Natalie Zemon Davis and Randolph Starn, 26 (Spring, 1989), 108.

19. German sources often refer to the former-colony as "Das Togogebiet," which translates as "the Togo territory."

20. Archival research in Europe was conducted at the Staatsbibliothek (State Library) in Berlin and the Staatsarchiv (State Archives) in Potsdam as well as at the Basel Missionary Society in Switzerland. In West Africa, research was carried out mostly at the Bibliothèque Nationale (National Library) in Lomé, Togo and the Ghana National Archives in Accra.

21. I am reluctant to apply the standard academic label of "research assistant" to these men, since their contributions to my research were extensive and invaluable. At the time, Adedze was a graduate student at the University of Ghana and a journalist with several years experience in historical and archaeological research. Asamoah, a Ho-based tour operator, had previously conducted research in local history. Dzokoto was a civil servant and journalist based in Ho and graduate of the University of Cape Coast. And Tamakloe, then a director of a governmental agency in Ho, was a graduate of the Universities of Ghana and Bergen (Norway) who had carried out historical fieldwork over several years. Each of these core-searchers was paid a monthly stipend for their work on the project.

22. Two of these oral historians, Seth Adu and Francis Yaotse Awuma, were also interviewed in 1995. N. K. Dzobo was interviewed during the 1995 fieldwork. All three of these oral historians resided in Ho.

23. Includes four pastors, one moderator, and a catechist.

24. Includes three chiefs, one linguist, and a historian.

25. Includes one each of the following: student, civil servant, blacksmith, carpenter, plumber, and soldier.

26. Several oral historians listed two occupations.

27. Three oral historians, all residents of Akpafu Todzi, were interviewed in Siwu while several interchanged Ewe and English in their interviews. One oral historian in Ho, Seth Adu, who was interviewed a total of four times, spoke Ewe and German during his first interview in 1995 (Seth Adu [oral historian], in interview with the author, August 8, 1995). Adu was a 102-year-old former-employee of the Evangelical Presbyterian Church who attended a German school in Lomé at the onset of the Allied invasion of Togoland.

28. These were Vivian Asempa and Olivia Baku, both based in Accra.

29. In fact, I was often the recipient of gifts from the oral historians, usually produce such as bananas.

30. For a summary of this methodology, see Douglas W. Hollan and Jane C. Wellenkamp, *Contentment and Suffering: Culture and Experience in Toraja* (New York: Columbia University Press, 1994), 7–10. Also, see the "Check Sheet for Psychodynamic Interviews" in Robert I. Levy, *Tahitians: Mind and Experience in the Society Islands* (Chicago: University of Chicago Press, 1973), 509–11.

31. The longest interviews lasted no more than ninety minutes and only a few respondents were interviewed more than once.

32. Only one oral historian, Seth Adu of Ho, was selected for extensive biographical interviews.

33. Tamakloe almost always led these in Ewe although, occasionally, such as in the presence of chiefs and elders, it was our hosts who presided over the formalities.

CHAPTER TWO

Cultural and Historical Contexts

The Volta Region, one of the ten administrative regions of Ghana, is located in the southeastern corner of the country and stretches from the Atlantic coast to approximately 275 kilometers (171 miles) north (Figure 2.1). It borders the nation of Togo to the east while the Volta River and Lake Volta form most of its western boundary. The Togo Mountains, emerging from the Akwapim hills to the southwest, run through the Volta Region toward the northeast.

The central Volta Region is neither an official governmental entity nor a strictly defined geographic zone. Nevertheless, beyond the fact the term easily identifies the area under discussion, there is a historic and cultural continuity to the central Volta Region, as will be explained below. The area is mostly rural, yet densely populated. The largest towns are Ho in the south; Hohoe, in the north; and Kpandu, in the west. These three serve as administrative, educational, and commercial centers to surrounding villages and towns. Ho is the capital of the Volta Region and, in recent years, has developed into a small city.

A varied agriculture, consisting of staples such as cassava, maize, and rice as well as the cash crops cocoa and coffee, characterizes the economy of the central Volta Region. Small-scale, nonindustrial crafts, including kente-weaving, carving, and pottery, also are pursued in many towns. Akpokope and Kpotoe, both of which are located to the southeast of Ho near the border with Togo, are particularly well-known centers of kente-weaving.

The Volta Region is perhaps the most ethnically and linguistically diverse region of Ghana. It includes several of the nation's major ethnic groups including, from north to south, speakers of the Guan, Akan, and Ewe languages. The largest ethnic group in the central Volta Region is the Ewe, but there are significant populations of speakers of most of the Central-Togo languages.

Ethnic Groups

Without reliable or recent data, it is difficult to estimate the number of speakers of the Central-Togo languages in the central Volta Region, but most likely it is above 50,000.[1] Also known as the *Togorestsprachen* (German for "Togo Remnant Languages"), this group constitutes 14 languages spoken in eastern Ghana, central Togo, and west-central Benin. While nearly two-thirds of these languages are spoken entirely within Ghana, the majority of speakers of Central-Togo languages reside in Togo. Eight Central-Togo languages are spoken in the central Volta Region, roughly from north to south: Buem, Siwu, Bowili, Sele, Likpe, Logba, Avatime, and Nyangbo-Tafi.[2]

Ewe serves as a *lingua franca* throughout the Central-Togo communities of Ghana, with the exception of the Buem-speaking area, which has no common border with the Ewe. However, proficiency in Ewe is not universal amongst speakers of Central-Togo languages in the central Volta Region. In the two interview sites in which Central-Togo languages are widely spoken, only 75% of speakers of Siwu (Akpafu) and 70% of speakers of Avatime (Amedzofe) claim to speak Ewe, according to a study by linguists. In Central-Togo speaking communities, knowledge of English generally is more widespread than proficiency in Akan, the most commonly spoken language in Ghana.[3]

Little research has been carried out on the history of the Central-Togo communities,[4] but based on oral traditions, it appears that many of the cultural and political practices of the Ewe as well as the Akan have been adopted by these ethnic groups.

The Ewe population of Ghana, which during the period of fieldwork probably numbered between approximately 2.5 and 3 million, resides mostly within the Volta Region.[5] Across the border, an even larger population of Ewe inhabits Togo, while a tiny group lives in Benin. The pan-Ewe area of West Africa, also known as "Eweland," stretches along the Atlantic coast from the Volta River in Ghana to the Mono River along the Togo-Benin border and extends north roughly 125 miles (200 kilometers). The Ewe have lived in this ecologically diverse area since at least the mid-seventeenth century.

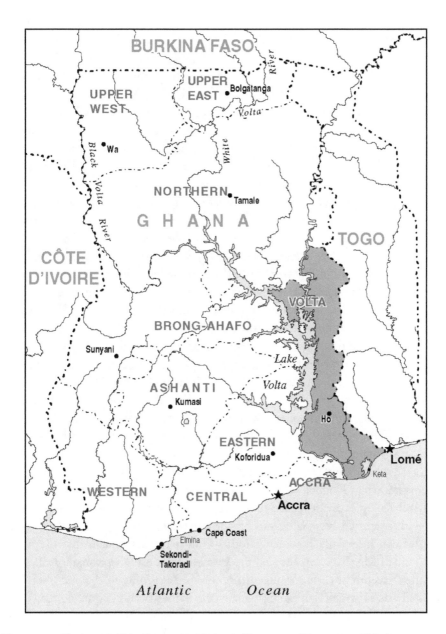

Figure 2.1 Ghana with Volta Region highlighted. (Courtesy of University of Madison-Wisconsin Cartography Lab)

Throughout their history of migrations and settlements, the Ewe demonstrated a remarkable ability to adjust to new environments. A notable example of this is the transformation of the Anlo Ewe of southeastern Ghana from a nonmaritime people into what Akyeampong calls the "quintessential sea fishermen of the West African coast." After their migrations in the mid-seventeenth century from areas further inland, the Anlo Ewe borrowed and adapted technologies from other Ewe and non-Ewe groups, allowing them to master the fishing and salt-making industries of the sea and lagoon environment along this stretch of the Atlantic coast.[6]

The Ewe trace their origins to a series of migrations which originated further east in what is today southwestern Nigeria and which also involved the Aja and the Fon. These three ethnic groups are often classified together in the historical literature under blanket terms such as the "Aja," the "Ajda-Ewe," or more recently, the "Gbe."[7] Although distinct from each other, the Ewe, the Aja, and the Fon share a common set of cultural beliefs and practices, their languages all belong to the Kwa subgroup of the Niger-Congo language family, and they have the collective history of migrations from areas to the east of their present locations. These migrations originated from Ketu, a walled city in present-day southeastern Benin, probably in the fifteenth century, according to oral traditions. It is believed that the migrations were spurred by the expansion of the Yoruba, historically the largest ethnic group in that part of West Africa.

Scholars have attempted to reconstruct the history of these migrations mainly based on oral traditions and, secondarily, archaeological evidence.[8] After their diffusion from Ketu, the migrants split into two main groups, the first moving toward the south. Part of this group founded a settlement near the Mono River called Tado where they became known as the Aja while others, who later formed some of the Ewe subgroups, established the town of Notsé in central Togo. The second group migrated to the Adele region along the central Ghana/Togo border. It is from this group that the Anlo Ewe, Be Ewe, and the Fon emerged. These latter Ewe groups later joined the others at Notsé where the various migrants collectively became known as Dogboawo, each occupying its own ward of the town.[9]

Archaeological evidence has indicated that Notsé probably was founded in the sixteenth century.[10] It grew into a city surrounded by a protective wall (*agbogbo*), parts of which are still in evidence today. Oral traditions explain that the tyrannical rule of King Agokoli I forced the Ewe once again to disperse, most likely in the late sixteenth or early seventeenth centuries. According to the oral traditions, Agokoli was a divine ruler, exercising absolute authority and commanding a powerful army, who imposed arbitrary and cruel punishments on his people. These traditions cite as an example that Agokoli forced his subjects to make rope out of clay and to mash earth laced with sharp thorns. While scholars speculate if Agokoli actually existed, archaeological excavations at Notsé and the uniformity of oral traditions across Eweland suggest the story should be regarded as factual.

In any event, it forms an essential myth in the history of the Ewe, one that was instrumental in the later formation of Ewe ethnicity and nationalism.[11]

The Ewe split into three distinct groups after their dispersal from Notsé. The first traveled in a northwesterly direction and settled the upland and valley regions and founded, among others, the Ghanaian towns of Hohoe, Kpandu, and Peki as well as Kpalimé in Togo. Ho and surrounding towns were settled by the Ewes who migrated westward from Notsé. Finally, the third group moved toward the south, with branches establishing settlements along the way, eventually reaching the coast, where the towns of the Be, which includes the Togolese capital of Lomé, and the Anlo were founded.

While it has been difficult to trace and date these Ewe migrations definitively, even more challenging has been ascertaining the identities of the people who were native to the areas the Ewe settled. Along the coast, the historical record largely remains silent about the original populations. Further inland, it is assumed that the aforementioned speakers of the Central-Togo languages were indigenous to the central and northern areas inhabited by the Ewe. According to M. E. Kropp Dakubu:

> The speakers of the various [Central-]Togo languages apparently have traditions of migration, but the migrations seem to have been more or less within the area they now occupy; there is no tradition of the entire group having arrived from anywhere.[12]

Amongst the oral traditions I collected, there are stories of migrations from afar amongst speakers of at least one of the Central-Togo languages, Avatime, spoken in Amedzofe and several surrounding villages.[13] It is probable these stories are inspired by the oral traditions of the Ewe who surround the Avatime-speaking area.[14]

The linguistic evidence indicates the speakers of the Central-Togo languages inhabited the central Volta Region before the arrival of the Ewe from the east as well as Akan and Guan groups from the west.[15] Kropp Dakubu and K. C. Ford explain:

> The term [Togo Remnant Languages] reflects the opinion of early writers that the people who speak these languages, whose towns are sometimes high up in the hills, represent populations that existed in the area before the arrival of the peoples who now occupy the plains around them. This may be true, at least in Ghana, since the Ewes of the Volta Region have strong traditions of fairly recent migration from further east, while the people who speak the [Central-Togo Languages] generally do not believe they came from outside the region.[16]

Moreover, Ewe oral traditions maintain that the areas in which they settled already were inhabited.[17]

It is impossible to reconstruct with the available data an overview of the histories and cultures of the speakers of the Central-Togo languages, but it is presumable that many aspects overlap with those of the Ewe, for which sources are far more detailed. It also is very likely that many of the indigenous peoples of the area were absorbed into the Ewe-speaking communities.[18]

After establishing their new communities in the mid-seventeenth century, the Ewe soon were joined by other migrants from west of the Volta River, including speakers of the Ga, Akan, and Guan languages. These migrants settled near the Mono River in the late seventeenth century and founded the towns of Aného (also historically known as Little Popo) and Glidji. They mixed with existing Watchi (or Ouatchi) Ewe communities to form the new Gun (or Ge) Ewe subgroup. The Gun Ewe are often referred to as the Mina, alluding to their sixteenth century origins in the Fanti (Akan) speaking coastal town of Elmina in Ghana. Amenumey states that about the same time Ga-speaking migrants from the area around Ghana's capital Accra settled around the Gbasa River to the west of Aného,[19] where they also were incorporated into the Gun Ewe. Later, so-called Brazilians, or freed slaves from the Americas and elsewhere, settled in Gun towns and became an important presence in local trade.

One hundred twenty Ewe subgroups could be identified by the turn of the twentieth century.[20] Together these subgroups form larger groupings, including the Anlo Ewe, the Central Ewe, and the Northern Ewe, all of which are found in Ghana.[21] Anloga is the "traditional capital" of the Anlo Ewe, who reside along the coast from the Volta River to Lomé. Between the Anlo Ewe and the Northern Ewe areas is the much smaller Central Ewe zone, which stretches between Akpokope, along the Togolese border, and Ho, with Kpotoe as its capital. The central Volta Region is inhabited by the Northern Ewes, who comprise the second largest grouping of Ewe in Ghana after the Anlo Ewe, and includes their capital of Ho. Among the Northern Ewe who reside in the central Volta Region are what Amenumey has termed "some of the more important subtribes" (subgroups) of the Ewe, including the Adaklu, the Ho, and the Kpandu.[22] The Krepi Ewe also belong to this group.

Political and Religious Institutions

Unlike their Akan and Fon neighbors, the Ewe never united into a centralized, single state. Instead, Eweland was comprised of numerous chieftaincies and small states throughout the precolonial period. Chieftaincies existed at the town level while several or numerous towns together constituted a state (*dukowo*), presided over by a paramount chief, who was elected patrilineally from one or two lineages of the founding families and advised by a council of elders.[23] Although the Ewe polities were independent from one another, their shared linguistic, cultural, and historical ties served to foster a common identity. Yet, due to the distance between states and the small territory each comprised, distinctions emerged, as evidenced by the diversity of Ewe dialects, cultural features (such as drumming styles and facial scarifications), and religious institutions.[24]

According to Diedrich Westermann, Ewe society was socially stratified into four groups: the nobility, the free citizens, the bondsmen, and the slaves. The nobility included the property-owning chiefs and the elders in each community, while the free citizens were comprised of peasants, traders, and skilled artisans, both poor and affluent. The "bondsmen" were non-Ewe who either were under the protection of a chief or paid a tribute in order to have the right to land use. Slaves were usually non-Ewe acquired through purchase or as the result of war.[25]

Each Ewe town was led by a chief (*dufia*) who was responsible for the administrative and judicial affairs of the community. The chief was supported in the administration by various sub-chiefs, including heads of lineages. He did not exercise absolute power but was advised by a council of elders drawn from various lineages (*fomewo*) and could be "de-stooled," or removed from office, for improper behavior or ineffective administration.[26] While the dufia was the "chief of the town," an *anyigbafia* was the "chief of the land" and was the religious leader of the community. The anyigbafia was often considered sacred and performed numerous ceremonies related to the spiritual world. Like many Niger-Congo cultures, Ewe religion encompassed beliefs in a supreme being (*Mawu*), lesser deities or spirits (*trowo*, *vodhun*), the presence of the ancestors (*togbewo*), and the mystical forces of nature. Regional variations existed, exemplified by the importance of ancestral cults and secret societies along the coast, which were less significant further inland.[27]

While it is necessary to point out that political and religious institutions developed regional particularities, it is likewise essential to emphasize the linkages across Eweland. Its economy was rooted in subsistence agriculture while small-scale manufacturing industries, such as kente-weaving, iron smelting, and salt making, were pursued in towns and villages across Eweland. A regular market cycle, whereby markets were held in specific towns on certain days, was a fundamental aspect of the economy. Traders from throughout Eweland and beyond bought and sold agricultural and manufactured goods—and, increasingly over time, human beings—at these markets.

Precolonial History

European trading posts already were established on the West African coast when the Ewes migrated to their present locations. Lacking the gold and ivory initially sought after by Europeans, most of Eweland did not directly participate in the

Atlantic trade, with the exception of the Anlo and the Gun, who resided on the coast itself. An obstacle to ocean commerce was the lack of natural harbors along the Ewe coast, forcing trade to be conducted aboard passing European ships. Yet Eweland was integrated into regional inland trading networks, to which it supplied agricultural and manufactured goods.

A trading network encompassing the lagoon system stretched along the coast from the Volta to Lagos. In the west, the Volta linked Eweland to another regional trading network, reaching from the Atlantic to the northern regions of present-day Ghana and Togo, where the commercial centers of Kete-Kratchi, Salaga, and Yendi were located. The main commodities traded in the southern part of this system were salt, fish, iron, and pottery.[28] Salt and fish were the primary products the Anlo Ewe exported to inland areas and across and along the Volta River, which served as an important commercial highway to areas further north.

The communities of speakers of the Central-Togo languages also were intertwined in this network. Akpafu Todzi, for instance, emerged as a key center of iron production.[29] Although iron is no longer produced or worked in Akpafu Todzi, the oral traditions of the town are replete with details of this precolonial industry. Iron tools, including hoes and machetes, were sold to neighboring as well as distant towns.[30] Thus, the central Volta Region was well incorporated into this regional trading system, linking the Ewe, Ga, and Akan areas with states and peoples further north.

Toward the east, the Ewe participated in trade heading north from Bagida on the coast to Kpalimé, Notsé, and Atakpamé in the interior and from there to the aforementioned commercial centers in the north. The main items exported from eastern Eweland were textiles, salt, and iron, and a common currency, the cowry shell, was widely in use. All these regional networks, of course, indirectly were linked to the continental Trans-Saharan trading system in the north.

These domestic networks likewise were transformed by the dynamics of Atlantic trade. In the eighteenth century, the Ewe-speaking areas became the source of increasing numbers of peoples who were enslaved by centralized, expansionist states, particularly the Akan kingdoms west of the Volta and Dahomey to the east of the Mono, and sold to Europeans. Slaving also occurred within Eweland as local traders acquired slaves at markets in Kpalimé, Notsé, and Atakpamé in exchange for salt and other commodities from the coast. The areas inhabited by the Northern Ewe in particular were convulsed by the slave trade.

While the slave trade clearly had devastating effects on individual lives, families, and communities, scholarly research has revealed that the general impact on Eweland was far more complex. The era was marked by regular invasions and slave raiding from outside and internal conflict and slave trading within Eweland yet subsistence agriculture was bolstered by the introduction of American crops such as cassava and maize via the Atlantic trade. These new staples fed a growing population, probably offsetting the loss of labor from the slave trade. Nevertheless, despite the possible economic growth associated with the coastal trade, the oral traditions of Ewe communities today highlight the disruptions, brutalities, and scars of the Trans-Atlantic Slave Trade.

The coast from the Volta to the Niger acquired the name "Slave Coast" by European cartographers as the Dutch, and later the English and the Danes, began to establish lodges along the Ewe part of this littoral. Keta and Aného became the two key towns through which the trade in human beings was conducted with Europeans although the numbers were significantly lower than the slave trade in major ports to the west (especially Elmina and Cape Coast) and east (Ouidah).[31] Trade in the Ewe towns increased during the eighteenth century, however, and in 1784, the Danes built a fort at Keta while Aného emerged as the secondary outlet (after Ouidah) for trade from Dahomey.[32] The enslavement and purchase of Ewes led to their dispersal across the Atlantic to the Americas, particularly to Brazil and Cuba, where they joined other ethnic groups in the formation of an African diaspora.

Access to and control of the slave trade fostered rivalry between Ewe polities and led to the formation of alliances with various non-Ewe states as well as European merchants. Competition over trade particularly was pronounced between the coastal Gun and Anlo who fought several wars in the 1680s for supremacy in the lagoon-trading network. For most of the eighteenth century, the Gun were the dominant power along the Ewe coast, exacting a monthly tribute from the Danes at Keta. At times, the Danes teamed up with Gun and Be forces in attacks on the Anlo who were also confronted by a hostile alliance of Krepi Ewes, including Peki, to the north. Gun-led alliances against the Anlo on occasion were joined by the Ada and the Akan-speaking Akwapim, both west of the Volta.

In response, the Anlo formed a long-lasting alliance with the Akan state of Akwamu and together they waged war against other Ewe polities. The Northern Ewe of the central Volta Region endured several invasions by the united Akwamu-Anlo Ewe forces during the early eighteenth century. At the turn of that century, the Akwamu crossed the Volta River and advanced eastward toward Dahomey. Two years later, they were forced to retreat from this area, only to return in 1707, when they successfully subjugated the Northern Ewe towns of Ho, Kpandu, and Peki.[33] Large numbers of Ewe were enslaved and forced from the area for sale at the European forts.[34] Akwamu exploited the discord which existed amongst the Northern Ewe and formed an alliance with the Peki Ewe, who provided assistance in the slave-raiding and military campaigns against other Ewe polities in the area.[35] The Akwamu were forced to leave the central Volta Region only in 1730 after their conquest by the Akyem, another expansionist Akan state, who themselves were defeated in 1742 by the Asante. The Akwamu-Anlo Ewe alliance, which provided the Anlo Ewe with military assistance in their local campaigns while granting Akwamu access to the coastal markets, persisted until the nineteenth century, despite the gradual decline of Akwamu's power.

To the east, the Gun also allied themselves sporadically with the Aja state of Allada against the latter's tributaries and, in the middle of the eighteenth century, Dahomey. The Gun attacked Dahomey's port, Ouidah, numerous times and signed and violated several peace treaties with the Fon kingdom. The overriding cause of all these inter-Ewe and regional conflicts was command of the trade in enslaved human beings in the interior and access to imported, mostly European goods, along the coast.

In the eighteenth century, Asante emerged as the most powerful state to the west of Eweland, eclipsing Akwamu and the other Akan kingdoms. The first Asante invasions across the Volta occurred in 1764, but their armies nearly were destroyed by the combined forces of the Dahomey and Oyo empires to the east. The political disunity of the Ewe benefited the Asante as they formed alliances with the Anlo in the late eighteenth century against the Ewe groups to the north on several occasions.[36]

The Asante state materialized in the late seventeenth century under the leadership of Osei Tutu, the first Asantehene (or king of the Asante). In about 1680, Kumasi was designated the capital and over the course of the following century, Asante gradually expanded its borders, defeating one state after another, including Denkyira in 1701,[37] Akwamu in 1731[38] and, again, Akyem during the following decade.[39] By this time, Opoku Ware was the Asantehene and Asante had extended its borders well beyond the Akan heartland,[40] fueled by its control of regional trading in kola to the north, gold to the south, and slaves in all directions, but particularly to the Europeans at the coast. By the middle of the nineteenth century, Asante's size exceeded that of Ghana at present, although the empire faced a formidable opponent in the British, who defeated the Asante armies at a battle at Katamansu (also known as the Battle of Dodowa) in 1826.

The wars waged by the Asante, and the related enslavement of the Ewe and other peoples, are well documented in the oral traditions of the central Volta Region. According to Gilbert Joel Nyavor of Kpandu, "... there was general insecurity [at this time]. This was because there was slave-raiding, robberies, and other crimes, coupled with constant Asante aggression on the Ewe states."[41] While details of the alliances between Ewe groups and non-Ewe states, such as Asante and Akwamu, are existent, the oral traditions emphasize the sporadic episodes of unified defense by the Ewe. John Vulie of Waya, for example, mentions that after the Asante-Anlo Ewe alliance had inflicted several defeats on the people of Ho and Peki, these two Northern Ewe subgroups "realized their folly ... [and] came together and that was how the scale changed in favor of Ho and her allies."[42]

Figure 2.2 Julius Agbigbi, an oral historian in Akpafu Todzi, with research assistants Divine Dzokoto (left) and Joseph Asamoah. (Photo by Dennis Laumann)

The Asante left lasting marks on the communities of the central Volta Region, particularly in terms of linguistic and cultural borrowings, but these are inconsistently attributed in the oral traditions. The Akan adaptations especially are evident in Akpafu Todzi, the Siwu-speaking town, where oral traditions state that Asante armies briefly settled in the town in order to regroup and secure much-needed iron products.[43] Linguistic and cultural traces of this short-lived Asante residence are apparent and acknowledged today. According to Julius Agbigbi (Figure 2.2):

> Within the years the Asante stayed with us while waging war on the Ewes, there was a lot of interaction between the two sides. We became one people and there developed one common drumbeat for us called *nfasu*.[44]

Emmanuel Amanku (Figure 2.3) continues:

> When the Asante stayed here close to three years, many things may have happened. Some of our people were fathered by the Asante. Some of these Asante children were left behind when their fathers finally left. Surely, we still have a few Akan words in our language.[45]

Fortified upon a mountain, Akpafu Todzi was able to escape the invasions and enslavement wrought upon the less fortunate Ewe-speaking populations on the plains and in the valleys below. Yet, distinctively Akan influences on the Siwu, introduced by the Asante during the height of their power, resulted from their momentary interaction.

Figure 2.3 Emmanuel Amanku, an oral historian in Akpafu Todzi. (Photo by Dennis Laumann)

Linguistic and cultural borrowings generally are not conceded in the Ewe-speaking towns of the central Volta Region, where the oral traditions are far more critical of the Asante. In Waya, the oral traditions accentuate the robust opposition the Asantes faced from the peoples of the central Volta Region. Hillarius Gikunu asserts:

> When [the Asante] turned toward the Ewes, they did not find it easy at all. Even then, they did not come to Adaklu directly, they went round until they came to Ho. Only a section of them came [to Waya]. They found it the toughest at Amed-zofe.[46]

The oral traditions of Waya depict at length the resistance the Asante faced in their attempts to conquer the Avatime. "At Amedzofe," Gikunu explains, "big stones were rolled down onto the Asante and their leader was killed."[47] Interestingly, oral traditions collected in Amedzofe itself do not place great emphasis on conflicts with the Asante.

Along the coast, the balance of power shifted as a civil war in Gun in 1821 diminished its power while Anlo benefited from expanded commerce with the Danes. The abolition of the slave trade by the British in 1807 led to the movement of Brazilian merchant families from Keta to Aného where the trade in human beings continued, albeit under the constant surveillance of British anti-slaving vessels.

As the slave trade gradually declined, the economies of the Ewe states, like others along the West African coast, shifted in the new era of so-called legitimate commerce. This was most evident in the expansion of oil palm plantations to satisfy demands for vegetable oils in Europe. The Brazilian families of Keta and Aného were instrumental in this development as they largely financed the new agricultural industry. In addition to oil palm, the growing of coconut palms expanded during this period and, toward the end of the century, cocoa cultivation spread throughout northern Eweland.

Commerce with Europeans, including the Germans who were relative newcomers to the trade, grew markedly by the middle of the nineteenth century. Beginning with the Friedrich M. Vietor Company in 1856, German firms were more active in the trade along the Slave Coast. Since the British dominated commerce along the Gold Coast and imposed increased duties on imported goods, the Germans were attracted to areas east of the Volta River, in their efforts to trade with "free ports." As a result, the Germans emerged as the principal European traders in (east to west) Grand Popo, Agoue, Little Popo (Aného), Beh Beach (Lomé), as well as Keta.

The Anlo Ewe continued to wage war during this period against the Ewe groups of the central Volta Region, often in union with the Asante, who were challenged by the British on the Gold Coast.[48] The boundaries of the British Gold Coast protectorate were extended in the 1850s to include the Peki Ewe state as well as the Akwapim and Krobo areas west of the Volta. This extension of British colonial occupation did not deter the Asante, who invaded the Krepi Ewe state in 1868 and in the following year subjugated Ho.

The expansion of European merchant (and missionary) activities clearly had ramifications in the political arena. European governments were increasingly answering calls from their bourgeoisie to officially declare protectorates over stretches of the West African coast in order to defend and monopolize trade. Coastal Eweland faced colonization by three European imperial powers: the British in Anlo; the Germans in the Bè, Watchi, and most of Gun areas; and the French in the extreme eastern part of Gun. Initially, the central Volta Region fell within the British sphere of influence.

British Colonial Occupation

The Asante and British fought several wars throughout the remainder of the nineteenth century, culminating in the British invasion of Kumasi in 1874, during which the British sacked the Asante capital. Later that year, the British signed a peace treaty with Asante and formally established the Gold Coast Colony, which included the Anlo Ewe and the Peki Ewe areas.[49] Asante imperial power was on the descent while the British gradually extended their occupation across other parts of the Akan and the Ewe areas. British power was further strengthened by the Treaty of Dzeukofe of 1874, in which the Anlo Ewe formally recognized British authority in the areas east of the Volta River. In 1880, the British regime created the Volta River District, which included the Krepi state, as well as the non-Ewe Krobo, Akwapim, and Shai groups. By this time, therefore, the Anlo Ewe state and most of the Northern Ewe territory were occupied by the British and incorporated into the Gold Coast Colony.

Besides the British imperial officers who subsequently assumed their posts in the towns of the central Volta Region, another group of Europeans, equally small in number but with a different self-proclaimed mandate, had resided in the area for several decades. These were the German missionaries who began proselytizing in the central Volta Region in the mid-nineteenth century and set up stations at Waya (in 1855) and Ho (1859). Indeed, the Ga, the Akan, and the Ewe speaking areas emerged as especially appealing and fruitful areas for proselytizing by Christians, and one missionary society after another established stations in the region.[50] Although the vast majority of the people in the central Volta Region did not embrace Christianity at this point, some interacted with the Germans; were introduced to their language, culture, religion, and technologies; and formed various kinds of relationships with Germans. By the end of the century, these missionaries were joined by other Germans, officials of the imperial regime based in Lomé, who were sent to occupy and administer the towns of the central Volta Region, creating a further series of introductions and relationships. Suddenly eager to follow the example of their competitors, the Germans joined the "scramble," leading to the imposition of a new and alien order in the central Volta Region.

Notes

1. I have based this estimate on the figures cited in M. E. Kropp Dakubu and K. C. Ford, "Central-Togo Languages," Chapter 6 in *The Languages of Ghana*, ed. by M. E. Kropp Dakubu (London: Kegan Paul International, 1988), 120–1.

2. Kropp Dakubu and Ford (*Ibid.*) divide the Central-Togo languages spoken in Ghana into three "clusters," one entirely and a second partly situated within the central Volta Region. The third cluster is found north of the area.

3. Kropp Dakubu and Ford, 124–6.

4. A condensed history of each of the speakers of the Central-Togo languages is provided in Bernd Heine, *Die Verbreitung und Gliederung der Togorestsprachen* (Berlin: Reimer, 1968).

5. A. S. Duthie lists a figure of 1.5 million (A. S. Duthie, "Ewe," Chapter 4 in *The Languages of Ghana*, ed. by M. E. Kropp Dakubu (London: Kegan Paul International, 1988), 92 while Amenumey claims that the combined Ewe population of Ghana and Togo is "a little over one million" (D. E. K. Amenumey, *The Ewe Unification Movement: A Political History* [Accra: Ghana Universities Press, 1989], 1). Although neither scholar lists the sources for their figures, these numbers are obviously dated. Based on the commonly accepted estimate that the Ewe constitute approximately 13%–15% of the Ghanaian population, which at the time of research was roughly 19–20 million, I arrived at this figure. According to the 2000 census of the Government of Ghana, the nation's population was 18,912,079 of which 12.7% were Ewe. The 2012 census lists a population of 24,658,823, with the Ewe constituting 13.9% of Ghana's people.

6. Akyeampong, 4–5.

7. This term derives from the common word for "language" in Ewe, Aja, and Fon (Edna G. Bay, *Wives of the Leopard: Gender, Politics, and Culture in the Kingdom of Dahomey* [Charlottesville: University of Virginia Press, 1998], 41).

8. The following chronology mostly is derived from D. E. K. Amenumey. *The Ewe in Pre-Colonial Times: A Political History with Special Emphasis on the Anlo, Ge and Krepi* (Accra: Sedco Publishing, 1986), and "A Brief History," Chapter 4 in *A Handbook of Eweland*, Vol. 1, *The Ewes of Southeastern Ghana*, ed. by Francis Agbodeka (Accra: Woeli Publishing Services, 1997), 14–27.

9. Amenumey, "A Brief History," 15. The group which later became known as the Fon separated from the Ewe groups and in the mid-sixteenth century established the town of Allada on the coast of Benin in the Aja-speaking area (Ansa K. Asamoa, *The Ewe of South-Eastern Ghana and Togo on the Eve of Colonialism: A Contribution to the Marxist Debate on pre-Capitalist Socio-Economic Formations* [Accra: Ghana Publishing Corp., 1986], 5). A series of migrations out of what became the kingdom of Allada to a plateau area of woodland savanna about 60 miles north of the coast occurred in the early seventeenth century. The migrants established the Fon kingdom of Dahomey in the 1620s. The kingdom gradually expanded into areas to the south and southeast of Abomey, the capital of Dahomey.

10. Amenumey, "A Brief History," 16.

11. See Sandra E. Greene, *Gender, Ethnicity, and Social Change on the Upper Slave Coast: A History of the Anlo-Ewe* (Portsmouth: Heinemann, 1996). For a version of the Agokoli legend, see Asamoa, 7–8. The flight from Notsé, also known as Amedzofe ("place of origin"), is commemorated in the annual Hogbetsotso festival.

12. M. E. Kropp Dakubu, "The Peopling of Southern Ghana: A Linguistic Viewpoint," Chapter 12 in *The Archaeological and Linguistic Reconstruction of African History*, ed. by Christopher Ehret and Merrick Posnansky (Berkeley: University of California Press, 1982), 245. The author's assertion is based on Heine's work.

13. Edward Kodzo Datsa details the migrations of the Avatime to their present-day locations from Notsé in the fourteenth century (Edward Kodzo Datsa [oral historian in Amedzofe], in discussion with the author, March 6, 1997 and April 17, 1997) while Johnson Agbemafle claims the Avatime migrated from the coast (Johnson Agbemafle [oral historian in Amedzofe], in discussion with the author, April 17, 1997).

14. As evidenced by Datsa's statement that "… the Avatimes are part of the Ewes" despite speaking a separate language (Edward Kodzo Datsa [oral historian in Amedzofe], in discussion with the author, April 17, 1997). On the politics of migration stories, see Paul Nugent, *Myths of Origin and the Origins of Myth: Local Politics and the Uses of History in Ghana's Volta Region* (Berlin: Das Arabische Buch, 1997).

15. Amenumey, *Ewe in Pre-Colonial Times*, 11–2.

16. Kropp Dakubu and Ford, 119–20.

17. Amenumey poses the following two questions related to the histories of the speakers of the Central-Togo languages: "Do they constitute the groups that successfully resisted Ewe hegemony? If so, do they have any memories of conflict with the Ewe immigrants and of other less fortunate neighbors who had succumbed to the Ewe?" (Amenumey, *Ewe in Pre-Colonial Times*, 10).

18. For studies on these communities, see Paul Nugent, "'A few lesser peoples,' The Central Togo minorities and their Ewe Neighbors," Chapter 8 in *Ethnicity in Ghana: The Limits of Invention*, ed. by Carola Lentz and Paul Nugent (New York: St. Martin's

Press, 2000) and, on Avatime specifically, Lynne Brydon, "Women in the Family: Cultural Change in Avatime, Ghana, 1900–80," *Development and Change*, Vol. 18 (1987), 251–269.

19. Amenumey, *The Ewe in Pre-Colonial Times*, 4.
20. Amenumey, *Ewe Unification*, 1.
21. An alternative categorization is as follows: (1) the Anlo Ewe and Some Ewe, who are situated along the coast; (2) the Tongu Ewe, who inhabit the lower Volta basin; and (3) the Ewedome (or Ewedometowo or Eweawo) Ewe, who reside in the area from Ho north to Hohoe (Kofi Baku, "The Asafo in Two Ewe States," *Transactions of the Historical Society of Ghana*, 2 [NS] [1998], 21–2).). In what is today southern Togo, the major subgroups along the coast (west to east) are the Bè, Gun, and Watchi. In the interior, they are (again west to east): the Agotime, Notsé, Atakpamé, and Tado. A very small population of Ewe, largely comprised of Gun, inhabits southwestern Benin.
22. Amenumey, *Ewe Unification*, 1. The Adaklu Ewe area includes Waya, one of the sites in which interviews were conducted.
23. The institution of paramount chief was more common and became more developed amongst groups in the western part of Eweland. Scholars have speculated that this may be attributed to the influences of Akan-speakers west of the Volta Region whose political systems included the paramount chiefship.
24. It has been argued that the decentralized nature of Ewe political institutions is a legacy of the reaction against the authoritarian rule experienced in Notsé. Amenumey, for example, writes that the Ewe "abhor tyranny" and characterizes Ewe polities as constitutional monarchies (Amenumey, *Ewe Unification*, 2). Distinctions between the "southern" Ewe (along the coast) and the "northern" Ewe (in the uplands region) are especially pronounced. For a succinct discussion of these differences, see Michel Verdon, *The Abutia Ewe of West Africa: A Chiefdom that Never Was* (Berlin: Mouton Publishers, 1983), 21–6. This division of the Ewe into southern and northern branches in the historical literature further complicates our understanding of Ewe history and culture for, as Verdon points out, the Tonu (or "middle" Ewe?) along the Volta are often ignored or subsumed with the Anlo Ewe.
25. Diedrich Westermann, *Die Glidyi-Ewe in Togo: Züge aus ihrem Gesellschaftsleben* (Berlin: Walter de Gruyter & Co., 1935), 125–6.
26. A stool is a symbol of chiefly authority, similar to a throne in the European royal tradition. Thus, being "de-stooled" is akin to a dethronement.
27. Verdon, 26.
28. A. Adu Boahen, "The states and cultures of the Lower Gunea Coast," Chapter 14 in *UNESCO General History of Africa, V, Africa from the Sixteenth to the Eighteenth Century*, ed. by B. A. Ogot (Berkeley: University of California Press, 1992), 404.
29. See F. Hupfeld, "Die Eisenindustrie in Togo," *Mitteilungen von Forschungsreisenden und Gelehrten aus den Schutzgebieten*, 12 (1899), 175–94; R. S. Rattray, "The Iron Workers of Akpafu," *Journal of the Royal Anthropological Institute*, XIX (NS) (1916), 431–5; and Leonard M. Pole, "Iron Working, Apparatus, and Techniques: Upper Region of Ghana," *West African Journal of Archaeology*, 5 (1975), 11–39.

30. Francis Agbewu (oral historian in Akpafu Todzi), in discussion with the author, June 17, 1997.

31. Along the Ewe coast, smaller slave markets also existed at Atoko, Blekusu, Adina, and Agoue.

32. According to calculations by Robert Harms, 40% of all slaves crossing the Atlantic in the early eighteenth century were shipped from Ouidah, making it the most active slave port in Africa (Robert Harms, *The Diligent* [New York: Basic Books, 2002], 92).

33. Boahen, "The states and cultures," 417. Before the Akwamu invasion, the Kwawu (or Kwahu) briefly had occupied parts of the Northern Ewe area in the late seventeenth century (Amenumey, *Ewe in Pre-Colonial Times*, 68).

34. Boahen, "The states and cultures," 408. The Northern Ewe states also were forced to pay tribute to Akwamu (Amenumey, *Ewe in Pre-Colonial Times*, 72).

35. Amenumey, *Ewe in Pre-Colonial Times*, 70.

36. Wars across the Volta basin continued in the early nineteenth century, when a Peki-led alliance of Krepi Ewes fought against a weakened Akwamu.

37. Denkyira was an Akan state that reached the zenith of power in the late seventeenth century, when it controlled areas of present-day southwestern Ghana as well as parts of Côte d'ivoire.

38. After its defeat, the Akwamu state repositioned itself east of the Volta River and established a new capital at Akwamufie.

39. Akyem earlier had defeated Asante at a battle on the Pra River in 1717, during which Asantehene Osei Tutu was killed. After the Asante victory, Akyem continued to remain one of the more powerful states in the region.

40. By 1745, both Gonja and Dagomba, two powerful states to the north, had become tributaries of Asante.

41. Gilbert Joel Nyavor (oral historian in Kpandu), in discussion with the author, March 5, 1997.

42. John Vulie (oral historian in Waya), in discussion with the author, June 16, 1997.

43. Francis Agbewu [oral historian in Akpafu Todzi], in discussion with the author, June 17, 1997. Another suggestion is that the Asante armies were waiting for supplies from Kumasi (Emmanuel Amanku (oral historian in Akpafu Todzi), in discussion with the author, June 17, 1997).

44. Julius Agbigbi (oral historian in Akpafu Todzi), in discussion with the author, June 17, 1997.

45. Emmanuel Amanku (oral historian in Akpafu Todzi), in discussion with the author, June 17, 1997.

46. Hillarius Gikunu (oral historian in Waya), in discussion with the author, June 16, 1997.

47. *Ibid.*

48. These wars between the Anlo Ewe and the Northern Ewe occurred during the following years: 1864–1865, 1868, and 1873–1874. The Anlo Ewe also formed an alliance in 1865 with the Asante against the Ada, who were supported by the British.

49. The Anlo Ewe state had been incorporated into the British sphere of influence in 1850, when the Danes sold all of their possessions along the coast, including the fort at Keta, to the British. As explained above, the Peki Ewe area became part of the protectorate in 1856.

In addition to these Ewe groups, the Gold Coast Colony also comprised a significant portion of the Akan areas (with the notable exception of Asante) as well as all of the Ga region. The capital of the Gold Coast Colony was Cape Coast until 1877, when it was moved to Christianborg (Osu in present-day Accra).

50. Several Christian missionary groups operated along the Gold Coast: the first missionaries from the Basel Missions arrived at Osu in 1828; the Methodists began their work along the Gold Coast in 1833; the Norddeutsche Missionsgesellschaft (or Bremen Mission) arrived in 1847; and the Roman Catholics established a mission at Elmina in 1881.

CHAPTER THREE

A Written History of the "Model Colony"

Misahöhe is a small Togolese town nestled in a mountainous, densely wooded area. It is not a significant place today, but Misahöhe had prominence in the German Togoland colony. It was from a hilltop here that Hans Gruner (Figure 3.1), the individual with whom many in the central Volta Region associate the German colonial period, administered the towns and villages near and far which comprised the Misahöhe Bezirk (German for "district"), an "enormous district," which Amenumey suggests encompassed "81 precolonial political units."[1]

Misahöhe is located approximately nine kilometers (about six miles) from the much larger town of Kpalimé and both are presently part of the Togolese prefecture of Klouto. While Kpalimé is the administrative center of the prefecture, Misahöhe was the "capital" of the German-era district. Today, at an altitude of 450 meters (1500 feet), one finds the remains of the German presence in Misahöhe, in the form of several dilapidated buildings, some in use by the local Togolese administration, others inhabited by families, and the rest entirely abandoned.[2] This is the station from which Gruner, the Bezirksamtsmann ("district commissioner") of Misahöhe for much of the German occupation (Table 3.1), ruled the area as a petty tyrant.

Gruner began his over 20-year, on- and off-again tenure in Misahöhe in 1892 but the Germans formally established the Togoland protectorate eight years earlier, when they occupied a 50-kilometer (31-mile) stretch of the West African coast between the Volta River estuary (controlled by the British) and the mouth of the Mono River (occupied by the French). In February 1884, a group of soldiers from the German warship "Sophie" kidnapped chiefs in Little Popo (Aného) and forced them into negotiations. This action resulted in a March "petition" to the German emperor to declare a protectorate ("Schutzgebiet" in German) over the town. Further west, a protectorate was proclaimed over the Lomé area in a treaty signed in July by Gustav Nachtigal, a German Imperial Commissioner, and Plakkoo, an official of the town of Togo, after which the new colony was named by the Germans.[3]

Table 3.1 District officials in Misahöhe[4]

Dates of posting	District official
May 1890–June 1892	Anton Bruno Herold
June 1892–May 1893	Hans Gruner
May 1893–June 1895	Ernst Baumann
June 1895–June 1897	Rudolf Plehn
June 1897–October 1899	Alexander Wegner
October 1899–November 1900	Hans Gruner
November 1900–February 1902	Julius Smend
February 1902–October 1904	Hans Gruner
October 1904–May 1905	Julius Smend
May 1905–April 1906	Rich Mühring
April 1906–December 1907	Hans Gruner
December 1907–July 1908	Gotthard Freude
July 1908–March 1909	Kurt von Parpart
March 1909–September 1910	Hans Gruner
September 1910–August 1911	Adam Mischlich
August 1911–January 1913	Hans Gruner
January 1913–August 1913	Wilhelm Mans
August 1913–August 1914	Hans Gruner

It was not until the 1890s, however, that the German regime began expanding their occupation to areas of central Togoland. The Misahöhe station was established on May 7, 1890 because of its proximity above the roads joining the commercial centers of neighboring Kpalimé and, approximately 105 kilometers (65 miles) to the northeast on the Volta River, Kete-Kratchi. The Germans hoped that an official presence in Misahöhe would force the redirection of Hausa-controlled commerce from areas in the north to Lomé instead of towards the coastal ports of Accra and Keta in the Gold Coast.[5]

Figure 3.1 Hans Gruner, from his collection. (Courtesy of Staastbibliothek zu Berlin—Preussischer Kulturbesitz, Handschriftenabteilung)

Like their imperialist counterparts elsewhere in Africa, the Germans preferred to set up their stations at higher altitudes for the more temperate climate and reduced prevalence of tropical diseases, such as malaria. Misahöhe was particularly attractive, according to historian M. B. K. Darkoh, because "under the protection of virgin forest, the harmattan was so modified as to be little felt, with a consequent gain in comfort and health."[6]

Misahöhe was designated a "scientific station" because its creation was financed at least partly by the Afrikafonds, a fund established by the German government in Berlin to sponsor agricultural research.[7] Most often the fund was used to cover the costs of the expansion of German-occupied territory. Sebald maintains "… this method made it possible to conceal the colonial objectives from the German people and to draw on the Afrikafonds, a fund set aside for scientific purposes, rather than on the colonial budget as a source of finance."[8] Thus, the decision to establish a station in Misahöhe was influenced by the German regime's paramount efforts to absorb territory and control commerce in Togoland, but was cloaked in a "scientific" disguise.

While Misahöhe and Kpalimé today are not situated in the central Volta Region, most of what was the Misahöhe district is presently part of that area of Ghana. Ho, Hohoe, and Kpandu were first occupied by the British as part of their Gold Coast colony, but were transferred to German Togoland through the Heligoland Treaty of July 1890.[9] Although all three of these towns were consigned to German occupation, the Krepi Ewe capital, Peki, remained part of the Gold Coast. As a result, this pact between European imperialists divided the Krepi state and, in the words of local historian A. K. Asem, "separated farms and lands from their owners, relatives from their families."[10]

Chiefs and Missionaries

In December of the same year, the Krepi King, Kwadzo Dei VI,[11] sent a letter to the Gold Coast governor in Christianborg (Osu in present-day Accra), William Brandford Griffith, protesting the new boundary agreement. In the correspondence, Kwadzo Dei VI derides the decisions by the chiefs of Ho and Kpandu to accept the German flag and maintains the issue is an internal Krepi matter, to be discussed between him and his subordinate chiefs.[12] Indeed, it appears the royal court at Kpandu viewed the new British-German boundary dividing the Krepi state as an opportunity to assert both its independence from Peki and its authority over surrounding Krepi Ewe towns and villages in the German territory.[13]

Dagadu II (or Dagadu Nyavor), the chief who ruled Kpandu from c.1866 to 1897, was allied with the British, but now his town was incorporated into German

Togoland (Figure 3.2). It was not until four years after the Heligoland Treaty, however, that the Germans attempted to forcibly occupy Kpandu and the surrounding area. In 1894, the newly reorganized and strengthened Polizeitruppe ("police troop") attacked and destroyed several towns in the area, confiscated property, and imposed fines on some of the inhabitants of the razed communities.[14] The following year, outright war erupted in the nearby Tove area, where the Germans put down an uprising which successfully blocked a road leading to Kete-Kratchi for several weeks. The *Gold Coast Chronicle* reported that German soldiers shipped the decapitated heads of those they killed to Germany, a common practice amongst German officers, as noted by historian Andrew Zimmerman, ostensibly for so-called anthropological study.[15] It was through such measures, "diplomatic," violent, and gruesome, that the Germans extended the areas they occupied and sought to impose the new colonial order.

A German station was established at Kpandu in 1897, the same year Dagadu III (Dagadu Anku) succeeded Dagadu II as chief, but according to Amenumey, it was not until 1903 that the Germans completely extended their authority over the area. The treaty negotiated by the British and the Germans, and the subsequent occupation by the German imperialists, drastically altered political relations in the area. Despite its partial success establishing independence from Peki, German colonization, Amenumey writes,

> dealt a blow to Kpandu's power and prestige by setting a number of Kpandu's former vassal villages up as independent of it. After this, Dagadu's position could not be compared with that of even a subchief in the neighboring Gold Coast.[16]

In the eyes of the Germans, Dagadu III simply was a chief who had to play his assigned role in the administration of the colonial state. Chiefs in the central Volta Region, and throughout southern Togoland, served a function similar to that of their counterparts in the British colonies, where the policy of "indirect rule" was practiced. According to Knoll, the Germans experimented with forms of direct and indirect rule, and the chiefs

> held court, publicized the orders of the [German] government, supervised the collection of taxes, reported contagious diseases, mustered villagers for tax work, and directed people to keep paths and roads clear.[17]

Figure 3.2 Dagadu II, from the collection of Hans Gruner. (Courtesy of Staastbibliothek zu Berlin—Preussischer Kulturbesitz, Handschriftenabteilung)

Chiefs received a minimal share of the taxes collected, were permitted to employ one police officer, and were issued "official garb" to wear, "even if it was only a replica of the caps worn by postal officials in Germany."[18] While they had jurisdiction over civil cases, criminal matters were handled by the German regime.[19] The chiefs were selected by the colonial government, and most were replacements for their predecessors who had signed "treaties" with the Germans. The new chiefs, generally younger and chosen for their "energy and obedience," often were viewed as illegitimate by the populations they presided over and "commanded little respect from the community elders."[20] But, with the financial and military backing of the German regime, these chiefs frequently exploited their newfound positions of authority.

Howusu, the chief of Ho, was one such individual.[21] Appointed by the Germans to his position, Howusu may not have been viewed as a legitimate chief by the people of Ho and the surrounding communities. As a result, in 1895, Howusu requested the use of the colonial police to intimidate neighboring villages, which he claimed wanted to declare independence from Ho. According to a German official, Howusu hoped the show of force would "make clear" their duties to him.[22]

The German regime formally established a station at Ho only in 1899, but there were Germans resident in the town for decades. The North German Missionary Society ("Norddeutsche Missionsgesellschaft" in German) set up a station there in 1859.[23] The Heligoland Treaty of 1890 not only resulted in the further division of the Ewe, the occupation of the area by the Germans, and the consequent realignment of relations between Ewe polities, but also solidified the position of the North German Missionary Society in the central Volta Region. This group was active in the general area since 1847, when it founded a station in Peki in what was to become the Gold Coast. By the end of 1890, the North German Missionary Society set up two additional stations, one in Ho and the other in Amedzofe, as well as nine secondary stations,[24] all of which were incorporated into Togoland. As a result, according to historian Ralph Erbar, the North German Missionary Society became, "against its will," a "national" mission in German-occupied territory and banned from the Gold Coast.[25] In the latter, the Swiss Basel Missionary Society ("Evangelische Missionsgesellschaft in Basel" in German) was largely responsible for missionary activities.

While both governmental and missionary stations were established in Ho and Kpandu, other important towns in the central Volta Region lacked the permanent presence of the German regime but nonetheless were the bases for missionary activities. Just as the German regime created capitals and "sub-capitals" in each of its districts, the missionary societies operated within a similar structure. The towns of Akpafu Todzi and Waya were the sites of two of the secondary stations of the North German Missionary Society,[26] but neither town had a governmental headquarters. Likewise Amedzofe was one of the two primary stations of the missionaries (along with Ho), but it lacked a German colonial office.[27] The North German Missionaries thus were active throughout the entire central Volta Region. In addition, the Roman Catholic Steyler Mission established stations in Kpandu, Hohoe, and Ho.[28]

Although these religious societies successfully opened stations, which included churches, schools, and missionary residences, the German regime had not yet completely "pacified" the central Volta Region or most of Togoland. By the end of the nineteenth century, the borders of Togoland finally were established by the European occupiers of West Africa,[29] and the German administration permanently was based in the capital of Lomé (Figure 3.3). Despite the recognition of Togoland's borders by European imperialists, roughly ninety percent of the Togolander population still lived in independent and free territories.[30] Through "scientific explorations," the establishment of government stations, and the display and use of military strength, the Germans strove to expand the areas under their control.

Resistance and Control

These German efforts were met with resistance, of course. While wars between the Germans and several African polities raged in the north of the colony,[31] the people of the central Volta Region opposed the German occupation by other methods. Only two years after the formal establishment of a German governmental presence in Ho, for instance, a petition was sent in April 1901 by residents of the town to the regime in Lomé. The petitioners complained about the forced labor imposed on them by the Germans as well as the government's interference in agriculture. The regime began pursuing aggressive economic policies in the areas it occupied in order to increase the export of cash crops from Togoland. As a result, the Germans attempted to force farmers to grow certain crops and change their agricultural practices. The petition from Ho cited the German ban on shifting (also known as "slash-and-burn") cultivation as an especially unpopular policy amongst the farmers. Additionally, Togolanders were forced to perform unpaid labor to construct the roads and railways intended to facilitate the delivery of agricultural products to the coast. The construction of roads as well as homes for Hausa merchants were two of the forced labor activities decried by the people of Ho in their petition. More general complaints about the German occupation also were listed in the document. According to Knoll,

> [the petitioners] maintained that recent events did not fulfill German promises of a mild and just government ... [they] said that some tribes blamed them for having originally supported German rule. [They] concluded that their burden of existence had increased since the Germans arrived.[32]

Jakob Spieth, one of the missionaries based at Ho and an author of several studies on the Ewe, wrote an accompanying letter of support. He addresses the forced labor issue and additionally describes the "momentous movement" of Togolanders to the

Gold Coast in order to avoid this burden. Interestingly, Spieth also recognizes the people of Ho "blamed the mission for their difficulties. They said the mission came to Ho first; it was then followed by the German government." When Gruner, the district commissioner in Misahöhe, again returned to his posting in February 1902, it appears relations between the people of Ho and the local German administration improved somewhat, but Gruner conceded in a report to the government in Lomé that emigration from his district to the Gold Coast continued unabated.[33]

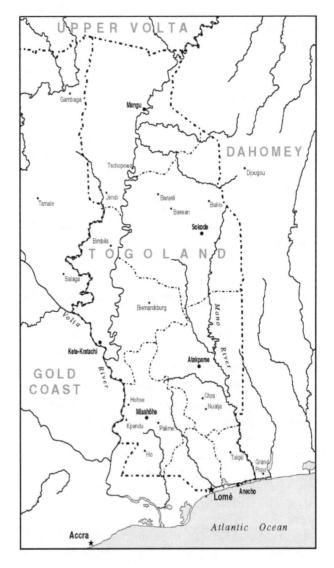

Figure 3.3 German Togoland. (Courtesy of University of Madison-Wisconsin Cartography Lab)

In fact, flight from the Misahöhe district assumed "enormous proportions," according to Amenumey.[34] He explains, "Emigration was not limited to ordinary citizens. Even chiefs joined in the stream. Emigration was usually in small parties and usually took place at night."[35] In fact, Howusu, the chief of Ho, was eventually granted asylum in the British-occupied territory, according to historian A. K. Asem.[36] The people of Ho had experienced British rule and many concluded, Asem argues, that "the treatment of citizens under the British protectorate was better than what obtained in the German protectorate, where conditions were rather harsh."[37] Knoll concurs:

> Lomé required much more of its people than Accra did. Government impinged on the [people of] Ho in its most coercive way; it required labor and taxes, and it hindered the movement of people. It regulated trade and it disrupted traditional modes of existence.[38]

Interference in the preexisting commercial systems especially was resented by the Togolanders. Merchants were prohibited by the regime from participating in the export of produce and manufactured goods and thus were restricted to the retail trade.[39] Despite the impact of these measures, Amenumey insists that emigration to the Gold Coast was not based on economic necessity, but "... was a reaction against authoritarianism."[40]

The exodus was considered such a serious problem by the Germans that they instituted a pass system in 1899. Zimmerman explains that those who violated its terms could be subject to large fines and lengthy prison sentences, including forced labor. He continues: "Under such restrictive regimes, many Togo[landers] surreptitiously crossed the border, often with the help of labor recruiters." He also notes that at least one German official argued emigration reduced agricultural output in the colony.[41]

Crucial in the process of imposing political and economic control were the small number of German district commissioners posted throughout the colony. These officials exercised nearly complete administrative, judicial, and military authority. Knoll describes this situation, using Misahöhe as an example:

> ... the district officer performed many tasks. He served as local court of appeal, explored his district, tended experimental gardens, encouraged the building of roads, supervised taxation, took the census, combated infectious diseases, made cartographical and weather measurements, and mustered workers.[42]

Despite this flattering portrayal, it was through sheer force that the district commissioners carried out orders from the German regime in Lomé. As Sebald argues "their rule was based on support by mercenary troops and on a judicial system with a preference for corporal punishment."[43] One Togolander writer claimed in a letter to the Reichstag that Gruner governed Misahöhe as a "Demi-god."[44]

The penal code of April 1896 granted district officers nearly absolute authority over the population they ruled.[45] They were allowed to punish Togolanders through flogging (or whipping), by delivering a sentence of hard labor, and by imposing fines. Only the administration in Lomé could issue death sentences, however, and these became increasingly rare toward the end of the occupation. Overall, flogging remained the most popular form of punishment amongst the district commissioners throughout the German period.[46]

A formal military was not established in Togoland. Instead, the regime relied on a "police contingent," the Polizeitruppe, which never exceeded 500 members (of which only several were European) throughout the occupation, to enforce its orders. The police were used in military engagements and to supervise forced laborers. In 1907, the German regime codified obligatory labor, which, until then, had not been regulated. The new decree specified that all compulsory labor should be salaried and used exclusively for public works projects. Despite these restrictions, flogging was still employed as the primary means of making Togolanders perform forced labor.[47] This measure not only served the purposes of building up the colonial infrastructure, but provided another source of revenue as Togolanders could opt to perform labor as an alternative to paying taxes.[48] Both direct and indirect taxes were imposed on the Togolanders, ranging from import duties, which remained the regime's main source of income throughout the occupation, to income, "urban," emigration, and dog taxes, as well as a tax for flying the German flag.[49]

Cash Crop Economy

The German officials in the Misahöhe district were notoriously zealous in their implementation of government policies. The central Volta Region was attractive to the Germans, due to its rich soil and thus its potential for cash crops, many of which were cultivated in the area long before the Germans arrived.

The regime primarily was interested in promoting the expansion of cotton cultivation, since they hoped to reduce Germany's dependence on imports from the United States. A flourishing trade in cotton throughout the central Volta Region existed well before the German occupation.[50] The Germans sought to expand cultivation and to control the buying and selling of cotton. In addition, the regime wanted to introduce new varieties of cotton to Togolander farmers.

In pursuing these goals, the Germans enlisted the services of African American scientists based at the Tuskegee Institute in Alabama.[51] This group of experts, who traveled from the segregated American south to colonized West Africa, began their work in January 1901 in Tove near Misahöhe. Their project was considered a great success by the Germans, despite the death of a number of the Americans and problems encountered with some of their experiments.[52] They operated several experimental farms, distributed seeds of new cotton species, and instructed Togolander farmers. Gruner also was actively involved in the cotton-growing schemes and wrote numerous articles on cultivation of cotton and other crops in the Misahöhe District.[53]

Gruner's enthusiasm for the cotton campaign was grounded not only in its economic potential, but also as a method of social control. As Zimmerman argues, "Gruner saw in cotton farming a means of establishing a patriarchal monogamy" as he sought "to make people less mobile, discouraging women from traveling as merchants and men from traveling as porters or for other work." This was not a hidden agenda but one which Germans officials sometimes publicly declared and certainly wrote about in reports and other official documentation. In a forum with African chiefs and missionaries, for example, Gruner promoted what he termed "orderly family relations" which he argued would result from German agricultural policies. Thus, like imperialists elsewhere, the Germans sought to impose their notions of domestic relationships and spaces and, in their estimation, cotton cultivation aided that process.[54]

The Togo Baumwollgesellschaft ("cotton society") operated ginning factories in the central Volta Region at Ho and Kpandu.[55] An agricultural school, specializing in cotton, was opened in 1904 in Notsé, located southeast of Misahöhe. The nearby district of Atakpamé also was a major producer of cotton, as evidenced by the nickname Baumwollbahn ("cotton railway") for the 163-mile rail link between Lomé and Atakpamé, which was completed in 1913.[56] Through the efforts of individual Togolander farmers, exports of cotton from Togoland increased dramatically, from 14,553 kilos in 1902 to approximately 502,000 in 1913.[57]

In addition to cotton, the Germans encouraged (and sometimes sought to force) the cultivation of cocoa, coconut, coffee, rubber, and sisal. Cocoa, however, was not introduced to the area by the Germans but was embraced by farmers in the central Volta Region on the recommendation of Togolanders who had worked in the Gold Coast.[58]

The Germans attempted to intensify the cultivation of these cash crops, partly through the establishment of plantations.[59] By the end of the German occupation, cocoa and coffee plantations were found throughout the central Volta Region, including in Avatime (the area around Amedzofe), Ho, and Kpandu, as well as in Kpalimé to the east.[60] In 1893, Gruner "negotiated" a 100-year rent-free lease for several hundred hectares of land from "King Date of Jo" for the creation of a coffee plantation.[61] Historian M. B. K. Darkoh claims nearly 86% of cultivation in the Misahöhe district was devoted to cocoa in the final years of the German period.[62] The 60-mile Kakaoeisenbahn ("cocoa railway"), linking Lomé and Kpalimé, was begun in 1904 and completed in 1907, its name attesting to the importance of the cash crop to the district.[63]

The cultivation and export of cocoa and coffee steadily increased during the German occupation. In addition, rubber collected from forests as well as maize emerged as important exports. The Germans introduced seedlings of teak imported from India and Thailand (then Siam), although there also were local species of this tree, in order to encourage its cultivation, partly for aesthetic purposes.[64]

Palm oil and palm kernels, however, consistently remained the top export crops from Togoland, and the production of these also gradually increased throughout the German period. Despite the expansion of palm cultivation, its share of the annual export totals declined sharply due to the growth of other cash crops. While palm products accounted for 89% of total exports from Togoland in 1895, by 1911 this figure had decreased to a still considerable 52%.[65] Kpalimé emerged as an extremely important palm kernel collection center and, according to historian Donna J. E. Maier, "the areas of Leklebi, Avatime, and Kpedze may have actually abandoned much food farming to devote themselves to palm kernel production."[66]

The central Volta Region therefore became an especially important area for the export of the cash crops, particularly cotton, which the German regime encouraged farmers to cultivate. As geographers Kwamina B. Dickson and George Benneh assert: "exports from [central Togoland] were more regular than those of the same crops from southern Ghana west of the Volta, where the British did not become involved in commercial agriculture to the same extent."[67]

A series of rail and road links were crucial in expeditious delivery of these agricultural products for export. Between 1900 and 1914, 766 miles of roads were built throughout German Togoland, mostly through the use of forced labor, in addition to three railways from the coast to the interior. These included the aforementioned Lomé-Kpalimé railway as well as several roads in the central Volta Region. Maier states that "the roads alone stimulated trade tremendously."[68] Moreover, communication and commercial connections were expanded. Ho, Kpandu, and Misahöhe all were linked to one another by telegraphic communications and post offices were established at Ho, Kpandu, and Kpalimé.[69]

In contrast, the regime invested minimally in social services. Health care was out of reach, since there were only a few hospitals in the entire colony and not all of these provided services to Togolanders.[70] After the completion of a new hospital in Little Popo in 1893, for example, the regime decided that only Germans could be treated there.[71] Nevertheless, like their fellow European imperialists in Africa, the Germans were obsessed with fighting contagious diseases, such as smallpox and sleeping sickness. Toward this effort, the Germans did provide some healthcare and enacted various, often draconian, measures. On the outskirts of Kpalimé, for example, a hospital was built for patients who the Germans diagnosed with sleeping sickness and forcibly interned during a suspected outbreak that was questioned by Togolanders.[72]

The Germans invested even fewer resources in education for the Togolanders, relying on the missionary societies to provide schooling at their stations. Toward the end of the occupation, the regime did establish several governmental schools, standardize the curriculum, and regulate the missionary schools.[73] However, educational opportunities remained extremely limited for the Togolanders, as few students were allowed to complete secondary school. By 1912, only two secondary schools, enrolling 180 students and operated by eight African and two German teachers, had been built by the regime. As a result, children often were sent by their families to the Gold Coast for post-primary education.[74]

The violence, burdens, and abuses, which characterized the German occupation, vitiated the potential benefits of any infrastructural development and social services to the population of the central Volta Region. As Maier succinctly asserts, "The public works projects were all completed with the use of forced labor."[75] Social services provided to the Togolanders were grossly inadequate. And the German regime failed to invest any significant sum in the development of industries in the colony.[76] Like true imperialists, virtually all expenditures by the German regime were directed towards the sole interest of the colonial state: the extraction of raw materials.

Resistance to the German regime continued unabated throughout the occupation, despite propaganda perpetuated in Germany (and elsewhere in Europe) that Togoland was a "model colony."[77] A notable exception to the German rhetoric was Gottlob Adolf Krause, a German merchant, linguist, and critic of colonialism, who authored numerous reports about German abuses in Togoland.[78] In a 1900 article in the Berliner Tageblatt, for instance, Krause claims:

> Each time a war with the natives breaks out through the fault of some official, the people back [in Germany] are told nothing but that a war has taken place, that it is over now and they have to foot the bill. There is never any mention of the whys and the wherefores ... According to the telegraphic message all is quiet in the protectorate. Everything is indeed quiet, the dead lie peacefully in their graves and the wounded on their sick-beds, and the rest have been put to rot.[79]

Since Togoland lacked a formal military force, Sebald explains, "Even major campaigns were described as police operations, which made it easier to conceal their true character from the German public."[80]

Model colony propaganda included praise for the Germans who ruled Togoland. Julius Graf Zech, who served as governor from 1903 to 1910, was referred to as the colony's "modernizer" and "lawmaker"[81] and was "a self-conceived humanitarian."[82] But, according to historian Woodruff D. Smith, this governor "created concentration camps for political prisoners and developed a means of assembling forced labor"[83]

The reality of daily life for many Togolanders during the German occupation included being forced to perform unpaid labor and being subjected to excessive and capricious punishment as well as rape, child molestation, and other violations of what we understand today to constitute basic human rights. The written record is replete with examples of these abuses in the central Volta Region. For example, the people of Ho complained about police tactics in 1909, stating the police "roamed their district with loaded rifles."[84] Knoll writes: "Many Togol[anders] felt they lived under an arbitrary and harsh regime. They could be disciplined with fifteen strokes for offenses as subjective and vague as 'perpetual laziness.'"[85] As Sebald argues:

> The general lack of rights, the practice of corporal punishment, the economic reprisals—indeed the whole of German colonial policy—led the Togo[landers] to conclude after 30 years of German rule that they wanted to get rid of the colonial power. The documents make nonsense of all subsequent attempts to glorify conditions in the 'model colony.'

In 1914, Sebald concludes,

> ... the Togol[anders] people showed their feelings very clearly. As soon as word came of the outbreak of the Great War, the inhabitants of the Volta region cast off the German yoke even before British soldiers appeared on the scene.[86]

The small German police force, after exploding the transcontinental radio station built at Kamina near Atakpamé, quickly surrendered on August 26 to the combined forces of the British and the French, which had invaded from their neighboring colonies. The people of the central Volta Region, some for the first time and others yet again, were now living under British occupation.

Notes

1. D. E. K. Amenumey, "German Administration in Southern Togo," *Journal of African History*, X: 4 (1969), 627. There were eight districts in Togoland: Lomé, Lomé-Land and Anécho along the coast; Misahöhe, Atakpamé, and Kete-Kratchi in central Togoland; and Sokode-Bassari and Mangu-Yendi in the north of the colony.

2. The buildings include the offices, residences, and jail of the Misahöhe station. For photographs of these structures and others, see Wolfgang Lauber (ed.), *Deutsche Architektur in Togo 1884–1914* (Stuttgart: Karl Krämer Verlag, 1993), 72–3.

3. For the German-language text of the "treaty," see Peter Sebald, *Togo 1884–1914: Eine Geschichte der deutschen "Muster-kolonie" auf der Grundlage amtlicher Quellen* (Berlin: Akademie-Verlag, 1988), 43–4.

4. Peter Sebald, "Der Berzirk Misahöhe" (unpublished manuscript), based on Staatsbibliothek Berlin File FA2/233 (Gruner, 7 Januar 1901), Staatsbibliothek Berlin File FA2/249 (Parpart, 17 April 1907, i.V), and Staatsbibliothek Berlin File FA2/24, s. 3 (ende September von Hirschfeld i.V.).

5. Misahöhe was promoted to a "Kaiserliches Bezirkamt" ("royal district headquarters") or district capital on January 7, 1904. The station was named by Jesko von Puttkamer, the Landeshauptmann ("chief of staff") of Togoland during the first half of the 1890s, after his former lover Misa von Esterhazy (Sebald, *Togo*, 87). The position of Landeshauptmann was replaced with the Governor in 1898. Kete-Kratchi is situated in the present-day Volta Region of Ghana and was located in the far west of German Togoland.

6. M. B. K. Darkoh, "Togoland under the Germans: Thirty Years of Economic Development— Part II," *Nigerian Geographical Journal*, 11:2 (December 1968), 153. Harmattan refers to the season, generally from December to February, when dry, dusty winds sweep across the West Africa coast.

7. Arthur J. Knoll, *Togo Under Imperial Germany* (Stanford: Hoover Institution Press, 1978), 42.

8. Peter Sebald, "Togo 1884–1900," Chapter 3 in *German Imperialism in Africa: From the Beginnings Until the Second World War*, ed. by Helmuth Stoecker (London: C. Hurst & Co., 1986), 89.

9. Knoll, 55. In return for the island of Heligoland in the North Sea as well as sections of the Volta River basin, Germany guaranteed Britain's exclusive right to occupy Uganda as part of this treaty. Other important areas in the Volta region which were ceded to the Germans were Adaklu, located south of Ho, and Buem, to the north of Hohoe. The transfer of Ho, Hohoe, and Kpandu to Togoland resulted in the increased importance of the Misahöhe station (Sebald, *Togo*, 87).

10. A. K. Asem, *A History of Awudome* (Tema: Ghana Publishing Corporation, 1973), 17.

11. Kwadzo Dei VI was king of Krepi from 1879 until 1901. "Kwadzo" is also written as "Kwadjo" in sources and "Dei" as "Deo."

12. The text of this letter appears in Asem, 48. Kwadzo Dei VI speculated that the British agreed to the division of Krepi because they owed money to the Germans for assistance in the war against Asante from 1873 to 1874 (Knoll, 34). Both the chiefs of Ho and Kpandu

signed the Bond of October 1886 incorporating Krepi into the Gold Coast. The text of the Bond appears in Asem, 40–5.

13. See David Brown, "Anglo-German Rivalry and Krepi Politics," *Transactions of the Historical Society of Ghana*, vol. XV (ii): 201–213.

14. Amenumey, "German Administration," 625.

15. Andrew Zimmerman, *Alabama in Africa: Booker T. Washington, the German Empire, and the Globalization of the New South* (Princeton: Princeton University Press, 2010), 131. In German South-West Africa, where the Germans committed genocide against the Herero from 1904 to 1907, women interned in concentration camps were forced to boil and scrape the skin off the heads of Herero who had been killed. Those skulls were then shipped off to Germany for museum displays and eugenics research.

16. Amenumey, "German Administration," 631. After continued protests about the German regime's policies, especially after a supposed outbreak of sleeping sickness discussed below, Dagadu III was deposed and deported to the Cameroons in March 1914. See Dennis Laumann, "Domination and Resistance: Epidemic and Exile in the German Togoland Colony," *Afrika Zamani*, No. 17 (2009): 1–16.

17. Knoll, 47.

18. *Ibid.*, 48. Sebald clarifies that only *some* chiefs were permitted the one police officer (personal correspondence).

19. Amenumey, "German Administration," 630. Only civil cases up to a value of 200 Marks could be decided by chiefs and all their decisions could be appealed to the German district commissioners. In judicial matters, the chiefs in Misahöhe, and other districts in central and northern Togoland, were allowed greater authority than their counterparts along the coast, where the German regime handled almost all civil cases, as well.

20. Knoll, 48.

21. Howusu also appears as "Hosu" and "Awoosoo" in various sources. Amenumey lists Kumi as the chief of the Dome stool in Ho during this period. Kumi, who was chief from 1886 to 1898, was the son of Ameko, who was also known as Wusu and served as chief from 1845 to 1852. It is possible that Howusu adopted the name of his father (i.e., Wusu), which may be a stool name. A second stool, the Banyakoe, also exists in Ho. For the lists of chiefs from these two stools, see Amenumey, *Ewe in Pre-Colonial Times*, 109.

22. Sebald, *Togo*, 169.

23. For a history of missionary activity in Togoland, see Hans W. Debrunner, *A Church Between Colonial Powers: A Study of the Church in Togo* (London: Lutterworth Press, 1965). The North German Missionary Society also is referred to as the "Bremen Mission" since it was based in the German city of Bremen. For accounts from this period by North German missionaries, see Gustav Müller, *Geschichte der Ewe-Mission* (Bremen: Verlag der Nordeutschen Missions-Gesellechaft, 1904) and Martin Schlunk, *Die Norddeutsche Mission in Togo*, Erster Band: *Meine Reise durchs Eweland* (Bremen: Verlag der Norddeutschen Missions-Gesellschaft, 1910).

24. These were in Kpewe, Akowieve, Matse, Abutia, Waya, Abudia, Wodze, Leglebi, and Anfoe.

25. Ralph Erbar, *Ein "Platz an der Sonne"?: Die Verwaltungs- und Wirtschaftsgeschichte der deutschen Kolonie Togo 1884–1914* (Stuttgart: Steiner, 1991), 239. As further proof of the

North German Missionary Society's new mandate, in July 1891 the German regime attempted to ban the use of English as a language of instruction in the missionary school in Ho, but this order was rescinded after a plea by one of the missionaries. The ban went into effect in 1904, however, as German colonial officials pressured missionaries to promote German language and culture. See Benjamin Lawrance, "Most Obedient Servants: The Politics of Language in German Colonial Togo," *Cahiers d'études africaines* 159/XL (2000): 489–524.

26. The station in Akpafu was established in 1905 and the one in Waya in 1855. Akpafu along with Kpandu were sites for proselytizing by the Basel missionaries, but after 1903 missionary work in those towns was transferred to the North Germans (Debrunner, 109).

27. The Amedzofe station was established in 1890.

28. The Steyler Mission was based in Holland and became active in the area in the early 1890s. The stations in Kpandu and Hohoe were established in 1904 and the one in Ho in 1908. See Debrunner as well as Müller. The latter history was published by the Steyler Mission.

29. In the east, Togoland shared the Mono River with the French colony of Dahomey up to the seventh parallel, where the river fell entirely into German-occupied territory. Togoland bordered the French colony of Haute-Volta (present-day Burkina Faso) in the north, while the Gold Coast was situated to the west. These borders were ratified by the European imperialists in the Treaty of Paris in 1897.

30. Sebald, "Togo 1884–1900," 92.

31. The Dagomba and Konkomba in northern Togoland opposed the efforts by the German regime to occupy their territories and to control and redirect trade in their areas. As a result, both peoples, sometimes in alliance, fought several wars with the Germans until the turn of the century.

32. Knoll, 55.

33. *Ibid.*

34. Emigration continued at high levels throughout the entire German occupation. In 1910, for example, an estimated 14,000 people left the Misahöhe district for the Gold Coast (Amenumey, "German Administration," 635).

35. *Ibid.*, 637.

36. Asem, 23. Howusu's emigration to the Gold Coast is not confirmed by other secondary sources. Asem states that Howusu was given asylum in Akuapim while Chief Yaw Takyi of Taviefe settled in Awudome after receiving asylum there. Asem explains: "The conditions on which asylum was granted were that they would conform to British Law and refrain from interfering with persons in the German protectorate. Chief Hosu (or Howusu) was also made to return his black stool to Ho in 1910, through His Excellency the Governor" (*Ibid.*, 24).

37. *Ibid.*, 23.

38. Knoll, 56.

39. Amenumey, *Ewe Unification Movement*, 4.

40. *Ibid.*, 8. In his study of the town of Have, Ken Kwaku argues that "ambitious individuals" traveled to the Gold Coast, "where the range of jobs and financial returns were considered greater," particularly in the mining and cocoa growing areas (Ken Kwaku, "Tradition, Co-

lonialism, and Politics in Rural Ghana: Local Politics in Have, Volta Region," *Canadian Journal of African Studies*, 10/1 [1976], 76).

41. Zimmerman, *Alabama in Africa*, 138.

42. Knoll, 43.

43. Sebald, "Togo 1900–1914," 175.

44. As quoted in Sebald, *Togo*, 660. The letter, dated 12 May 1914, was signed by "Herald Patriot Diasempa."

45. The only limitations to this policy was that approval from the governor was required for fines over 300 Marks, prison sentences over six months, and execution (Amenumey, "German Administration," 628).

46. *Ibid.*

47. *Ibid.*, 630.

48. Sebald, "Togo 1900–1914," 176.

49. Amenumey, "German Administration," 632 and Amenumey, *Ewe Unification*, 4.

50. See Donna J. E. Maier, "Persistence of precolonial patterns of production: cotton in German Togoland, 1800–1914," Chapter 4 in *Cotton, Colonialism, and Social History in Sub-Saharan Africa*, ed. by Allen Isaacman and Richard Roberts (Portsmouth: Heinemann, 1995), 71–95.

51. See Kendahl Radcliffe, *The Tuskegee-Togo Cotton Scheme, 1900–1909*, unpublished PhD dissertation (Los Angeles: University of California, Los Angeles, 1998); Andrew Zimmerman, "A German Alabama in Africa: The Tuskegee Expedition to German Togo and the Transnational Origins of West African Cotton Growers," *The American Historical Review*, vol. 110, no. 5 (December 2005): 1362–1398; and Zimmerman, *Alabama in Africa*.

52. Togolese scholar Ali Napo, however, concludes that the project was unsuccessful since only one of the Tuskegee scientists remained in Togoland for any considerable amount of time. See Ali Napo, *Le Togo à l'époche allemande: 1884–1914*, unpublished doctoral dissertation (Paris: Sorbonne, n.d.).

53. These appeared in the *Amtsblatt für das Schutzgebiet Togo*, an official government publication.

54. Zimmerman, *Alabama in Africa*, 142.

55. M. B. K. Darkoh, "Togoland under the Germans: Thirty Years of Economic Development—Part I," *Nigerian Geographical Journal*, 10:2 (December 1967), 122. Elsewhere in the Misahöhe district, the organization had a factory at Kpalimé. The structure in Kpandu remains today but no longer serves the same function. For a study of the German remains in Kpandu, see Wazi Apoh, "The Archaeology of German and British Colonial Entanglements in Kpando-Ghana," *International Journal of Historical Archaeology* 17 (2013): 351–375.

56. Darkoh, "Togoland under the Germans: Thirty Years of Economic Development—Part II," 158.

57. Amenumey, "German Administration," 634.

58. Sebald, "Togo 1900–1914," 181.

59. After an early debate within the regime about whether to organize a plantation economy, that option was ruled out and the Germans chose to encourage small-scale farming by Togolanders though some plantations were established (Sebald, "Togo 1900–1914," 180).

60. Darkoh, "Togoland under the Germans—Part I," 120.

61. Sebald, *Togo*, 89.
62. Darkoh, "Togoland under the Germans—Part I," 120.
63. Darkoh, "Togoland under the Germans—Part II," 158.
64. *Ibid.*, 154. Teak and mango trees were usually planted along the roads built during the German occupation.
65. Amenumey, "German Administration," 634.
66. Maier, "Persistence," 78. Maize often was grown between palm trees, according to the author.
67. Kwamina B. Dickson and George Benneh, *A New Geography of Ghana* (London: Longman, 1970), 165.
68. Donna J. E. Maier, "Slave Labor and Wage Labor in German Togo, 1885–1914," Chapter 5 in *Germans in the Tropics: Essays in German Colonial History*, ed. by Arthur J. Knoll and Lewis H. Gann (Westport, Connecticut: Greenwood Press, 1987), 77. Sebald maintains the rail and road links between the Central Volta Region and the rest of German Togoland were negligible, an argument later articulated by those Togolanders in favor of integration with the Gold Coast (Sebald, personal correspondence).
69. Darkoh, "Togoland under the Germans—Part II," 159.
70. Amenumey, "German Administration," 635. In addition to Kpalimé, these hospitals were located at Lomé, Little Popo, and Atakpamé. According to Amenumey, governmental employees and "bona fide paupers" were treated without charge.
71. Sebald, "Togo 1900–1914," 183. Little Popo was renamed Anecho in 1904 and today is the Togolese town of Aného.
72. See Laumann, "Domination and Resistance."
73. Amenumey, "German Administration," 635.
74. However, in the same year, there were 342 mission schools with 13,098 students, or three percent of the school-age population of Togoland (Sebald, "Togo 1900–1914," 182).
75. Maier, "Slave Labor," 78.
76. The little "industry" which existed in Togoland consisted of ten cotton ginneries, three palm oil refineries, a sisal refinery, a soap factory, and a lime kiln. Despite the presence of significant iron and bauxite deposits, no mining industries were established (Sebald, "Togo 1900–1914," 181).
77. European imperialists maintained that Togoland was a "model colony" because they believed the German regime produced balanced budgets after a limited period of "pacification" devoid of any major wars. For an analysis of the "model colony" hypothesis, see Dennis Laumann, "A Historiography of German Togoland, or the Rise and Fall of a 'Model Colony,'" *History in Africa*, 30 (2003): 195–211.
78. Krause, who filed a protest with the Reichstag in 1898 about slavery in Togoland, was later prosecuted by the German government for slander (Maier, "Slave Labor," 76). Sebald wrote a book about Krause subtitled (in German) "explorer, scientist, and humanist." See Peter Sebald, *Malam Musa, G. A. Krause 1850–1938: Forscher, Wissenschaftler, Humanist: Leben und Lebenswerk eines antikolonial gesinnten Afrika-Wissenschaftlers unter den Bedlingungen des Kolonialismus* (Berlin: Akademie-Verlag, 1972).

79. From the January, 1 1900 issue (13–4) as quoted in Carol Aisha Blackshire-Belay, "German Imperialism in Africa: the Distorted Images of Cameroon, Namibia, Tanzania, and Togo," *Journal of Black Studies*, 23:2 (December 1992), 241.

80. Sebald, "Togo 1900–1914," 175.

81. Knoll, 61.

82. Woodruff D. Smith, *The German Colonial Empire* (Chapel Hill: The University of North Carolina Press, 1978), 68.

83. *Ibid.*

84. Knoll, 40.

85. *Ibid.*, 71.

86. Sebald, "Togo 1900–1914," 184.

CHAPTER FOUR

An Oral History of "Gruner's Time"

"I know [the Germans] brought Christianity first before governance,"[1] Mosis Kofi Asase explains, underscoring the notion among oral historians that the arrival of missionaries marked the start of German influence in the central Volta Region. In fact, oral historians often do not distinguish between the activities of missionaries, on the one hand, and officials of the colonial regime, on the other. "There was some kind of cooperation between the two, the missionaries and the administrators," Edward Kodzo Datsa maintains. "They were all Germans, so I think there was cooperation between the two."[2] Gilbert Joel Nyavor concurs, stating: "The Germans came with the missionaries and the government. [The government] had a hand in everything the missionaries did."[3] Indeed, "it was the missionaries who recommended the people [of the area] go to the German government," argues Hillarius Gikunu.[4] He also asserts that "in 1854, the German government came to Togo," further evidence of the blurred line between the pursuits of the missionaries and the administrators in the recollections of oral historians, since that was the approximate year the first missionaries arrived, according to the oral history. Oswald Kwame Klutse even suggests that "in a way, the government was subject to the missionaries," since it was the latter who "recommended the good practices."[5] As a whole, despite the emphasis on missionary influence, the German period often is termed "Gruner's Time" by oral historians, in reference to Hans Gruner, the district commissioner who served for most of the German colonial occupation in the central Volta Region.[6]

After establishing churches in nearby areas of the Gold Coast with mixed results,[7] the missionaries slowly expanded their activities within the central Volta Region. The first missionaries arrived in Peki in 1847, moved to Keta, then Anyako, all in the Gold Coast, and continued to Waya before reaching Ho.[8] Togbe Kuleke offers the following chronology of how the Germans settled in Waya: "Concerning the coming of the Germans, they came in 1855 from Keta through Mamfe and Torda, where they were not taken on. They returned [to Waya] in 1856, secured a piece of land, and started building schools and mission houses."[9] The chief of Waya, Togbe Adisatsi, allowed the missionaries to work in the town, according to Gikunu.[10] Similarly, in Ho, the missionaries reached an agreement with the chief there. Klutse describes the negotiations:

> On November 29, 1859, two priests arrived in Ho-Axoe and asked to buy land from the paramount chief, Owusu Mote Kofi I. The priests desired to settle on the hill, but the chief declined, saying that a stranger does not stay far from the natives lest anything adverse happens to him. This explains why the mission is situated where it is now at Ho-Kpota. Construction of the mission at Ho was very fast because the chief supported them in many ways.[11]

While oral historians speak frequently of German missionaries and administrators in the same breath, the work of the former is recognized to have impacted the lives of the Togolanders to a greater degree. Indeed, during the German occupation, the missionaries were more extensively settled throughout the area than their governmental counterparts, as missions were established at Akpafu, Amedzofe, Ho, Kpandu, and Waya, among other places. In general, oral historians credit the missionaries with the introduction of "civilization" to the area, and they apply this term largely in reference to Christianity and commerce.[12] For example, in describing the work of (first name?) Danpinger, a missionary in Ho, Klutse states:

> [Danpinger] preached the Christian message to the people. [He] brought civilization. Where the Christian message had not reached, he sent it there. He went to Tanyibe, Sokode, Abutia. He built mission houses in all these places and taught the word of the Christian god. Some of the evil practices which were prevalent in those days ... such as slavery and killing ... [the Germans] stopped once and for all. They took up these issues very seriously.[13]

The names of several other missionaries prominently feature in the oral history. The most cited is Hermann Schosser, who was based in Akpafu during the

German occupation and is recalled by historians from that town and elsewhere.[14] Schosser is recognized as having played a central role in the spread of Christianity in the area. As Abra Janet Kumordzi explains:

> The German who came to stay, that I know of, was Reverend Schosser. He came as an evangelist and established a church. He also introduced education ... Reverend Schosser did not only help the people of Akpafu Todzi, he helped the people of Jasikan, Kpalimé, and central Eweland. He was, however, headquartered in Akpafu Todzi.[15]

Schosser, who is buried together with his wife in Akpafu, supervised the construction of his own house,[16] in addition to several other structures, including the church and the catechist's home.[17] Kumordzi furthermore maintains that Schosser taught the raising of domesticated animals, including cattle, and provided western medicine.[18] Schosser's predecessor in Akpafu was (first name?) Fiesel,[19] another missionary who is mentioned in the oral history of the town, and who is credited with the construction of the school in Akpafu.[20]

In Amedzofe, the work of Matthew Schlegel in particular is recalled by oral historians. Although he was Swiss, he is associated with the Germans, with whom and under whom he worked. Schlegel had many talents, according to Datsa:

> He was the first missionary to arrive [in Amedzofe]. He was a missionary, an architect, a mason. He was training masons, carpenters—the same man. When he realized the job was too much, he sent an appeal home and [the North German Missionary Society] started sending specialists.[21]

Schlegel settled in Amedzofe in 1890 and also taught at the seminary which was later established in the town.[22] The construction of several buildings in Amedzofe, including a small chapel[23] and a missionary residence, are attributed to him.[24]

While missionaries such as Danpinger, Schosser, Fiesel, and Schlegel have assumed an important place in the oral history of the period, the religion they practiced initially was met with indifference. Among the first converts to Christianity were slaves, partly because "it was difficult for people to accept Christianity."[25] Many of the present-day descendants of these converted slaves have Germanic names, as Seth Adu explains:

> There are German names like Lemgo, Burge, Dentmack, etc. [The Germans] named their houseboys after them[selves]. Some of these boys were slaves. The aim of the missionaries was to propagate the gospel, so when the slaves were brought, the healthy and strong ones were selected and paid for. These slaves were taught to read and write so that they would help [the Germans] spread the gospel.[26]

In general, many Togolanders who resided at the missions adopted Germanic names. Asase states that these names "are common to the people of Ho-Hliha," one of the present-day sections of Ho, "because that was where the whitemen settled." He continues: "It was from Hliha that the first local priests emanated. Priests like Ankama, Anku, all came from there."[27]

While missionaries were the first to introduce Christianity to the central Volta Region, the Togolander men who attended the mission schools played a leading role in spreading Christianity in the area. According to Klutse, the brothers Cornelius Klutse Kodzo and William Akpobi, who attended school in Waya, "really brought Christianity to Ho."[28] Although he was not able to recall their names, Johnson Agbemafle in Amedzofe also singled out the efforts of two men from Gbadzeme, a village to the northwest, who proselytized in that part of the region.[29]

German Colonization

As the numbers of German missionaries and Togolander converts to Christianity steadily increased in the central Volta Region, the German government began to colonize the area, as well. Residents of some towns, including Waya, Ho, and Amedzofe, had interacted with missionaries for several decades, but the initial contact with Germans for other communities was through the establishment of colonial stations. For example, the first Germans to settle in Kpandu in 1890 were governmental officials, not missionaries.[30] It was not until 1892 that the first Bremen missionaries arrived in Kpandu, while the Catholic mission was established in the town only in 1902.[31] And, unlike those towns which were settled and influenced by Germans through the work of the missionaries, Kpandu was forced under German colonial rule. Nyavor narrates the circumstances:

> When the Germans first came in 1889, Togbe Dagadu [II, the chief of Kpandu] was trading and the Germans gave his brother, Nyavo Dagadu, a flag. This chief threatened his brother not to accept the flag or [he would have to] deal with him. In fact, [the brother] couldn't accept the flag in 1889, but when the chief went to trading missions, which took five to six months before returning home, the Germans returned again. This time they brought armed soldiers. The Germans gave a condition: either the Kpandus accept the German flag or Kpandu would be shelled with bullets. So, Nyavo sent a messenger to Williams, the English colonial administrator for help. The English sent word to him that they had already handed over Kpandu area to the Germans, so they could not help the situation. It was then that the Kpandus accepted the flag, thereby bringing Kpandu under German rule.[32]

Figure 4.1 Dagadu II with German colonial officials, from the collection of Hans Gruner. (Courtesy of Staastbibliothek zu Berlin—Preussischer Kulturbesitz, Handschriftenabteilung)

Nyavor explains that Dagadu II and British officials had "a cordial relationship" and "a bond of friendship" before the German occupation.[33] But, as a result of agreements between the British and the Germans, Kpandu fell under German rule, and relations between the chieftaincy in the town and the colonial regime in Lomé were strained (Figure 4.1).

While the threat of violence preceded the occupation of Kpandu, oral historians depict a more evolutionary process elsewhere. Klutse describes what amounts to a negotiated occupation of Ho:

> The Germans said they wanted to introduce their system of government. Our grandfathers made it clear to them that they were not going to tolerate any bad governance. Earlier on, [the Germans] had asked to buy some land, but none was sold to them. They were told that the land was the people's heritage and shouldn't be sold away. They were, however, allowed to occupy part of the land. The elders also warned the Germans that they would sack them if their way of life and commercial activities did not suit them.[34]

These consultations continued even after the Germans formally established themselves in Ho. They proceeded to create an administrative code, which, according to Asase, drew at least partly from existing laws:

> When the government came, they listed all our traditional customs and religions with their days and uses. Those considered evil were stuck off. Those thought good were maintained. They respected our will, so there was no problem.[35]

As more and more of the central Volta Region was occupied by the German imperialists, governmental stations were set up in several towns, including Ho and Kpandu, as well as Kpalimé and Misahöhe to the east.[36] The latter two towns are recognized by oral historians as especially important centers of German administration, and one district commissioner who was based in Misahöhe, the aforementioned Gruner, is well-remembered by oral historians. Datsa discusses Gruner's reputation:

> Amedzofe wasn't a seat of government. The nearest seat of government was at Kiruko Kpalimé and there stayed the Provincial Commissioner. The name that we came to hear of, in our early childhood, was Dr. Gruner. He is said to have been a very strong administrator, very disciplined.[37]

The district commissioner performed many functions in the German administration and wielded almost absolute power. Citing the example of Gruner, Datsa states the district commissioner "was both a magistrate, administrator, minister for roads and transport, agriculture and virtually everything."[38] He further explains that the district commissioner's decisions were absolute. "This place was governed by decrees from the Kaiser," Datsa asserts, "You dared not question the District or Provincial Commissioners on this, as to their legality."[39] According to Adu, the "highest authorities" were based at Misahöhe and "whenever a case was beyond the jurisdiction of the authorities of Ho," for example, "it was referred to Misahöhe."[40]

While Misahöhe was the seat of the district commissioner, other German officials were based within the central Volta Region, including at Ho. Here, the Germans built a governmental station atop a hill,[41] which was soon named after one of the administrators posted to the town. Today, the hill is still called "Galenkui," an Ewe term for "wearer of eyeglasses"[42] or "glasses on the eyes"[43] that was the nickname of the German in charge of the station there.[44] Most oral historians do not recall his actual name, but Adu suggests it was (first name?) Foss.[45] He not only was responsible for governing Ho, but also nearby towns, including Waya, according to Simon Kugbleadzor.[46]

Like Gruner, Galenkui is considered a strict administrator, as Eugenia Kodzo Yawa explains: "That man was not a person to joke with. You could not get near him and chat with him, you are already scared of him."[47] Adu, however, paints a more sympathetic portrait of Galenkui:

He understood a little Ewe. Sometimes he went round the town to check on one or two things. If he found something going amiss, he would call the people's attention, comment on it, and order that it was put right.[48]

But, in a reference to the authority district commissioners enjoyed, Adu elaborates: "He supervised projects. For instance, if a road was being constructed from here to Adaklu, he took part in the construction so those who were idling about were whipped and disciplined."[49] Besides Gruner and Galenkui, one official based in Kpandu, (first name?) Pearl, is remembered by oral historians.[50]

Despite all the power wielded by these individual Germans officials, they relied heavily on Togolander chiefs to implement their policies and uphold order in the towns of the central Volta Region. "[The Germans] carried on with some form of indirect government," Datsa explains. "They used the chiefs and heads of villages. That was how they enforced their discipline."[51] A present-day chief in Waya, Togbe Lavi V, agrees: "The chiefs formed an integral part of the German administration. [The Germans] worked together with the chiefs and the chiefs had special powers. That is why [the Germans] had a smooth stay."[52]

Among the primary duties of the chief was supervising the maintenance of roads connecting the towns of the area.[53] The district commissioner repeatedly would order the clearing of roads in order to expedite travel and trade. The chief of any given town was held responsible for assuring the completion of such a project, or face various sanctions. Datsa provides an example:

> The people of Amedzofe could be told to make sure the road from their town to Kane was cleared in a week's time and [if] they fail to do it and the commissioner came, it was the chief who had to answer. If he did not give a tangible explanation, he was asked to report at Kloto the next morning at 7 a.m.[54]

Oral historians in Ho and Waya also state that if a chief failed to properly maintain a road, he was ordered to report to officials at Ho.[55] In Togbe Kuleke's words, "The chief was locked up until his subjects weeded the road and kept it clean before he was released."[56]

German officials were quite insistent that the roads remain well maintained. The chiefs thus mustered laborers from their towns to clear the roads whenever an official from the German regime was anticipated. John Vulie of Waya explains:

> If you were told that the "big man" [the district commissioner] will be coming, the people had to use hoes to dress the road nicely before he came. He was the only person who had a bicycle. On his way, if he should see one weed, that weed was uprooted and the chief who was responsible for that part of the road was in deep trouble.[57]

Another oral historian in the town, Gikunu, corroborates this assertion:

> The road was like a path. The paths were kept very neat. Now, the towns along the path, such as Waya, Kpodzi, Torda, all had a portion of the path which they took care of ... there had to be no weed on the path. Each chief had to make sure of that. If Galenkui, on a journey from Ho, finds any weed on the road, the chief was held responsible. So, many towns had to sweep the road with brooms so that the bicycle would not jump at any point of the journey.[58]

In addition to overseeing road maintenance, the chief served a role in the colonial judicial system. In these matters, too, a chief could be punished if his German superiors were not satisfied with his performance. "If anybody stole any government property here, it was the chief who had to answer for it," Datsa explains. "If he could not discover the thief and the lost article, it was the chief who must report at Kloto at a given time to account for the loss."[59] In cases of murder, according to Klutse, the chief himself could face capital punishment. He offers the following scenario:

> The fact is that some tribes did not get along well with others, so if a hunter, for instance, happened to find himself in an enemy's camp, he was killed. Anytime this happened, the Germans persuaded the chief of the murderer's town to give up the person. If the chief refused, he was killed. So, the chief would do everything to find the killer. That was how the Germans administered justice.[60]

Nyavor supports this latter statement: "If somebody commits a serious crime in any town, the Germans would hold the chief responsible until he presents the criminal. This ensured that the chief insisted that people behave with public decorum."[61]

The chiefs therefore served as an important link in the German administrative system, responsible for road maintenance and upholding public order, in addition to other duties. While they were supervised by German officials at the various governmental stations, they still exercised a degree of autonomy in their polities. According to Nyavor, "The chiefs were also revered. What the chief said was final."[62]

In order to implement the policies of the colonial regime, German officials relied not only on the chiefs, but also a police force almost entirely comprised of Africans.[63] These policemen were stationed throughout the central Volta Region, including at Kpandu[64] as well as at Misahöhe, but generally did not originate from the towns in which they were posted. Describing the police force at Kpandu, for example, Nyavor states: "They were citizens of other places. They were Africans or blacks drafted or recruited into the army to assist the German colonial administration. They were just transferred to Kpandu to execute their job."[65] Togbe Kuleke states there were no Germans in the force, "only black soldiers trained by the Germans."[66] The responsibilities of the police ranged from enforcing orders of the German administrators, assisting in medical campaigns, patrolling the roads in the area,[67] escorting agricultural shipments,[68] and transporting money for the regime.[69]

Once the German occupation was extended to most of the central Volta Region, governmental stations were established, and the guidelines by which the Germans would govern in some circumstances were negotiated between the Germans and Togolanders, the colonial authorities began to implement policies designed to reorder the economy of the area. The regime sought to achieve this goal through dictates, force, and education, and most often were joined in their efforts by the missionaries. While many sectors of the economy remained outside their regulatory power, the Germans concentrated their efforts on enforcing agricultural policies.

Agriculture and Technology

The Germans attempted to significantly change agriculture in the central Volta Region, but their success was limited to the adoption of several new plants and the modification of some practices. Many oral historians credit the Germans with the introduction of mango,[70] teak,[71] and the avocado.[72] Two historians claim the Germans also brought a new type of coffee to the area.[73] In addition, the Germans became actively involved in the processing and selling of shea butter[74] and rubber.

The promotion of rubber as a cash crop in the westernmost and northernmost parts of the central Volta Region is recalled by some oral historians as especially important. For example, Kwami Asamani singles out the following three introductions of the Germans: "when the Germans came here, they brought education, Christianity, and the art of harvesting latex rubber." According to him, it was the Germans who "taught our people how to harvest to get rubber for sale."[75] Tegbe also credits the Germans with introducing additional species of trees from which "more rubber was produced."[76] It is unclear from the oral history whether rubber extraction occurred before the German occupation.

The expansion of cotton cultivation also was strongly encouraged by the German regime.[77] Oral historians are in disagreement as to whether cotton had long existed in the central Volta Region. Nyavor believes the Germans "introduced the cotton seed and they distributed them among the farmers,"[78] but most oral historians maintain cotton had been cultivated before the German occupation. As Asase states, "The cotton tree existed long before the Germans came, but they brought new varieties."[79]

Whether or not cotton was introduced by the Germans, its importance as a cash crop to the regime was evident. As Togbe Kuleke states, "Cotton was to [the Germans] what cocoa is to Ghana today."[80] The Germans established a cotton ginnery in Kpandu,[81] one of the centers of cotton production in the central Volta Region. Togbe Kuleke explains that after cotton was weighed by German officials it was "carried on the head" and transported by foot to Kpalimé and Lomé, accompanied by "German soldiers."[82]

In contrast to what it says about cotton, the oral history consistently credits individuals from the Gold Coast with the introduction of cocoa to the central Volta Region. Although Kwami Asamani singles out the British,[83] others uphold the widely accepted belief in present-day Ghana that it was Tetteh Quarshie, an African farmer in the Gold Coast, who brought cocoa to the British colony before its cultivation expanded to Togoland.[84] As with cotton, however, oral historians suggest the Germans encouraged the expansion of cocoa farming, which had been embraced by Togolander farmers before the occupation.[85] Adu details the German involvement in cocoa farming, which included the distribution of seeds. He furthermore states that "if you decided to make a cocoa farm, the agricultural officers would come to advise you on how you should do it."[86] Kpalimé was the local center for purchasing cocoa from farms throughout the central Volta Region.[87] As Tegbe explains:

> In those days, people went to Lomé to collect money to buy cocoa. There were people to carry the cocoa in loads to Kpalimé. There were no roads. The journey to Kpalimé was by foot. The journey on the mountain can be compared to the distance from Hohoe and Kpoeta. When the cocoa gets to Kpalimé, it was carried by train to Lomé.[88]

In addition to the possible introduction of several plants as well as their efforts to encourage the cultivation of certain cash crops, the Germans attempted to alter the agricultural technology employed in the region. In particular, they banned shifting agriculture in Togoland, a practice which was developed by Niger-Congo peoples over several thousand years. This technology also involved the burning of secondary growth areas, often referred to as "bush burning," which the Germans likewise sought to terminate. At least on one occasion, however, a German administrator recognized the rationale for bush burning. Tegbe offers the following story:

> I also heard from my parents that bush burning was not allowed in those days as it is today. Listen very carefully. There is a creeping plant in the forest that bears fruit. This fruit gives a very severe itching. One day, the people plucked one of the fruits and took it to the German official of the time, telling him it was the reason they had to burn the bush grasses. Taking the fruit, the official folded one sleeve of his shirt and rubbed it on his arm. Within a few seconds, he had removed his shirt in order to

scratch his skin. The whiteman asked, "Is this what caused this level of itching?" The people replied in the affirmative. From then onward, he allowed them to use the slash and burn method of farming.[89]

Besides attempting to change farming practices, the Germans introduced new imported agricultural tools, which were "easier to use" than those manufactured locally.[90]

The Germans also promoted the expansion of some agricultural staples. Adu explains, for example, how the cultivation of cassava spread during the German occupation: "When the missionaries realized there was no cassava at certain areas, they would send cassava sticks to those areas to be distributed to the farmers under the supervision of government officials. As a result, cassava was in abundance."[91]

The German governmental stations established throughout the central Volta Region not only served as administrative centers, but engaged in agricultural activities, as well. According to Adu, the station at Ho cultivated seedlings of cocoa and kola, which were, along with mango, disbursed to farmers in the area.[92]

Some oral historians suggest the Germans had little or no impact on farming during the period. Nyagbe and Yawa, for example, maintain the Germans did not introduce any crops into the local agriculture.[93] Togbe Kuleke states the German regime offered "minimal"[94] or "no help"[95] in the improvement of agriculture. Adu explains "there was no compulsion" to plant any cash crops,[96] although there existed "a decree that very farmer should grow kola and cocoa because these were the cash crops."[97] In any event, Agbewu argues the Togolanders continued to emphasize subsistence agriculture over the cultivation of cash crops.[98]

In general, it appears the German occupation impacted the economy of the central Volta Region in divergent, but not transformative, ways. While the colonial regime sought to impose its dictates on farmers, the result was merely an expansion of certain cash crops which already were cultivated in the area. Most agriculturists continued to work their own farms, as there were no plantations established by the Germans in the area.[99] The routing of some trade was altered, with agricultural goods from the central Volta Region sold in Kpalimé and other towns with an official German presence and ultimately destined for Lomé. As a result, Kpalimé emerged as a regional commercial center. According to Catherina Ama Kwadzo Kugbleadzor, "My mother and her people carried things from [Waya] to Kpalimé for sale and it was from there that they purchased other things to come and sell here."[100] Beyond agriculture, the Germans neither introduced new technologies nor deeply affected existing ones, with two exceptions, cotton weaving and iron making.

Technology

Knowledge of cotton-weaving probably was brought into the central Volta Region from areas of present-day northern Ghana hundreds of years before the German period,[101] but oral historians credit the Germans with introducing new techniques, such as the spinning of cotton using machines.[102] "The men could weave cloths," Vulie states. "So, in the German time, it was a form of occupation which the Germans brought to our people."[103] The "new dimension" of cotton weaving during the German era, according to Nyavor, was "the commercialization which was introduced."[104] Although the Germans encouraged cotton spinning and weaving, the flow of imported cloth into the local economy adversely affected the already-existing cotton-weaving industry. "Even the coming of European-made cloths stopped us from weaving our type of cloth," Klutse explains.[105]

Iron production clearly was not introduced by the Germans, but definitely impacted by their occupation. Akpafu, for example, was a center of iron making for at least several centuries before the German occupation. According to oral historians, particularly but not limited to those in Akpafu Todzi, the Germans either directly or indirectly damaged this industry, primarily by saturating the market with imports of iron products from Europe. Klutse argues local iron production ceased because:

> (1) When the European brought plenty of their tools, we did not need to make ours again; (2) Our people became lazy. They did not want to go through that long process of digging rocks, extracting iron, and molding iron. That was why we lost the art; (3) Also, our land was so good and we had a lot to eat. So, we started buying the European-made goods and stopped ours.[106]

Agbewu concurs, explaining "The Germans brought along tools that we already knew, so there was no need to go through the trouble of mining and extracting iron to make our tools." As a result, he says the Germans "came to destroy" the iron industry of Akpafu.[107] Concurrent with their flooding of the local market with cheap imports, the Germans likewise failed to encourage iron production in Akpafu. Kwami Asamani states:

> When the Germans came, they did not help us in any way at all. Later on, our people explained that there must be a reason why the Germans did not help us, that it could be that because they themselves were blacksmiths where they came from. They should have given us a form of help to improve our smelting industry. They did not do.[108]

While the new colonial economy undermined the iron industry of Akpafu, several oral historians do credit the Germans with introducing new blacksmithing techniques.[109] Moreover, outside of Akpafu, iron working was not widespread in the area, so it appears the Germans were responsible for promoting this technology.[110] Asase suggests the following:

> In Kpandu, we were told that the Germans taught the people the art of blacksmithing ... [a] a few people who stayed with the Germans as househelps learned blacksmithing from them ... I would therefore say it was the Germans who taught the craft of blacksmithing.[111]

Additionally, the German regime contracted work to local blacksmiths, such as Komla Asamani of Kpandu. Komla Asamani and his father were taught European blacksmithing techniques by the Germans, although their family manufactured guns and repaired imported arms before the occupation. Komla Asamani was hired to supervise the construction of bridges designed by the Germans, including one at Gbefi, near Kpandu (Figure 4.2), and another at Aného. Asamani's son, Nicholas (Figure 4.3), describes how the bridge at Gbefi was constructed by his father:

> [The Germans] brought the plan and the materials and they were also there to show [Komla Asamani] where the bridge was to be constructed. The workers were housed somewhere and the Germans visited them ... [The tools] were bought in Lomé, for example, the anvils and roofing sheets. German-made goods are strong.[112]

The Germans introduced other crafts to the area, according to oral historians, including carpentry,[113] masonry,[114] and tailoring.[115] Tegbe maintains that "it was the Germans who brought craftsmanship to this land,"[116] but Nyavor argues that the Germans "just admired the existing handicrafts so they did not provide any technological improvements."[117] The majority of historians do credit the Germans with these introductions, however, and especially carpentry appears to have been promoted during the occupation.[118] Datsa explains, "Our people were not carpenters. [The missionaries] came to teach what carpentry was."[119] Adu also singles out the efforts of missionaries, explaining "The Bremen missionaries came with artisans such as carpenters, blacksmiths, and sawyers. There were nationals of the West Indies who worked for them. So, our people had the opportunity to learn these trades from them."[120] Gikunu concurs, stating: "All the missionaries who came were pastors, but at the same time they all had various personal skills. Some were cobblers, others were carpenters, sawyers, and various other forms of work, such as tailoring."[121] As a result, the Germans "came to teach us how to build fortified houses" which Asase claims were meant to protect homes from wild animals.[122]

Figure 4.2 The bridge at Gbefi, from the collection of Hans Gruner. (Courtesy of Staastbibliothek zu Berlin—Preussischer Kulturbesitz, Handschriftenabteilung)

Figure 4.3 Nicholas Asamani, a blacksmith in Kpandu. (Photo by Dennis Laumann)

The German regime established centers, at Agu and Nyangbo[123] as well as Lomé,[124] where the aforementioned crafts were taught. Those Togolanders who studied there were later employed by the regime in the construction of buildings throughout the central Volta Region. "The Germans taught the people vocations like masonry, carpentry, carving, and many others," explains Togbe Kuleke. "These people actually helped the Germans to do the building works."[125] Adu states that the vocational center in Lomé offered training in "tailoring, shoe-making, black-smithing, goldsmithing, and several others. Whatever one wanted to learn was taught."[126]

Education and Health Care

In addition to these trades, the Germans introduced western education to the central Volta Region. Togbe Kuleke maintains: "[The Germans] brought education so that literacy came into our part of the world, too."[127] Oral historians highlight the efforts of the missionaries, not the German regime, in promoting education. "As for the German government, I do not know anything," Gikunu asserts. "But the missionaries, they established schools for people to attend."[128] Datsa states that the German administrators allowed the missionaries "free hands in anything they wanted to do, especially concerning education."[129] While Nyavor confirms "the government did not establish schools per se," he argues that the German regime cooperated with the missionaries in promoting education.[130]

Schools were founded by missionaries throughout the central Volta Region,[131] the impact of which extended beyond the towns where the missions were based. For example, Tegbe asserts that "[a] very big school was established at Gbla. People came from far and near for this education ... People came from Keta, Kpalimé, and Lomé to school here."[132] But, according to another oral historian, it required a concerted effort on the part of the Germans to draw students to the schools. "Schooling was a new thing so people were not interested," Alfred Adinyra explains, continuing:

> [The Germans] therefore went round the villages themselves after people had returned from the farm to tell the small boys to come to school. People were at first not interested. So, the first thing [the Germans] did was to give out uniforms. In those days, the children did not have [European style clothing]. Any child who wanted to attend school never said so, he only had to say he wanted a [uniform] and that was understood.[133]

Adu states that these uniforms were referred to as "all of us" and were representative of the assistance the Germans provided to students without parents or guardians. He elaborates:

> Those who could not get money to buy books were given minor jobs to do. The money got from doing these odd jobs was used in buying books and stationary. The odd jobs included clearing the hen coops, watering, and cleaning the house.[134]

Students in these schools were instructed in a variety of subjects by both German and Togolander teachers.[135] The curriculum was intensive and strictly enforced, as Adinyra details:

> Their teaching was with iron hands and the cane rod was the agent of discipline. It was easy, therefore, to learn to read. Anybody who schooled for three years could write a letter. By the time you enter the seventh class, it means you've become a complete teacher and you could be sent to a new station where a teacher was needed.[136]

Only a select few students managed to obtain education beyond the primary level. German was not taught in the schools but, according to Tegbe, "those who were educated to a higher level could speak a little German."[137] "In those days," Adu explains, "if you managed to school up to the seventh class, then you have attained a lot of education."[138] Many of these advanced students, as Adinyra points out above, served as instructors in new or expanding schools throughout the area, while others joined the colonial administration or attended the seminary at Amedzofe.[139] Those who continued their education at the latter would become either pastors or teachers or attain both positions. Adu expounds:

> One could enter the seminary at Amedzofe, which was and still is, a teacher training school. At the training college, the student was taught German and religion. At the end of the course, an examination is conducted. Any student who passed was posted as a teacher to teach and to preach.[140]

Another option for students who completed the secondary level, according to Adu, was to attend a college administered by Catholic missionaries in Lomé.[141] Admission to this college was based on passing an examination, which Adu describes from personal experience:

> After the seventh class, we went to do an exam at a place that had been chosen for us. It was the same [exam] for anybody who had completed the seventh class. The exam took place at Lomé, Kpalimé, or Ho. If you passed this exam, you could decide what you want to do.

The examination, Adu adds, included translation from German into Ewe and vice-versa.[142]

Reverend (first name?) Galevo of Akpafu was one of the students who attended the seminary. Educated at the Amedzofe Training College under the leadership of Reverend Hermann Schosser, he went on to assume senior church positions, eventually becoming a Moderator of the Evangelical Presbyterian Church. His ascent is recalled by Kumordzi, his sister:

> Reverend Schosser took my brother as his own and gave him all the training that a man must go through. He had his education as he stayed with Reverend Schosser. He schooled to a high level, got married, and had children. His children also grew up to occupy responsible positions.[143]

While a small number of men were able to obtain some higher education and pursue a limited variety of careers, women were denied these opportunities during the German occupation partly since "… it was feared they might get pregnant along the way," explains Nyagbe.[144] Additionally, men simply were deemed better candidates for receiving western education. Kumordzi, for example, assumed a supporting role in Galevo's education. She explains:

> At that time, my brother, Reverend Galevo, was schooling and another brother was learning a trade. I was the only person left to help my mother. When my parents went to farm, I had to prepare food and send [it] to them on the farm. This was the reason why I could not get formal education. When my brother, the late Reverend Galevo, was at Amedzofe Training College, I had to take care of his food and other needs any time he was leaving for school. I carried part of his luggage, saw him off to Amedzofe, and returned alone to Akpafu Todzi.[145]

The missionaries did operate a few schools exclusively for women but, according to oral historians, the curriculum at these institutions was restricted to domestic skills[146] and religion.[147] The former included "sewing, making bread, housekeeping, home management, decent living, and how to be good wives"[148] as well as "how to take proper care of babies."[149] A vocational school was opened for girls in Waya that offered instruction in the aforementioned subjects.[150]

Within these constraints, there were limited opportunities for women to extend their education at other missions in the central Volta Region. For example, Gikunu states: "My mother also attended 'girls' school' [in Waya] and even went on to Ho to continue the school."[151] Catherina Ama Kwadzo Kugbleadzor concurs, saying her mother and other women from Waya were taught by the German missionaries in Keta on "how to stay with whites."[152] Some of the women converts to Christianity resided at the mission stations, apparently as prospects for marriage to the men attending seminary. Adinyra explains:

> The girls were made to live in the mission house so that they could be trained in the handling of day nurseries for children. They were also trained in needlework and cookery. Any teacher who had finished the seminary and wanted to get married could get the best girls from among these young girls.[153]

While most of women's education was provided by the missionaries, Adu states even the spouses of government officials also taught domestic skills. For instance, the wife of Galenkui, the administrator at Ho "was responsible for domestic affairs." Adu continues:

> She would move from house to house advising the women to keep their homes tidy. For example, she would advise them to cover their waterpots, paint their hearths and the floors of the kitchens ... She would point out their mistakes to them and advise them not to repeat such mistakes.[154]

In addition to domestic training and religion, various skills related to agriculture were taught to the women, particularly cotton spinning.[155] Jane Atakumah, discussing the activities women pursued during the German occupation, recalls:

> As a child, at the time, I only knew of cotton-spinning and this trade was very popular everywhere at the time. This cotton was brought and sent elsewhere. Women also gathered shea-nut, which they sold to [the Germans]. The women also learnt how to prepare shea butter for the Germans.[156]

Thus, the regime's efforts to influence agriculture through education extended to women, who were encouraged to learn the techniques necessary for the production of cash crops.

Besides providing educational opportunities, the missionaries often offered the only access to western medicine.[157] At Akpafu, Schosser is remembered by Kumordzi for giving basic medical care and drugs, not only for the residents of that town, but from neighboring villages, as well.[158] Although there were hospitals at Lomé and Kpalimé, no doctors were based in the central Volta Region.[159]

The regime did not entirely neglect health care, but concentrated its efforts on combating infectious diseases and epidemics, usually by administering what oral historians term vaccinations.[160] Those afflicted with leprosy, for example, were "isolated and camped in Lomé" and could be visited only with permission from German authorities, Adu explains.[161] Anyone entering the leprosy center was vaccinated and "could neither eat nor drink anything there."[162] During an epidemic of sleeping sickness, the government dispatched "special doctors who went about treating the afflicted by giving them injections."[163] Another quarantine center was established at Kpalimé, according to Tegbe, who asserts the Germans were consistent in their campaigns against infectious diseases. "Any time there was an epidemic," he says, "the people attacked were quarantined in order to prevent the diseases from spreading any further ... Those quarantined who became healed, returned to their communities."[164]

In their efforts to contain infectious diseases, the Germans also enforced border controls, which prevented travelers afflicted with any of these diseases from entering Togoland. During an epidemic in Dahomey, for example, people coming from the French colony were prevented from going into the central Volta Region.[165] When an outbreak of smallpox occurred in the Gold Coast, residents of the area were not allowed to cross the border into the British colony.[166] Atafe Badasu claims that whenever a traveler passed the border between the colonies in either direction, they were vaccinated.[167]

In addition to the vaccination programs, the quarantines, and the border controls, the Germans regulated the sale of foods. According to Adu, there were "sanitary inspectors" who visited the markets and disposed of food that was "found to be unwholesome."[168]

Western medicine, particularly the vaccinations, often was not welcomed by the Togolanders. Adu states that some Togolanders refused vaccinations, but they simply were "arrested and vaccinated" by officials, who were escorted by the police. He explains that "some people thought the injections were lethal, that is why they didn't want to be vaccinated."[169] An outbreak of cerebro spinal meningitis in Kpandu in 1912, in which many of those injected by the Germans died, led to a direct challenge to the German occupation. Nyavor describes the events surrounding the epidemic:

> There were mass protests or complaints during the crisis period. [In addition to cerebro spinal menigitis] others also suffered from sleeping sickness and strangely, too, all these ailments attracted the same treatment, which caused deaths. The people protested to Chief Dagadu [III], who was considered as the person who could champion their cause against the mass deaths.[170]

Atakumah corroborates these events, stating: "many people died and many people stood against [the Germans] because they were responsible for those deaths."[171]

After traveling to Lomé to meet with German officials, explains Nyavor, Dagadu III and his advisors "rejected the law which prescribed the injection treatment." Gabriel Kofi Bakotse elaborates:

> Whenever the disease was detected on you, you were sent to Kpalimé, not for treatment, but to be isolated until you died. So our chief Togbe Dagadu Anku decided enough was enough. He was not going to allow anybody to test the neck of his subjects anymore to find out if he had the disease or not.[172]

But, Nyavor argues, "The German colonial government did not like the protest." Gruner, the district commissioner at Misahöhe, furthermore was incensed that Dagadu III did not consult him before presenting his grievances to the colonial administration in Lomé. Nyavor details the altercation between the two men:

> This over-jumping of channel by Dagadu to the governor brought a conflict between Dagadu and Gruner. Gruner claimed Dagadu was disrespectful. So, he decided to punish him. He fined Dagadu and the Kpandu state an amount of 10,000 pounds. This official imposed the fine in order to incite the people of Kpandu against Dagadu, but the Kpandu people did not agitate and even when the law was repealed, the people jubilated extremely. This heightened Dr. Gruner's anger towards Dagadu.[173]

Not long after, on accusation that he had written a letter maligning the German monarch, Dagadu III was destooled, that is, stripped of his authority and rights as ruler, and imprisoned for three months at Misahöhe by Gruner, with the assistance of Pearl, the German official based at Kpandu, and a police detachment. Nyavor states that "there was complete uproar in Kpandu on that fateful day." Although he "vehemently denied" authoring the document, Dagadu III was told by Gruner that his case had been tried and that his punishment would be permanent exile in Cameroon.[174]

According to Nyavor, Dagadu III was "just arbitrarily tried, found guilty, and sent on exile," which was "his punishment for insulting Kaiser Wilhelm the Second and also because it was realized he preferred English rule to German rule." He explains Dagadu III, on several occasions, "... revealed certain bad practices by the Germans against the people of Kpandu" in his communications with the British, his former allies.[175] Atakumah, Dagadu III's granddaughter who presently lives in Kpandu, concludes "it was a bitter experience to the people because he was a great ruler who helped his state" (Figure 4.4).[176]

Figure 4.4 Jane Atakumah, granddaughter of Dagadu III. (Photo by Dennis Laumann)

Forced labor and punishment

The public, coordinated opposition of Dagadu III and the people of Kpandu against the German regime was in many ways an isolated episode. Oral historians do not cite many instances of direct challenges to the German occupation in the central Volta Region. Yet, in their numbers and over the years, residents of the area protested German occupation merely by emigrating to the Gold Coast. A primary motivation often was economic, but "[a] lot of people," Nyavor tells us, "left the colony for the Gold Coast and others also left for present-day northern Ghana in order to avoid German high-handedness."[177]

Most of these emigrants traveled to the British colony to seek employment on cocoa farms,[178] to tap palm wine,[179] to harvest palm nuts,[180] to work on road and rail construction projects,[181] and to mine gold, silver, and diamonds.[182] In order to cross the border, travelers were required to seek permission from the German administration,[183] which granted permits for stays in the Gold Coast ranging from a few days to several months.[184] The necessary permits were issued by colonial officials at Kpeve, according to Tegbe.[185]

Togolanders regularly violated the travel restrictions imposed by the Germans. Catherina Ama Kwadzo Kugbleadzor maintains, "Many people went to stay there for a long time before coming back,"[186] while Gikunu says "Some stayed for a number of years, others never came back."[187] Once one of these travelers who transgressed the permit returned to Togoland, they were "severely punished," according to Badasu, and either lashed by colonial officials[188] or made to pay a penalty.[189] Yawa reveals her uncle was repeatedly imprisoned for his visits to the Gold Coast. She explains the circumstances:

> The people who went to the Gold Coast always sought permission for a specific number of days and came back before or on the last day. But, this uncle of mine would always overstay his permit. He could take a permit for three months and stay for four months. The moment he came back, he was arrested.[190]

In addition to crossing the border in search of wage labor, many Togolanders traveled to the Gold Coast to conduct trade. Preexisting commercial links between Kpandu and Accra continued during the German occupation, as agricultural goods were traded across the Volta River to the Gold Coast capital. A "small tax" had to be paid by traders at the customs point at Kpandu. But, according to Nyavor, the Germans often punished residents of Kpandu when they returned from "their economic activities" in the Gold Coast, imposing a one pound fine and a one-month jail term on each offender.[191]

While some Togolanders decided to leave the colony for economic pursuits and others to escape the harshness of life under the Germans, the majority endured the demands placed on them by the regime in Lomé. Foremost amongst the most oppressive aspects of the occupation, according to oral historians, was the German's reliance on forced labor. This was mandated usually for road construction projects and for the transport of goods across the colony, as Gikunu asserts "the German government used force for all her works."[192] Togolander men were required to contribute their labor to the colonial state or risk punishments, ranging from flogging to imprisonment. Adinyra succinctly states: "Anybody who failed to comply was taught how to do so."[193]

During the German occupation, a series of roads were constructed throughout the colony, including in the central Volta Region, largely to facilitate the movement of agricultural products toward the coast. These routes were built entirely through the use of forced labor. Tegbe explains that the workers were not paid for their work, since it was "like a communal labor,"[194] which Datsa states "was very much encouraged" by the German regime.[195] Catherina Ama Kwadzo Kugblead-zor, however, emphasizes the coercive nature of these projects: "When [the Germans] came, they constructed roads with force. There was no way one could refuse to do so."[196] Badasu confirms this: "As for the construction of roads, it was by force. If you refuse, you will not go scot free."[197]

Laborers were taken from their towns to other parts of the colony to work on the road-building projects. Men from Akpafu Todzi, for example, were ordered to Kpalimé and Agormetodzi,[198] while laborers from Hohoe worked on roads in Dafor, Kame, and Tornu.[199] But, despite the hardships associated with the construction of these routes, Agbewu suggests the projects were supported by the communities. He explains that in Akpafu Todzi, "we wanted the roads so that lorries could come up here. That is why we constructed the roads ... The nature of the road determined whether [the lorries] came or not."[200] Furthermore, Tegbe suggests that, although the Togolanders were not paid for their labor, the German supervisors were somewhat benevolent:

> The Germans knew we had no roads, so they wanted to build roads in our area ... I heard from my parents that anytime people went to construct roads, the Germans gave any form of help they were capable of giving. Otherwise, there was no form of payment.[201]

Nyagbe disputes the idea that the people of the central Volta Region desired or even needed the roads planned by the Germans:

> Nobody told me that the Germans built roads because, naturally, before they came there were routes linking the various villages. [The Germans] were not the first to start the building of roads. Do you think the people will sit down for the European to construct roads for them? [The Germans] also traveled on the routes used by the local people.[202]

While most oral historians identify the links between towns constructed during the German period as "roads," others argue they were more akin to "paths." Vulie describes the typical road in the area of Waya: "[The Germans] did not drive cars on the road, but the roads were neat. Trees were planted on each side of the roads. The roads were just like footpaths."[203] Likewise, Togbe Kuleke claims the roads were "just footpaths ... only wide enough for bicycles to use,"[204] and Gikunu also says "the road was like a path."[205]

Besides serving as the routes that German officials traveled in order to visit towns surrounding their stations, the main purpose of the roads was to facilitate the movement of goods throughout the colony. Agricultural products were transported, as mentioned above, from towns in the central Volta Region to region-al purchasing centers, such as Kpalimé,[206] and then to coastal towns, particularly Lomé, from which they were exported to Europe and elsewhere. Many individual farmers, along with their families and hired laborers, transported the crops them-selves. But, as with the actual construction of the roads, the Germans relied heavily on forced labor to ship the goods across the colony.

Togolanders also were forced to carry the belongings of individual Germans. "In those days," Adinyra explains, "because there were no cars, people carried the luggage of the Germans from town to town."[207] He continues that those the Ger-mans considered not to be "idle" were often singled out to perform this task: "For example, if the whiteman was on a journey to Kpedze and his luggage needed to be carried, it was those who loitered about who were made to carry such luggage."[208] Simon Kugbleadzor corroborates this account:

> In those days, there were no vehicles. When [the Germans] moved from place to place, they made people carry those loads. In the olden days, people spent their leisure periods staying under trees. So, when [the Germans] move from one village to the next, people from here were also made to carry the load to the other village. This they did until they got to Daklu.[209]

Nyavor makes clear "[the Germans] did not tolerate laziness. If you were a lazy person, then you would send loads to Lomé on foot. The Germans would not pay you any wage but would give food on the way."[210] Nyagbe also states that "any time news came that a European was in a nearby village, people were hand-picked to go and carry his luggage to our place [Hohoe]."[211] As a result, Asase argues, "our people thought the Germans were trying to be bossy."[212]

Those who refused to perform forced labor or violated any of the other orders of the regime faced a variety of punishments meted out by the German officials, but flogging[213] and lashing[214] are the two that are most often cited by oral histori-ans. Togolanders could be flogged for simply showing "disrespect,"[215] spanked for disobeying colonial laws,[216] or even lashed for "quarreling at a funeral."[217] Yawa states that "even the act of roaming about in town is considered by [the Germans] as committing a crime."[218] Adu describes one of the ways German officials deter-mined the extent of punishment: "Listen! Every offense merited its punishment. In some cases, you were lashed 25 times depending on your physical fitness and in other cases the culprits were lashed 15 times."[219] Datsa recalls that offenders were given 24 strokes of the cane and a "twenty-fifth one was for the Kaiser."[220] These punishments often were arbitrarily applied, as Adu explains: "At their courts, the magistrate would watch you, especially your face and mouth to find out if you would tell lies or the truth. If you were suspected of not telling the truth, you would be slapped severely from behind."[221] Another method of punishment was chaining, which Adu illustrates:

[The Germans] chained offenders together according to crimes committed. For example, if three people were involved in a stealing case, they were chained together, so that if one of them wanted to attend to nature's calls, others were compelled to go with him. So also was the case of farming and weeding. When the sun was high up, the chain absorbed its heat and, in order their skins were not burnt, [the Germans] supplied them with rags to cover their necks. The chains were only removed from their necks when it was time for meals. After the meals, they went back to work.[222]

Besides all the aforementioned corporal penalties, some Togolanders were sentenced to a few days of forced labor. "If you did something wrong, such as failing to pay your poll tax," Adinyra explains, "you were taken to Kamina to stay there for three or four days to work, after which you were brought back."[223]

Men more likely than women received the punishments of flogging and lashing, but Yawa asserts women "were also beaten."[224] Adu maintains the regime applied different punishments to women, however. "That of the women was not so severe as the men," Adu states. "Different people lashed both the men and the women."[225]

Clearly, oral historians recollect a host of negative aspects of the German occupation of the central Volta Region. Among others detailed above, men were forced to perform unpaid labor, traders were denied access to markets across the border, and farmers were punished for failing to follow the agricultural policies mandated by the colonial regime. At times, Togolanders resisted the Germans by electing to leave the colony or by refusing to submit to the dictates of the administration, as in the case of the vaccination campaign in Kpandu. But, generally, organized resistance against the German occupation failed to materialize in the central Volta Region. The very harshness of the regime may provide one explanation for this situation. "There was no resistance," Nyavor offers, "because the Germans were a very tough people and they used very tough laws in ruling the colony."[226]

But oral historians claim the benefits of German rule far outweighed what may be considered to be the negative experiences of the occupation. Gikunu, for example, states:

I can say that [the Germans] did not do any bad thing but the forced labor which they liked so much. They were well-respected so they had every love for the people. In those days, they used forced labor but, today, looking back, people realized that they were actually good. If somebody fails to understand something, just apply a little force and that will do the trick.[227]

This idea that German "firmness" is a positive attribute is repeated by many oral historians. Datsa, like Gikunu, suggests that forced labor had a beneficial end result. During the German occupation, Datsa maintains, besides farming,

> all other things were done either by manual or forced labor. No complaints. This was the picture our grandfathers gave us of how it was like. The good things left behind were done by forced or communal labor.[228]

Nevertheless, while forced labor exacted a heavy toll on the Togolanders, oral historians tend to accentuate the positive aspects of the German occupation. They furthermore seek to de-emphasize the arbitrary and harsh punishments imposed by the Germans by suggesting that the recipients may have been deserving of such treatment. Yawa, for example, claims that "although [the Germans] were troublesome, they never worried anyone who was engaged in productive work to earn a living. But, if you are not careful in your activities, they would arrest you." She concludes that "some aspects [of the German occupation] are good, that is the disciplinary measures instill some sort of fear into the people which deters them from misbehaving."[229]

Honesty, Order, and Discipline

The introduction of Christianity undoubtedly is attributed to the Germans, a fact that influences oral historians' impressions of the later colonial occupation itself. This is evident in Klutse's summation of the general impact of the German presence in the central Volta Region: "[The Germans] taught us how to live by the word of God. They explained to us the implications of wars, conflicts, murders, etc. They taught us to do away with wickedness and forgive one another's sins."[230] Gikunu also emphasizes the religious activities of the Germans when he states: "The main thing they brought was the gospel or word of God. They were not so involved in any physical development."[231]

While many oral historians do acknowledge the infrastructural projects which occurred during the German occupation, they most accentuate, in addition to the beginning of local Christianity, the "honesty,"[232] "order,"[233] and "discipline"[234] which they believe characterized the German period. Nyavor states that "honesty and truth were virtues which were practiced to the letter during the German colonial occupation." He cites as an example the fact that if someone found money on a road, it would be hung on a pole, until the rightful owner retrieved it since "people were law-abiding and respectful" during the German period.[235] Adinyra explains that "the Germans did not like liars and they always made sure that people worked."[236] This adherence to order, Adu argues, extended to the colonial administration itself:

> There was no bribery or corruption during the German era. It was unheard of, for even you dared not tell lies … For the Germans, if you accepted bribe, especially if you were a government employee, you would be lashed for 25 times, whether you could bear it or not.[237]

Besides the honesty and order which predominated society during the German period, oral historians discuss the discipline the Germans instilled in the Togolanders. Asase elaborates:

> German discipline was not a bad thing … It wasn't the master-slave kind of relationship. It was rather the kind of discipline that made us stand up to our responsibilities … the Germans were quick and straight to the point about doing things.[238]

Datsa adds: "Our fathers and grandfathers who [the Germans] met here seem to have some likeness for this type of discipline."[239] He continues:

> There was nothing like laziness. If you were a farmer, you were a serious farmer. You couldn't sit under the shade of a tree for the whole day chatting for Gruner to come and see. As a farmer, you must be on your farm. Therefore, theft was hardly heard of. Nobody went to steal from another's farm because everybody had enough food in his/ her farm.[240]

These qualities of honesty, order, and discipline influenced all aspects of community life, leading to a general respect for authority[241] and, in particular, the elderly,[242] among others.

Therefore, the overall German presence in the central Volta Region is viewed in mostly favorable terms by oral historians. During the period, "everyone lived in godliness, oneness, love, peace, happiness, and brotherhood and merrymaking," Klutse gushes. "The Germans brought literacy and formal education. Wars and conflicts ceased and we lived in peace … [the Germans] lived together in harmony with us."[243] Togbe Kuleke summarizes the sentiments of most of the oral historians when he states: "There was truthfulness and adherence to public order. There was no indiscipline."[244] The dual impact of Christianity and German occupation has influenced subsequent generations in the central Volta Region, according to Asase. "We have the German spirit in us," he explains. "By the German spirit, I mean honesty, humility, and godliness. These are the virtues that the Germans imparted on our parents and they in turn imparted on us."[245] Considering all the positive influences attributed to the Germans, it is not surprising Tegbe concludes "… when [the Germans] left, it was considered a great loss."[246]

In 1914, the British invaded Togoland and, according to Gikunu, "pushed the Germans to the wall at a place called Kamina in present-day Togo"[247] while Vulie claims that the battle was fought at Agbeluvhoe "in French Togo."[248] "When the war broke out," Togbe Kuleke offers, "some of our people became soldiers."[249] In Waya, those residents who originated from the Anlo Ewe area quickly left the central Volta Region. According to Catherina Ama Kwadzo Kugbleadzor, when the residents of Waya asked the Anlos why they were fleeing, "they said there was a war going on."[250] Even Galenkui, the German official at Ho, "had to run away to Lomé, their capital,"[251] maintains Gikunu. Other German administrators, Tegbe asserts, were seized and taken away by the British.[252]

The Germans were defeated, partly because of the actions of an informer, as Vulie explains:

> The Germans were betrayed by someone who showed the English where the Germans had hidden their arms and ammunition. During the war, the Germans got short of arms, so they decided to go for more. Not knowing that the railway line had been cut, the train got involved in an accident. There was no way of sending arms and ammunitions to the soldiers. That was how they were defeated.[253]

Tegbe makes clear the First World War was the result of rivalries between the European imperialists: "You see, this land belonged to the Germans. They were envied by other world powers at the time. They were thus dislodged during the 1914 world war."[254] As a result, according to Gikunu, the defeat "distorted all [the German] plans" for the central Volta Region.[255]

Immediately following the defeat of the Germans, an epidemic affected the central Volta Region, according to two oral historians, one in Waya and the other in Akpafu Todzi. "There was [an epidemic] our people called dzameza ("attack in the night")," explains Vulie. "They called it Asian flu. It was believed that the smoke from the guns shot during the First World War was responsible for that epidemic."[256] Agbewu confirms this account stating, "[The epidemic] they said was caused by the smoke from the guns. A lot of people died." Agbewu, however, believes there were outbreaks of both smallpox and influenza at the time.[257]

Within weeks, the collective group of German administrators who had resided in the central Volta Region for nearly three decades was replaced with British officials. And, as suddenly, the German missionaries were ordered to leave the area, abandoning their stations, thus disrupting an order which had evolved over nearly half a century in many of the communities.

Notes

1. Mosis Kofi Asase (oral historian in Ho), in discussion with the author, April 15, 1997.
2. Edward Kodzo Datsa (oral historian in Amedzofe), in discussion with the author, April 17, 1997.
3. Gilbert Joel Nyavor (oral historian in Kpandu), in discussion with the author, March 5, 1997.
4. Hillarius Gikunu (oral historian in Waya), in discussion with the author, June 16, 1997.
5. Oswald Kwame Klutse (oral historian in Ho), in discussion with the author, April 16, 1997.
6. Datsa, for example, contrasts the present with "Gruner's Time" (Edward Kodzo Datsa [oral historian in Amedzofe], in discussion with the author, April 17, 1997).
7. Togbe Kuleke (oral historian in Waya), in discussion with the author, February 19, 1997.
8. Based on Mosis Kofi Asase (oral historian in Ho), in discussion with the author, April 15, 1997 and Oswald Kwame Klutse (oral historian in Ho), in discussion with the author, April 16, 1997.
9. Togbe Kuleke (oral historian in Waya), in discussion with the author, February 19, 1997. Gikunu concurs that the first Germans in Waya were missionaries (Hillarius Gikunu [oral historian in Waya], in discussion with the author, June 16, 1997), while Catherina Ama Kwadzo Kugbleadzor maintains that German traders arrived in Waya before the missionaries (Catherina Ama Kwadzo Kugbleadzor [oral historian in Waya], in discussion with the author, June 16, 1997).
10. Hillarius Gikunu (oral historian in Waya), in discussion with the author, June 16, 1997.
11. Oswald Kwame Klutse (oral historian in Ho), in discussion with the author, April 16, 1997. Ho-Axoe and Ho-Kpota are sections of the town of Ho.
12. Jane Atakumah (oral historian in Kpandu), in discussion with the author, March 5, 1997; Johnson Adinyra (oral historian in Amedzofe), in discussion with the author, April 17, 1997; Oswald Kwame Klutse (oral historian in Ho), in discussion with the author, July 17, 1997; and Togbe Kuleke (oral historian in Waya), in discussion with the author, February 19, 1997.
13. Oswald Kwame Klutse (oral historian in Ho), in discussion with the author, July 17, 1997.
14. Francis Agbewu (oral historian in Akpafu Todzi), in discussion with the author, June 17, 1997; Julius Agbigbi (oral historian in Akpafu Todzi), in discussion with the author, June 17, 1997; Francis Agbewu (oral historian in Akpafu Todzi), in discussion with the author, June 17, 1997; Oswald Kwame Klutse (oral historian in Ho), in discussion with the author, July 17,1997; Abra Janet Kumordzi (oral historian in Akpafu Todzi), in discussion with the author, June 17, 1997; and Mathias Yevu Tegbe (oral historian in Hohoe), in discussion with the author,17 June 1997.
15. Abra Janet Kumordzi (oral historian in Akpafu Todzi), in discussion with the author, June 17, 1997.
16. Francis Agbewu (oral historian in Akpafu Todzi), in discussion with the author, June 17, 1997.
17. Julius Agbigbi (oral historian in Akpafu Todzi), in discussion with the author, June 17, 1997. These structures still stand at present.

18. Abra Janet Kumordzi (oral historian in Akpafu Todzi), in discussion with the author, June 17, 1997.
19. Francis Agbewu (oral historian in Akpafu Todzi), in discussion with the author, June 17, 1997.
20. Adzoa Asase (oral historian in Akpafu Todzi), in discussion with the author, July 16, 1997. Sebald suggests this might be a corruption of the German surname "Fies," as there were several Germans with this name working in the colony (personal correspondence).
21. Edward Kodzo Datsa (oral historian in Amedzofe), in discussion with the author, April 17, 1997.
22. Alfred Adinyra (oral historian in Amedzofe), in discussion with the author, April 17, 1997.
23. *Ibid.*
24. Edward Kodzo Datsa (oral historian in Amedzofe), in discussion with the author, April 17, 1997. These buildings remain today, but serve different functions.
25. Oswald Kwame Klutse (oral historian in Ho), in discussion with the author, April 16, 1997. For example, Klutse asserts it was only on December 13, 1868, that "the first batch of Christians were baptized," nearly ten years after the arrival of the missionaries in Ho.
26. Seth Adu (oral historian in Ho), in discussion with the author, March 7, 1997. Adu adds: "The German names are very difficult to be pronounced by the people. For instance, a man from Lemgo was called thus. Other names included Schlegel, Westermann, Diel, Kofinger, and Funcker." Sebald proposes the German surnames Diehl, Kopfinger, and Funke for the last three (personal correspondence) which may have been mispronounced by the oral historian or incorrectly transcribed afterwards. Among the former slaves who were educated by the missionaries and became pastors was (first name?) Quist, according to Adu.
27. Mosis Kofi Asase (oral historian in Ho), in discussion with the author, April 15, 1997.
28. Oswald Kwame Klutse (oral historian in Ho), in discussion with the author, July 17, 1997 and April 16, 1997. In the July interview, Klutse also refers to William Akude, who was one of the first Christians from Ho. Akude served as an assistant to Stefano Kwami, who moved to Peki in 1883 to work as a cathechist (Debrunner, 99). Kwami held the same position in Ho since 1871, while Akude worked as an evangelist in Amfoe, one of the secondary stations, in 1883 (Staatsbibliothek, Berlin, File FA 1/358, 65–6).
29. Alfred Adinyra (oral historian in Amedzofe), in discussion with the author, April 17, 1997. Gbadzeme is a village immediately to the northwest of Amedzofe. Adinyra states these two men "took their communion at Ho."
30. Nyavor states the first North Germans missionaries arrived in Kpandu in 1892 (Gilbert Joel Nyavor [oral historian in Kpandu], in discussion with the author, March 5, 1997).
31. *Ibid.*
32. *Ibid.*
33. *Ibid.* In fact, according to Nyavor, Dagadu on several occasions met with British officials in nearby Peki as well as in Accra, while Williams, the district commissioner in Peki, also visited Kpandu.
34. Oswald Kwame Klutse (oral historian in Ho), in discussion with the author, April 16, 1997.
35. Mosis Kofi Asase (oral historian in Ho), in discussion with the author, April 15, 1997.
36. Misahöhe was identified as the seat of the local district commissioner by Francis Agbewu (oral historian in Akpafu Todzi), in discussion with the author, June 17, 1997; Gilbert

Joel Nyavor (oral historian in Kpandu), in discussion with the author, March 5, 1997; and Mathias Yevu Tegbe (oral historian in Hohoe), in discussion with the author, June 17, 1997. Outside of the station at Kpandu, Tegbe states the nearest German official was at Yor, which is "between Hohoe and Kpalimé," that is, in the area of Misahöhe.

37. Edward Kodzo Datsa (oral historian in Amedzofe), in discussion with the author, April 17, 1997.

38. *Ibid.*

39. *Ibid.*

40. Seth Adu (oral historian in Ho), in discussion with the author, June 15, 1997. Furthermore, cases which fell outside Misahöhe's jurisdiction were sent to Atakpamé, "the seat of the governor's special assistant," Adu asserts.

41. The Germans built many of their stations, both governmental and missionary, atop hills because of the climate, according to Alfred Adinyra (oral historian in Amedzofe), in discussion with the author, April 17 1997 and Mosis Kofi Asase (oral historian in Ho), in discussion with the author, April 15, 1997.

42. Simon Kugbleadzor (oral historian in Waya), in discussion with the author, June 16, 1997.

43. Hillarius Gikunu (oral historian in Waya), in discussion with the author, June 16, 1997.

44. Seth Adu (oral historian in Ho), in discussion with the author, March 7, 1997; Mosis Kofi Asase (oral historian in Ho), in discussion with the author, April 15, 1997; Edward Kodzo Datsa (oral historian in Amedzofe), in discussion with the author, April 17, 1997; Hillarius Gikunu (oral historian in Waya), in discussion with the author, June 16,1997; Simon Kugbleadzor (oral historian in Waya), in discussion with the author, June 16, 1997; and Eugenia Kodzo Yawa (oral historian in Ho), in discussion with the author, June 16, 1997.

45. Seth Adu (oral historian in Ho), in discussion with the author, March 7, 1997. However, "Galenkui" will be used here, since this is the name used by oral historians. Sebald indicates he has come across this nickname in reference to the German administrator Hupfeld and that "Foss" probably is a corruption of Voss, a German official at Ho (personal correspondence).

46. Simon Kugbleadzor (oral historian in Waya), in discussion with the author, June 16, 1997.

47. Eugenia Kodzo Yawa (oral historian in Ho), in discussion with the author, June 16, 1997. Datsa also states Galenkui was "another very strong man" (Edward Kodzo Datsa [oral historian in Amedzofe], in discussion with the author, April 17, 1997).

48. Seth Adu (oral historian in Ho), in discussion with the author, March 7, 1997.

49. Seth Adu (oral historian in Ho), in discussion with the author, June 15, 1997.

50. Gilbert Joel Nyavor (oral historian in Kpandu), in discussion with the author, March 5, 1997 and Mathias Yevu Tegbe (oral historian in Hohoe), in discussion with the author, June 17, 1997. Atakumah also describes the station at Kpandu, but does not mention Pearl (Jane Atakumah [oral historian in Kpandu] in discussion with the author, March 5, 1997). The German administrator was named Perl, according to Sebald (personal correspondence).

51. Edward Kodzo Datsa (oral historian in Amedzofe), in discussion with the author, April 17, 1997.

52. Togbe Lavi V (oral historian in Waya), in discussion with the author, February 19, 1997.

53. Seth Adu (oral historian in Ho), in discussion with the author, March 7, 1997; A. Y. Daldi (oral historian in Waya), in discussion with the author, February 19, 1997; Edward Kodzo Datsa (oral historian in Amedzofe), in discussion with the author, April 17, 1997; Togbe Kuleke (oral historian in Waya), in discussion with the author, February 19, 1997; and John Vulie (oral historian in Waya), in discussion with the author, June 16, 1997.

54. Edward Kodzo Datsa (oral historian in Amedzofe), in discussion with the author, April 17, 1997.

55. Seth Adu (oral historian in Ho), in discussion with the author, March 7, 1997 and Togbe Kuleke (oral historian in Waya), in discussion with the author, February 19, 1997.

56. Togbe Kuleke (oral historian in Waya), in discussion with the author, February 19, 1997.

57. John Vulie (oral historian in Waya), in discussion with the author, June 16, 1997.

58. Hillarius Gikunu (oral historian in Waya), in discussion with the author, June 16, 1997.

59. Edward Kodzo Datsa (oral historian in Amedzofe), in discussion with the author, April 17, 1997.

60. Oswald Kwame Klutse (oral historian in Ho), in discussion with the author, April 16, 1997.

61. Gilbert Joel Nyavor (oral historian in Kpandu), in discussion with the author, March 5, 1997.

62. *Ibid.*

63. Seth Adu (oral historian in Ho), in discussion with the author, June 15, 1997 and March 7, 1997; Gilbert Joel Nyavor (oral historian in Kpandu), in discussion with the author, March 5, 1997; and Catherina Ama Kwadzo Kugbleadzor (oral historian in Waya), in discussion with the author, June 16, 1997. According to Adu, "The whites didn't have time for that kind of job." It is not clear from the oral history whether non-Togolander Africans were members of this force.

64. Gilbert Joel Nyavor (oral historian in Kpandu), in discussion with the author, March 5, 1997.

65. *Ibid.*

66. Togbe Kuleke (oral historian in Waya), in discussion with the author, June 16, 1997.

67. Seth Adu (oral historian in Ho), in discussion with the author, June 15, 1997 and March 7, 1997.

68. Togbe Kuleke (oral historian in Waya), in discussion with the author, June 16, 1997.

69. Catherina Ama Kwadzo Kugbleadzor (oral historian in Waya), in discussion with the author, June 16, 1997.

70. Alfred Adinyra (Amedzofe), in discussion with the author, April 17, 1997); Seth Adu (oral historian in Ho), in discussion with the author, March 7, 1997; Mosis Kofi Asase (oral historian in Ho), in discussion with the author, April 15,1997; Hillarius Gikunu (oral historian in Waya), in discussion with the author, June 16, 1997; Togbe Kuleke (oral historian in Waya), in discussion with the author, June 16, 1997 and February 19, 1997; Simon Kugbleadzor (Waya), in discussion with the author, June 16, 1997; and Catherina Ama Kwadzo Kugbleadzor (oral historian in Waya), in discussion with the author, June 16, 1997 and February 19, 1997 . Asase explains that "mango trees were planted along the roads to provide shade" and Adinyra concurs. Klutse maintains that mangoes "grew as wild trees before [the Germans] came" (Oswald Kwame Klutse [oral historian in Ho], in discussion with the author, April 16,

1997) and Yawa also states that mangoes were in existence before the German occupation (Eugenia Kodzo Yawa [oral historian in Ho], in discussion with the author, April 18, 1997).

71. Seth Adu (oral historian in Ho), in discussion with the author, March 7, 1997; Togbe Kuleke (oral historian in Waya), in discussion with the author, June 16, 1997; and Catherina Ama Kwadzo Kugbleadzor (oral historian in Waya), in discussion with the author, June 16, 1997.

72. Alfred Adinyra (oral historian in Amedzofe), in discussion with the author, April 17, 1997; Togbe Kuleke (oral historian in Waya), in discussion with the author, June 16, 1997; and Catherina Ama Kwadzo Kugbleadzor (oral historian in Waya), in discussion with the author, June 16, 1997. Avocado is referred to as "pear" in Ghana.

73. Edward Kodzo Datsa (oral historian in Amedzofe), in discussion with the author, April 17, 1997 and Mathias Yevu Tegbe (oral historian in Kpandu), in discussion with the author, June 17, 1997. Datsa identifies the introduction as "the small type" of coffee.

74. Jane Atakumah (oral historian in Kpandu), in discussion with the author, March 5, 1997.

75. Kwami Asamani (oral historian in Akpafu Todzi), in discussion with the author, July 16, 1997.

76. Mathias Yevu Tegbe (oral historian in Kpandu), in discussion with the author, June 17, 1997.

77. Togbe Kuleke (oral historian in Waya), in discussion with the author, June 16, 1997.

78. Gilbert Joel Nyavor (oral historian in Kpandu), in discussion with the author, March 5, 1997.

79. Mosis Kofi Asase (oral historian in Ho), in discussion with the author, April 15, 1997. Atafe Badasu concurs: "cotton work was common before the Germans came to add theirs to it" (Atafe Badasu [oral historian in Waya], in discussion with the author, June 16, 1997).

80. Togbe Kuleke (oral historian in Waya), in discussion with the author, June 16, 1997. Cocoa remains one of the primary exports of Ghana, a legacy of the colonial economy of the Gold Coast.

81. Gilbert Joel Nyavor (oral historian in Kpandu), in discussion with the author, March 5, 1997. These structures, long in disuse, still stand in Kpandu.

82. Togbe Kuleke (oral historian in Waya), in discussion with the author, June 16, 1997.

83. Kwami Asamani (oral historian in Akpafu Todzi), in discussion with the author, July 16, 1997. Asamani states: "The kind of farming we do now, it was the English who brought cocoa. They taught us how to cultivate that and palm-fruits."

84. Gilbert Joel Nyavor (oral historian in Kpandu), in discussion with the author, March 5, 1997 and Mathias Yevu Tegbe (oral historian in Hohoe), in discussion with the author, June 17, 1997. Datsa, however, maintains "cocoa was brought to this place not by Tetteh Quarshie; it was the missionaries and the administrators who introduced cocoa" (Edward Kodzo Datsa [oral historian in Amedzofe], in discussion with the author, April 17, 1997).

85. Sebald disputes this point. His research indicates the Germans did not encourage small-scale cocoa farming since they feared competition for the cocoa plantations they established in Togoland and Cameroon (personal correspondence).

86. Seth Adu (oral historian in Ho), in discussion with the author, March 7, 1997.

87. Gilbert Joel Nyavor (oral historian in Kpandu), in discussion with the author, March 5, 1997 and Hillarius Gikunu (oral historian in Waya), in discussion with the author, June 16, 1997. The latter states that cocoa from Waya was shipped to Kpalimé.

88. Mathias Yevu Tegbe (oral historian in Hohoe), in discussion with the author, June 17, 1997.

89. *Ibid.*

90. Oswald Kwame Klutse (oral historian in Ho), in discussion with the author, July 17, 1997.

91. Seth Adu (oral historian in Ho), in discussion with the author, March 7, 1997.

92. *Ibid.*

93. Theresa Nyagbe (oral historian in Hohoe), in discussion with the author, June 17, 1997 and Eugenia Kodzo Yawa (oral historian in Ho), in discussion with the author, June 16, 1997. Yawa states: "[The Germans] brought nothing. All these [crops] were here before they came."

94. Johnson Agbemafle (oral historian in Amedzofe), in discussion with the author, April 17, 1997.

95. Yafet Togbe Kuleke (oral historian in Waya), in discussion with the author, June 16, 1997.

96. Seth Adu (oral historian in Ho), in discussion with the author, March 7, 1997.

97. Seth Adu (oral historian in Ho), in discussion with the author, June 15, 1997. Those who refused to obey this order were punished at Misahöhe, according to Adu, contradicting his assertion in the March interview.

98. Francis Agbewu (oral historian in Akpafu Todzi), in discussion with the author, June 17, 1997. Agbewu explains that the residents of Akpafu primarily were engaged in blacksmithing, "so farming was done on subsistence basis."

99. Togbe Kuleke (oral historian in Waya), in discussion with the author, June 16, 1997.

100. Catherina Ama Kwadzo Kugbleadzor (oral historian in Waya), in discussion with the author, June 16, 1997. Among the items sent from Waya to Kpalimé were groundnuts (or peanuts) and maize.

101. Nyavor asserts: "Cotton-weaving was well-known in the northern part of this country. Our forefathers learnt it from northern Ghana before the Germans arrived" (Gilbert Joel Nyavor [oral historian in Kpandu], in discussion with the author, March 5, 1997).

102. Jane Atakumah (oral historian in Kpandu), in discussion with the author, March 5, 1997.

103. John Vulie (oral historian in Waya), in discussion with the author, June 16, 1997.

104. Gilbert Joel Nyavor (oral historian in Kpandu), in discussion with the author, March 5, 1997.

105. Oswald Kwame Klutse (oral historian in Ho), in discussion with the author, July 17, 1997.

106. *Ibid.* Tegbe mentions German imports of "cutlasses, knives, and the like" (Mathias Yevu Tegbe [oral historian in Hohoe], in discussion with the author, June 17, 1997).

107. Francis Agbewu (oral historian in Akpafu Todzi), in discussion with the author, June 17, 1997.

108. Kwami Asamani (oral historian in Akpafu Todzi), in discussion with the author, July 16, 1997.

109. Seth Adu (oral historian in Ho), in discussion with the author, June 15, 1997 and March 7, 1997; Mosis Kofi Asase (oral historian in Ho), in discussion with the author, April 15,

1997; and Mathias Yevu Tegbe (oral historian in Hohoe), in discussion with the author, July 17, 1997.

110. Adu asserts that before the Germans "it was only at Akpafu where they practiced blacksmithing" (Seth Adu [oral historian in Ho], in discussion with the author, March 7, 1997).

111. Mosis Kofi Asase (oral historian in Ho), in discussion with the author, April 15, 1997.

112. Nicholas Asamani (oral historian in Kpandu), in discussion with the author, March 5, 1997.

113. Alfred Adinyra (oral historian in Amedzofe), in discussion with the author, April 17, 1997; Seth Adu (oral historian in Ho), in discussion with the author, March 7, 1997; Johnson K. Agbemafle (oral historian in Amedzofe), in discussion with the author, April 17, 1997; Mosis Kofi Asase (oral historian in Ho), in discussion with the author, April 15, 1997; Togbe Kuleke (oral historian in Waya), in discussion with the author, June 16, 1997 and February 19, 1997; and Mathias Yevu Tegbe (oral historian in Hohoe), in discussion with the author, July 17, 1997.

114. Alfred Adinyra (oral historian in Amedzofe), in discussion with the author, April 17, 1997; Johnson K. Agbemafle (oral historian in Amedzofe), in discussion with the author, April 17, 1997; Togbe Kuleke (oral historian in Waya), in discussion with the author, June 16, 1997 and February 19, 1997; and Mathias Yevu Tegbe (oral historian in Hohoe), in discussion with the author, July 17, 1997.

115. Seth Adu (oral historian in Ho), in discussion with the author, June 15, 1997 and March 7, 1997 and Mathias Yevu Tegbe (oral historian in Hohoe), in discussion with the author, July 17, 1997.

116. Mathias Yevu Tegbe (oral historian in Hohoe), in discussion with the author, July 17, 1997. Adu agrees: "All handicrafts were introduced by the Germans" (Seth Adu [oral historian in Ho], in discussion with the author, March 7, 1997).

117. Gilbert Joel Nyavor (oral historian in Kpandu), in discussion with the author, March 5, 1997.

118. Alfred Adinyra (oral historian in Amedzofe), in discussion with the author, April 17, 1997. Adinyra is a retired carpenter.

119. Edward Kodzo Datsa (oral historian in Amedzofe), in discussion with the author, April 17, 1997.

120. Seth Adu (oral historian in Ho), in discussion with the author, March 7, 1997. In listing the German names adopted by Christian converts, as discussed above, Adu explains: "Some 'Quists' are not Germans, they are West Indians. Even my uncle, Agripah, is named after one West Indian who was a carpenter. So, Agripah has become his surname."

121. Hillarius Gikunu (oral historian in Waya), in discussion with the author, June 16, 1997.

122. Mosis Kofi Asase (oral historian in Ho), in discussion with the author, April 15, 1997.

123. John Vulie (oral historian in Waya), in discussion with the author, June 16, 1997.

124. Seth Adu (oral historian in Ho), in discussion with the author, June 15, 1997.

125. Togbe Kuleke (oral historian in Waya), in discussion with the author, February 19, 1997.

126. Seth Adu (oral historian in Ho), in discussion with the author, June 15, 1997.

127. Togbe Kuleke (oral historian in Waya), in discussion with the author, June 16, 1997. Nyagbe concurs: "I heard [the Germans] were the first to introduce education to our area" (Theresa Nyagbe [oral historian in Hohoe], in discussion with the author, June 17, 1997).

128. Hillarius Gikunu (oral historian in Waya), in discussion with the author, June 16, 1997.
129. Edward Kodzo Datsa (oral historian in Amedzofe), in discussion with the author, April 17, 1997.
130. Gilbert Joel Nyavor (oral historian in Kpandu), in discussion with the author, March 5, 1997.
131. Seth Adu (oral historian in Ho), in discussion with the author, July 17, 1997; Francis Agbewu (Akpafu Todzi), in discussion with the author, June 17, 1997; Kwami Asamani (oral historian in Akpafu Todzi), in discussion with the author, July 16, 1997; Atafe Badasu (oral historian in Waya), in discussion with the author, June 16, 1997; Hillarius Gikunu (oral historian in Waya), in discussion with the author, June 16, 1997; and Mathias Yevu Tegbe (oral historian in Hohoe), in discussion with the author, June 17, 1997.
132. Mathias Yevu Tegbe (oral historian in Hohoe), in discussion with the author, June 17, 1997.
133. Alfred Adinyra (oral historian in Amedzofe), in discussion with the author, April 17, 1997. Asase also asserts that the Germans provided free uniforms to school children (Mosis Kofi Asase [oral historian in Ho], in discussion with the author, April 15, 1997).
134. Seth Adu (oral historian in Ho), in discussion with the author, March 7, 1977.
135. *Ibid.*
136. Alfred Adinyra (oral historian in Amedzofe), in discussion with the author, April 17, 1997.
137. Mathias Yevu Tegbe (oral historian in Hohoe), in discussion with the author, June 17, 1997. Asase maintains that "those who attended schools built by the Germans studied both German and English" (Mosis Kofi Asase [oral historian in Ho], in discussion with the author, April 15, 1997). Adu, who was a student in these German schools, states "I entered the fourth class before I started learning German" at a school in Kpeme (Seth Adu [oral historian in Ho], in discussion with the author, July 17, 1997).
138. Seth Adu (oral historian in Ho), in discussion with the author, July 17, 1997.
139. Mosis Kofi Asase (oral historian in Ho), in discussion with the author, April 15, 1997.
140. Seth Adu (oral historian in Ho), in discussion with the author, July 17, 1997.
141. *Ibid.* Adu states there were also colleges in Aného and Ho, although he does not specify whether these too were affiliated with the Catholic Mission.
142. *Ibid.*
143. Abra Janet Kumordzi (oral historian in Akpafu Todzi), in discussion with the author, June 17, 1997.
144. Theresa Nyagbe (oral historian in Hohoe), in discussion with the author, June 17, 1997.
145. Abra Janet Kumordzi (oral historian in Akpafu Todzi), in discussion with the author, June 17, 1997.
146. Mosis Kofi Asase (oral historian in Ho), in discussion with the author, April 15, 1997 and Oswald Kwame Klutse (oral historian in Ho), in discussion with the author, April 16, 1997.
147. Hillarius Gikunu (oral historian in Waya), in discussion with the author, June 16, 1997.
148. Oswald Kwame Klutse (oral historian in Ho), in discussion with the author, April 16, 1997.
149. Mosis Kofi Asase (oral historian in Ho), in discussion with the author, April 15, 1997.
150. Hillarius Gikunu (oral historian in Waya), in discussion with the author, June 16, 1997 and Togbe Kuleke (oral historian in Waya), in discussion with the author, February 19, 1997.
151. Hillarius Gikunu (oral historian in Waya), in discussion with the author, June 16, 1997.

152. Catherina Ama Kwadzo Kugbleadzor (oral historian in Waya), in discussion with the author, February 19, 1997). This included cooking and sweeping, according to Kugbleadzor.
153. Alfred Adinyra (oral historian in Amedzofe), in discussion with the author, April 17, 1997.
154. Seth Adu (oral historian in Ho), in discussion with the author, March 7, 1997.
155. Mosis Kofi Asase (oral historian in Ho), in discussion with the author, April 15, 1997; Jane Atakumah (oral historian in Kpandu), in discussion with the author, March 5, 1997); and Eugenia Kodzo Yawa (oral historian in Ho), in discussion with the author, June 16, 1997 and April 18, 1997.
156. Jane Atakumah (oral historian in Kpandu), in discussion with the author, March 5, 1997.
157. Abra Janet Kumordzi (oral historian in Akpafu Todzi), in discussion with the author, June 17, 1997 and Mathias Yevu Tegbe (oral historian in Hohoe), in discussion with the author, June 17, 1997.
158. Abra Janet Kumordzi (oral historian in Akpafu Todzi), in discussion with the author, June 17, 1997.
159. Mathias Yevu Tegbe (oral historian in Hohoe), in discussion with the author, June 17, 1997.
160. Seth Adu (oral historian in Ho), in discussion with the author, June 15, 1997 and Mathias Yevu Tegbe (oral historian in Hohoe), in discussion with the author, June 17, 1997. The diseases treated by the Germans included leprosy, sleeping sickness. smallpox, and influenza.
161. Seth Adu (oral historian in Ho), in discussion with the author, March 7, 1997.
162. Seth Adu (oral historian in Ho), in discussion with the author, June 15, 1997.
163. Seth Adu (oral historian in Ho), in discussion with the author, March 7, 1997.
164. Mathias Yevu Tegbe (oral historian in Hohoe), in discussion with the author, June 17, 1997. He asserts that there were additional quarantine centers.
165. Seth Adu (oral historian in Ho), in discussion with the author, June 15, 1997 and March 7, 1997.
166. Seth Adu (oral historian in Ho), in discussion with the author, June 15, 1997.
167. Atafe Badasu (oral historian in Waya), in discussion with the author, June 16, 1997.
168. Seth Adu (oral historian in Ho), in discussion with the author, March 7, 1997.
169. Seth Adu (oral historian in Ho), in discussion with the author, June 15, 1997.
170. Gilbert Joel Nyavor (oral historian in Kpandu), in discussion with the author, March 5, 1997.
171. Jane Atakumah (oral historian in Kpandu), in discussion with the author, March 5, 1997.
172. Gabriel Kofi Bakotse (oral historian in Kpandu), in discussion with the author, July 2001.
173. Gilbert Joel Nyavor (oral historian in Kpandu), in discussion with the author, March 5, 1997.
174. *Ibid.*
175. *Ibid.* Despite his continued resistance to the Germans, however, Nyavor claims that Dagadu "condemned each colonial power to the other," and also criticized British policies in the Gold Coast.
176. Jane Atakumah (oral historian in Kpandu), in discussion with the author, March 5, 1997. For an expanded discussion of this episode, see Laumann, "Domination and Resistance."
177. Gilbert Joel Nyavor (oral historian in Kpandu), in discussion with the author, March 5, 1997.

178. Seth Adu (oral historian in Ho), in discussion with the author, June 15, 1997; Francis Agbewu (oral historian in Akpafu Todzi), in discussion with the author, June 17, 1997; Atafe Badasu (oral historian in Waya), in discussion with the author, June 16, 1997; Togbe Kuleke (oral historian in Waya), in discussion with the author, June 16, 1997; and Catherina Ama Kwadzo Kugbleadzor (oral historian in Waya), in discussion with the author, June 16, 1997.

179. Atafe Badasu (oral historian in Waya), in discussion with the author, June 16, 1997; Hillarius Gikunu (oral historian in Waya), in discussion with the author, June 16, 1997; Togbe Kuleke (oral historian in Waya), in discussion with the author, June 16, 1997; and Catherina Ama Kwadzo Kugbleadzor (oral historian in Waya), in discussion with the author, June 16, 1997.

180. Catherina Ama Kwadzo Kugbleadzor (oral historian in Waya), in discussion with the author, June 16, 1997.

181. Francis Agbewu (oral historian in Akpafu Todzi), in discussion with the author, June 17, 1997.

182. Seth Adu (oral historian in Ho), in discussion with the author, June 15, 1997.

183. Francis Agbewu (oral historian in Akpafu Todzi), in discussion with the author, June 17, 1997; Atafe Badasu (oral historian in Waya), in discussion with the author, June 16, 1997; and Mathias Yevu Tegbe (oral historian in Hohoe), in discussion with the author, June 17, 1997.

184. Seth Adu (oral historian in Ho), in discussion with the author, June 15, 1997; Mathias Yevu Tegbe (oral historian in Hohoe), in discussion with the author, June 17, 1997; and Eugenia Kodzo Yawa (oral historian in Ho), in discussion with the author, June 16, 1997 and April 18, 1997. Badasu claims the permits were limited to a few days only (Atafe Badasu [oral historian in Waya], in discussion with the author, June 16, 1997). Gikunu maintains travelers simply needed to ask for permission at the border and then the length of their stay in the Gold Coast was not restricted (Hillarius Gikunu [oral historian in Waya], in discussion with the author, June 16, 1997).

185. Mathias Yevu Tegbe (oral historian in Hohoe), in discussion with the author, June 17, 1997.

186. Catherina Ama Kwadzo Kugbleadzor (oral historian in Waya), in discussion with the author, June 16, 1997.

187. Hillarius Gikunu (oral historian in Waya), in discussion with the author, June 16, 1997.

188. Atafe Badasu (oral historian in Waya), in discussion with the author, June 16, 1997.

189. Eugenia Kodzo Yawa (oral historian in Ho), in discussion with the author, April 18, 1997.

190. Eugenia Kodzo Yawa (oral historian in Ho), in discussion with the author, June 16, 1997.

191. Gilbert Joel Nyavor (oral historian in Kpandu), in discussion with the author, March 5, 1997. Adu argues that very little trade took place between the German and British colonies, except for individuals dealing in "contraband goods like guns and gunpowder," who were arrested by the German authorities. Furthermore, he claims the movement of people seeking employment also followed the opposite direction. According to this oral historian, opportunities in carpentry, goldsmithing, and blacksmithing abounded in Togo. Adu continues: "In the Gold Coast, there were no such job opportunities because the English were only concerned with mining gold. People therefore crossed over from the Gold Coast

to Togo in pursuit of jobs" (Seth Adu [oral historian in Ho], in discussion with the author, March 7, 1997).

192. Hillarius Gikunu (oral historian in Waya), in discussion with the author, June 16, 1997.

193. Alfred Adinyra (oral historian in Amedzofe), in discussion with the author, April 17, 1997.

194. Mathias Yevu Tegbe (oral historian in Hohoe), in discussion with the author, June 17, 1997.

195. Edward Kodzo Datsa (oral historian in Amedzofe), in discussion with the author, April 17, 1997.

196. Catherina Ama Kwadzo Kugbleadzor (oral historian in Waya), in discussion with the author, June 16, 1997.

197. Atafe Badasu (oral historian in Waya), in discussion with the author, June 16, 1997.

198. Francis Agbewu (oral historian in Akpafu Todzi), in discussion with the author, June 17, 1997.

199. Mathias Yevu Tegbe (oral historian in Hohoe), in discussion with the author, June 17, 1997. These towns are located elsewhere in the central Volta Region.

200. Francis Agbewu (oral historian in Akpafu Todzi), in discussion with the author, June 17, 1997.

201. Mathias Yevu Tegbe (oral historian in Hohoe), in discussion with the author, June 17, 1997.

202. Theresa Nyagbe (oral historian in Hohoe), in discussion with the author, June 17, 1997.

203. John Vulie (oral historian in Waya), in discussion with the author, June 16, 1997. Vulie states there were roads connecting Waya to Kpeve, Ho, and Ziope.

204. Togbe Kuleke (oral historian in Waya), in discussion with the author, June 16, 1997.

205. Hillarius Gikunu (oral historian in Waya), in discussion with the author, June 16, 1997.

206. Atakumah states men were forced to carry goods from Kpandu to Kpalimé (Jane Atakumah [oral historian in Kpandu], in discussion with the author, March 5, 1997).

207. Alfred Adinyra (oral historian in Amedzofe), in discussion with the author, April 17, 1997.

208. *Ibid.*

209. Simon Kugbleadzor (oral historian in Waya: February 19, 1997). When Kugbleadzor made this comment, another oral historian, Togbe Kuleke, added: "I just want to correct [Kugbleadzor] … It was not the missionaries who forced the people to carry loads. It was the German administrative workers" (Togbe Kuleke [oral historian in Waya], in discussion with the author, February 19, 1997).

210. Gilbert Joel Nyavor (oral historian in Kpandu), in discussion with the author, March 5, 1997.

211. Theresa Nyagbe (oral historian in Hohoe), in discussion with the author, June 17, 1997.

212. Mosis Kofi Asase (oral historian in Ho), in discussion with the author, April 15, 1997.

213. Edward Kodzo Datsa (Amedzofe), in discussion with the author, April 17, 1997 and Theresa Nyagbe (oral historian in Hohoe), in discussion with the author, June 17, 1997.

214. Seth Adu (oral historian in Ho), in discussion with the author, March 7, 1997; Atafe Badasu (oral historian in Waya), in discussion with the author, June 16, 1997; and Togbe Kuleke (oral historian in Waya), in discussion with the author, June 16, 1997 and February 18, 1997.

215. Theresa Nyagbe (oral historian in Hohoe), in discussion with the author, June 17, 1997.

216. Mathias Yevu Tegbe (oral historian in Hohoe), in discussion with the author, June 17, 1997.
217. Seth Adu (oral historian in Ho), in discussion with the author, March 7, 1997.
218. Eugenia Kodzo Yawa (oral historian in Ho), in discussion with the author, April 18, 1997.
219. Seth Adu (oral historian in Ho), in discussion with the author, March 7, 1997.
220. Edward Kodzo Datsa (oral historian in Amedzofe), in discussion with the author, April 17, 1997.
221. Seth Adu (oral historian in Ho), in discussion with the author, March 7, 1997.
222. *Ibid.*
223. Alfred Adinyra (oral historian in Amedzofe), in discussion with the author, April 17, 1997.
224. Eugenia Kodzo Yawa (oral historian in Ho), in discussion with the author, April 18, 1997.
225. Seth Adu (oral historian in Ho), in discussion with the author, March 7, 1997.
226. Gilbert Joel Nyavor (oral historian in Kpandu), in discussion with the author, March 5, 1997.
227. Hillarius Gikunu (oral historian in Waya), in discussion with the author, June 16, 1997.
228. Edward Kodzo Datsa (oral historian in Amedzofe), in discussion with the author, April 17, 1997.
229. Eugenia Kodzo Yawa (oral historian in Ho), in discussion with the author, April 18, 1997.
230. Oswald Kwame Klutse (oral historian in Ho), in discussion with the author, April 16, 1997.
231. Hillarius Gikunu (oral historian in Waya), in discussion with the author, June 16, 1997.
232. Mosis Kofi Asase (oral historian in Ho), in discussion with the author, April 15, 1997; Togbe Kuleke (oral historian in Waya), in discussion with the author, June 16, 1997; and Gilbert Joel Nyavor (oral historian in Kpandu), in discussion with the author, March 5, 1997.
233. Togbe Kuleke (oral historian in Waya), in discussion with the author, June 16, 1997 and Togbe Lavi V (oral historian in Waya), in discussion with the author, February 19, 1997.
234. Alfred Adinyra (oral historian in Amedzofe), in discussion with the author, April 17, 1997; Mosis Kofi Asase (oral historian in Ho), in discussion with the author, April 15, 1997; Edward Kodzo Datsa (oral historian in Amedzofe), in discussion with the author, April 17, 1997; Togbe Kuleke (oral historian in Waya), in discussion with the author, June 16, 1997; and Eugenia Kodzo Yawa (oral historian in Ho), in discussion with the author, April 18, 1997.
235. Gilbert Joel Nyavor (oral historian in Kpandu), in discussion with the author, March 5, 1997.
236. Alfred Adinyra (oral historian in Amedzofe), in discussion with the author, April 17, 1997.
237. Seth Adu (oral historian in Ho), in discussion with the author, March 7, 1997.
238. Mosis Kofi Asase (oral historian in Ho), in discussion with the author, April 15, 1997.
239. Edward Kodzo Datsa (oral historian in Amedzofe), in discussion with the author, April 17, 1997.
240. *Ibid.*
241. Hillarius Gikunu (oral historian in Waya), in discussion with the author, June 16, 1997.
242. Catherina Ama Kwadzo Kugbleadzor (oral historian in Waya), in discussion with the author, June 16, 1997.
243. Oswald Kwame Klutse (oral historian in Ho), in discussion with the author, April 16, 1997.
244. Togbe Kuleke (oral historian in Waya), in discussion with the author, June 16, 1997.
245. Mosis Kofi Asase (oral historian in Ho), in discussion with the author, April 15, 1997.

246. Mathias Yevu Tegbe (oral historian in Hohoe), in discussion with the author, June 17, 1997.

247. Hillarius Gikunu (oral historian in Waya), in discussion with the author, June 16, 1997.

248. John Vulie (oral historian in Waya), in discussion with the author, June 16, 1997.

249. Togbe Kuleke (oral historian in Waya), in discussion with the author, June 16, 1997.

250. Catherina Ama Kwadzo Kugbleadzor (oral historian in Waya), in discussion with the author, June 16, 1997.

251. Hillarius Gikunu (oral historian in Waya), in discussion with the author, June 16, 1997.

252. Mathias Yevu Tegbe (oral historian in Hohoe), in discussion with the author, June 17, 1997.

253. John Vulie (oral historian in Waya), in discussion with the author, June 16, 1997.

254. Mathias Yevu Tegbe (oral historian in Hohoe), in discussion with the author, June 17, 1997.

255. Hillarius Gikunu (oral historian in Waya), in discussion with the author, June 16, 1997.

256. John Vulie (oral historian in Waya), in discussion with the author, June 16, 1997.

257. Francis Agbewu (oral historian in Akpafu Todzi), in discussion with the author, June 17, 1997. Agbewu claims "the symptoms were feverish conditions and growing lean. People died within two or three days after the symptoms."

CHAPTER FIVE

Nostalgia, Neglect, and Nationalism under the British

In contrast to the oral history, written sources suggest those who lived under German occupation enthusiastically welcomed their new British rulers.[1] E. D. K. Daketsey claims that in the Ewe areas of Togoland, "the villages were thrown into jubilation, with chiefs publicly burning the loathsome German flags."[2] F. K. Buah argues that during the First World War the people of "… Eweland lent their support to the victory of the British over the Germans."[3] Amenumey explains that assistance to the Allied forces especially was forthcoming from the Anlo Ewe, most of whom resided in the Gold Coast, as they offered soldiers, covert information, and material aid to the British forces invading Togoland in August 1914.[4] And Nugent points out that "[t]he British forces were struck by the warmth of the reception that greeted their arrival in towns and villages across Togoland."[5]

Support for the British partly was based on the hope of resolving what was to become known as the "Ewe Question." Since the occupation of Eweland by the British, Germans, and French at the end of the nineteenth century, and particularly as a result of the Heligoland Treaty of 1890 which separated the Krepi Ewe, the Ewe remained a people divided by colonial boundaries. While in precolonial times the Ewe never came together in a centralized state, many viewed the disruption of the colonial order caused by the First World War as an opportunity to agitate for the unification of the Ewe under British administration. This effort was organized and led mainly by the Anlo Ewe elite of the Gold Coast, who were encouraged by the expulsion of the Germans and the subsequent Allied seizure of Togoland. The Ewe Question was to be the predominant political issue in the area until the return to independence of Ghana.

British Occupation

The central Volta Region, along with most of the former German colony, including Lomé, was occupied by the British even before the capitulation of the German colonial forces on August 14, 1914. The remaining areas of Togoland, that is, those districts stretching along the border with Dahomey, were seized by the French. This tentative arrangement, dubbed the "Lomé Convention," was formalized by the Governor of the Gold Coast, Hugh Clifford, and M. Nouflard, the Lieutenant-Governor of Dahomey, at a hastily arranged meeting on August 31.[6]

The wartime administration of the newly occupied areas by the British took the form of martial rule. Some colonial officials from the Gold Coast were transferred to the former German stations at Ho, Kpandu, and Misahöhe, while Lomé was administered by the military commanders based in the town. The British-occupied areas of Togoland quickly were brought under the monetary authority of the West African Currency Board, which was established by the British imperial authorities in 1912.[7]

The German presence in Togoland was phased out by the British. At first, the schools at Akpafu, Amedzofe, and Kpandu and elsewhere were allowed to continue teaching in German, but by 1917 most of the German missionaries were expelled from the British-occupied areas, following the sinking of a boat by the German military off the coast of Accra. The British administration also issued a German Firms Closure and Liquidation (Togoland) Proclamation Order of 1916, which seized all German-owned property.[8]

To the Togolanders affiliated with the German churches and educated in the German schools, and to others who had held positions in the German missionary and governmental structures, the period following the First World War was one of uncertainty and frustration. Despite the permission granted by British military rulers for instruction in German to continue, for example, western education was disrupted in the central Volta Region, especially after the German missionaries were ordered to leave the area. "There was a lapse in education when the British came," Klutse maintains. "For a long time, there were no teachers."[9] Togbe Kuleke explains that when the war began the German missionaries remained in Waya as if "... they were not concerned with government business." But, shortly thereafter, these missionaries "... were gathered together and little by little" sent back to Germany.[10] As a result, the supervision of missionary activities was left to Togolanders who had worked under the Germans at the various schools and missions in the area. Debrunner claims that "the Christian quarters were gradually abandoned, no doubt because their care and control by missionaries and teachers declined."[11] He cynically concludes: "It became evident that the work had depended too much on the missionary."[12] The flow of financial support from abroad also was interrupted by the war, as money from the Bremen headquarters was blocked from entering Togoland.[13] Debrunner asserts that there was "… a revival of open paganism [sic]" as a result of the First World War, since African religious institutions, suppressed by the former-German regime, were publicly reactivated.[14]

Due to the disturbances caused by the war and the subsequent expulsion of the German missionaries, 97 of the North German schools were abandoned in 1915 and the number of students at mission institutions dropped to a third of prewar enrollment levels.[15] Agbodeka states "general decline set in and most schools all but disintegrated."[16] Some Togolander students, according to Adu, prepared for the change in colonial rulers by transferring to British schools in Keta during the war,[17] probably a relatively easy move since English and Ewe were the main languages of instruction in North German schools.[18] Moreover, Debrunner explains that students no longer wanted to study German, and demand for English instruction grew after the defeat of the Germans.[19] In any event, the British government prohibited German as a language of instruction in January 1918.[20]

Beyond the realms of religion and education, the departure of the Germans also had economic ramifications in the central Volta Region. Tegbe states the occupation of the area by a new imperial power modified the source of imported goods. "When the Germans left," Tegbe explains, "the things they imported, like cutlasses, knives, and the like, also vanished" and were replaced by items from elsewhere.[21] More significantly, the British reversed the German prohibition on African involvement in the export and import of goods in Togoland. Accordingly, Asase argues "it was the British who introduced commerce."[22] Indeed, despite the world war, trade in British-occupied Togoland increased dramatically, and Debrunner refers to the period immediately after the war as "… the golden age for trade in Togo."[23] In terms of agriculture, the most notable change was the expansion of cocoa farming in Togoland. Debrunner explains that "cocoa was planted with zest, a thing the Germans had obstructed."[24] Some of the most oppressive measures perpetuated by the Germans, such as the use of forced labor and the imposition of direct taxes, were discontinued by the British.[25] Even some unpopular chiefs installed by the German regime were removed from office.[26]

As a result of this latest European partition, most of the Ewe population, with the exception of a minority under French rule in Dahomey and the areas of

Togoland the French occupied, lived under the administration of a single colonial power, that is, the British regime of the Gold Coast. According to Amenumey, the Anlo Ewe elite, not only the "literate"[27] population but also the "non-literate" chiefs, agitated for the whole of Eweland to be united and placed under British administration. Indeed, historians of this period place great emphasis on the claim that the majority of Ewe preferred British colonial rule to that of the Germans and the French. Amenumey epitomizes this argument when he writes:

> On the eve of the First World War, the overall picture was that the Ewe in German Togo[land] looked enviously at the Gold Coast while those there pitied their kinsmen in Togo[land] … By 1914, therefore, there was already in existence amongst most Ewe peoples a general preference for the type of regime in force in the Gold Coast as opposed to that in German Togo[land].[28]

Buah asserts the same, stating that the Ewe favored the British "… whose colonial administration the people considered safeguarded native institutions and was more favourable."[29]

As explained in Chapter 2, the general area, and in particular the central Volta Region and areas to its north, was multiethnic, comprised of speakers of Ewe, Central-Togo, Guang, and Akan languages, among others. This desire for Ewe unification under British rule not only appears to have been limited to the Ewe, but even amongst the Ewe themselves, was a position especially popular with the Anlo Ewe, the majority of whom already lived under British administration in the Gold Coast. The Anlo Ewe elite benefited from the British military occupation of Togoland, in terms of trade and positions, and thus were motivated by a desire to protect their economic and political interests in the face of the possible transfer of the area to French rule.[30] These Anlo Ewe served as the vanguard of the Ewe unification movement. As it grew and became better organized and more vocal, however, steadfast opposition to its aims emerged, particularly in the central Volta Region and areas further north.

The merchants, civil servants, intellectuals, and chiefs who lobbied for the British administration of Eweland cloaked their Ewe nationalist agenda in the rhetoric of keeping the former German colony whole. They also tried to appeal to British feelings of imperialist superiority. A delegation of these men met in October 1918 with the Officer-in-Charge of the British forces in Togoland. Amenumey's summary of their points gives us the gist of the delegation's agenda:

> This deputation emphasized the need for Togo[land] to remain intact and to be amalgamated with the Trans-Volta district of the Gold Coast under British rule. It pointed out that the section of Togo[land] taken over by Britain was largely dependent on Anécho and on the area occupied by France for good supplies. It also stressed the

preference of the entire population for British as opposed to French rule and its dis-like of the prospect of amalgamation of any party of the territory with Dahomey. The deputation recalled the ethnographic, linguistic and historical unity of the Ewe and asked that they be united under British rule. It concluded that "the Ewe people can never develop properly if they are again put under different flags."[31]

The Anlo Ewe elite encouraged the Allied powers to formalize the earlier agreement between Clifford and Nouflard and to add the remaining Ewe ar-eas under French rule (specifically, the part of Togoland they occupied) to the British Gold Coast, thus uniting all of Eweland. In Lomé, a group of Anlo Ewe men organized "A Committee on behalf of Togoland natives," which in March 1919 petitioned the Allied Powers to allow the "natives of Togoland," which they characterized as "sentimentally British," to remain under British rule.[32] They alluded to the promises of the League of Nations, established by the Allies during the war, which specified that the inhabitants of all of the former German colonies would be consulted before the selection of a future administrating power of each territory. Interestingly, these Anlo Ewe purported to campaign on behalf of all the people of Togoland and did not characterize their efforts as a strictly Ewe affair.

Nevertheless, in May 1919, the Supreme Council of the League of Nations decided that Britain and France should determine how they wished to divide and administer Togoland. During the Versailles Peace Conference, in which the Allied Powers dictated the terms for peace in Europe and beyond, the Germans were singled out amongst the imperialist nations for criticism of their colonial record. Germany was forced to renounce its claims to Togoland when it signed the Treaty of Peace in June 1919. "The Germans were punished," Datsa explains, "and dis-possessed of their territories overseas."[33]

It was resolved that the Allies should assume control of all the former Ger-man colonies as "mandates" on behalf of the League of Nations. The British and French were charged with administering areas of Togoland in "sacred trust" and in accordance with Article 22 of the League of Nations Covenant, which specified neutrality, non-militarization, and open-door economic policies for the mandated territories.[34] The Simon-Milner Declaration of July 1919 laid down the bound-aries between the British and French Togolands, an international border that re-mains to this day.

Roughly two-thirds of German Togoland was mandated to the French, while the remainder was given to the British. The total area placed under British admin-istration amounted to 33,777 square kilometers (13,041 square miles). The regime in the Gold Coast further divided its share of Togoland, placing the northern part of their mandate under the jurisdiction of the neighboring Northern Territories, while southern British Togoland, which included the central Volta Region, was administered as part of the Gold Coast Colony.[35]

These new colonial borders divided Eweland in new ways. Both the Anlo Ewe and the Northern Ewe, the latter including the Ewe population of the central Volta Region, were separated by the British-French Togolands boundary, with additional populations of Anlo Ewe and others both in the Gold Coast and Dahomey. While the entire Northern Ewe population resided in the former German colony, now they were separated by the mandates border. James S. Coleman explains the predicament that faced the Northern Ewe:

> The British westward withdrawal in 1919 from what was roughly the eastern boundary of Eweland to the present boundary of British Togoland meant not only that the Ewe in French Togoland were obliged to learn their third European language, but also that Ewe groups not previously divided found themselves straddling a new international boundary.[36]

After the Simon-Milner Declaration was approved by the British and French governments, the two Togolands were transferred from military to mandated occupation. In British Togoland, the formal beginning of mandate rule did not occur until 1922. In the interim, from 1919 to 1922, the territory experienced a "provisional mandatory period." According to Daketsey, the years immediately following the formal beginning of mandate rule were marked by a British policy of "accommodation and adaptation." This policy was terminated in 1928, when the British regime sought to completely integrate British Togoland into the Gold Coast. Coleman explains:

> This policy found expression not only in specific measures making British Togoland for all practicable purposes an indistinguishable part of the Gold Coast but also in a general disinclination to erect institutions or take measures which would in any way tend to endow British Togoland with a separate status.[37]

As Nugent explains, "British policy was overtly imperialist, in the sense that it ultimately worked towards the absorption of the western half of Togoland into the Gold Coast."[38] In violation of the spirit of the League of Nations Covenant, indirect rule was introduced to British Togoland, and the territory slowly was amalgamated with the Gold Coast. In fact, the British repudiated the provisions of Article 22 and directly applied the ordinances of the Gold Coast to British Togoland. "From thence," argues Daketsey, "the mandate more and more took on the features of a normal British colony."[39]

Most of the former Misahöhe District was situated in British Togoland and constitutes today's central Volta Region. The smaller part of the former Bezirk, including the capital of Misahöhe as well as Kpalimé, was incorporated into French Togoland. The new border did not completely sever links between the central Volta Region and neighboring towns in French Togoland, but it did result in a host of inconveniences for the local population. The boundary, viewed as arbitrary and intrusive by residents of the area, divided families and communities and thus to various degrees affected longstanding economic, social, and political ties. For example, some families in the general area had their farms split by the border. Additionally, as with any international boundary, customs regulations hindered the free flow of people and products.[40] As a result of European partition, Agbewu explains, the people of the central Volta Region found themselves "... on the English side of the divide."[41] Across the border, in the towns around the former German district capital of Misahöhe, the residents opposed the British-French agreement since, according to Daketsey, they "... resented the thought of being severed from those in Ho and Kpando sub-districts and handed over to a power [i.e., the French] they had come to identify with harsh rule."[42]

After nine years of occupying the area, the British attempted to rectify the disorder that had descended on European religious and educational activities during the First World War. In 1923, they allowed German missionaries to return to British Togoland, although English remained the sole European language of instruction in the schools.[43] During the Germans' absence, the British placed the Bremen mission schools under the authority of the Gold Coast Education Department. Then, in the same year the Germans came back, the British regime transferred supervision of the North German missions to the United Free Church of Scotland, locally based in Accra.[44] According to Datsa, the Scottish missionaries were sent to the area "... to exercise a kind of supervisory role over our church until the Germans returned."[45] It was during this period that the Africanization of the local variant of Christianity deepened.

Ewe Nationalism

A new era in the history of Christianity in the area was initiated with the creation of the Ewe Evangelical Church in Kpalimé in May 1922.[46] At their formative meeting, delegates from all the missions established by the North German Missionary Society were in attendance, including those located in British Togoland (i.e., the Akpafu, Amedzofe, and Ho districts), French Togoland (Agu, Atakpamé, Kpalimé, and Lomé), and the Gold Coast (Keta and Peki). All the participants in this first synod were Africans; not a single European attended the proceedings. The meeting resolved that the church would continue its affiliation with the Bremen mission, which would receive regular reports and be consulted on important doctrinal issues.[47]

The establishment of the Ewe Evangelical Church was significant in several ways. First, it marked the transfer of authority in missionary activities from the Bremen-based North German Missionary Society to the African pastors, catechists, church elders, and teachers working on the ground. But, just as important, the new church did elect to maintain its links with the Bremen mission.[48] The formation of this church also coincided with the general emergence of Ewe nationalism, again, particularly among the Anlo Ewe. Debrunner states that the church "... felt itself strongly to be an Ewe church" and furthermore argues "... it was actually more than that, it was the first public manifestation of the Ewe people as such."[49] The church used Ewe as the language of worship and operated on both sides of the British-French border. It held a general synod (termed the "great synod") with representatives from the two Togolands every few years, while divisional synods ("little synods") met separately in the individual mandates on an annual basis.[50] The two branches of the church were autonomous from one another, but they maintained a close relationship, as evidenced by the synods, and they used the same Ewe religious texts.[51]

Amenumey highlights the influence of the mission schools in the development of Ewe nationalism during this period. While previously the North German Missionary Society, which operated in both German Togoland and the southeastern part of the Gold Coast, provided "some degree of unity" amongst the Anlo Ewe and the Northern Ewe and others, the Ewe Evangelical Church played a leading role in the construction of a common Ewe ethnic identity. In its schools, a particular dialect of Anlo Ewe was adopted as the language of instruction, thereby providing a standard Ewe for at least one segment of society (i.e., those who received western education) throughout Eweland. Additionally, students in these schools all read the same text of Ewe oral traditions, further accentuating the concept of a shared past and identity. Thus, Amenumey concludes "... this meant that a fair proportion of the Ewe population—and more important, the literate class—was exposed to the idea of Ewe unity."[52]

The economy of the area proved to be another impetus to the construction of this Ewe nationalism. As discussed in previous chapters, a longstanding economic network linked the communities of Eweland before and during the European occupation, particularly since each of the subregions specialized in different products. Amenumey emphasizes that during the mandate period, despite the imposition of yet another colonial boundary, "an intense commercial activity in both locally produced and imported goods bound all the Ewe towns together." This economic interdependence in his view "... helped to sustain the concept of Ewe unity."[53] All these economic and social factors joined together with a rising political consciousness during the following decades to nurture an Ewe nationalism, one encouraged by the Anlo Ewe.

The Anlo Ewe elites who during the First World War agitated for the unification of the Ewe under British rule continued their campaign, somewhat indirectly, throughout the 1920s. Since the Permanent Mandates Commission of the League of Nations accepted petitions from peoples residing in the mandates, the Ewe nationalists took advantage of this avenue for publicizing their concerns. These men did not necessarily articulate an Ewe unification plank, but issued a series of petitions and memoranda which detailed the hardships the new border had caused in their communities.[54] Furthermore, they submitted complaints about the policies implemented by the regime in French Togoland, including the imposition of new taxes.[55] The commission, entirely composed of representatives of the mandate powers themselves, remained largely indifferent to these communications. Neither the French nor the British were willing to reconsider the boundary they created, nor would they risk embarrassing the other by acknowledging African resistance to the administration of the mandates.

Despite the series of petitions sent to the League of Nations in the 1920s, the push for Ewe unification subsided during the following decade. The movement remained almost exclusively driven by the Anlo Ewe, since the Northern Ewe did not actively support its aims, and no lasting formal organization promoting Ewe unification materialized. Additionally, the British regime in the Gold Coast made clear its reluctance to revisit the border issue, particularly in reference to the Ewe question. Amenumey cites a speech in front of the Permanent Mandates Commission by a former district commissioner in British Togoland, Captain Lilley, who questioned whether the Ewe had ever considered themselves a single "tribe," since they had long constituted independent "clans."[56] This remark was indicative of the regime's dismissive attitude toward the campaign by the Anlo Ewe elite.

As the concept of an Ewe nationalism developed, an often opposed, but sometimes parallel movement emerged, agitating for the re-unification the two Togolands. The first group to push this agenda after the wartime activities of the Anlo Ewe elite was the Bund der Deutschen Togolander (German for "Union of German Togolanders"), also known as the "Togobund." Although there was speculation that the group originally was constituted by the German regime during their occupation of Togoland, the Togobund was established in the 1920s[57] by a group of German-educated African civil servants in Accra who, according to Amenumey, "found themselves out of work because they were literate only in German."[58] The purpose of the organization was "to watch over the welfare of our country, to keep close liaison with Germany and to defend the interests of Togo."[59]

The Togobund filed numerous petitions with the League of Nations asking for the return of German administration, but, interestingly, its primary activity was to protest mandate rule in French Togoland. Benjamin N. Lawrance depicts the group's activities as follows:

> Bundists maintained contact with journalists and former German colonial officials in the "Fatherland." They held regular meetings, circulated propaganda, collected membership dues, and invited Germans to assist in the development of Eweland.[60]

Their consistent efforts to file petitions were increasingly stifled by the French authorities in Lomé who viewed the Togobund "... as revolutionary, subversive, and after 1933, pro-Nazi."[61] Echoing this characterization, Coleman claims the organization had "... the hope that under Hitler the Germans would return to a reunited Togoland and the Bund members would regain their former jobs and status."[62]

British Policies

As the groups who supported either the unification of the Ewe or the reunification of the two Togolands filed their grievances with the League of Nations, the British carried on with the administration of their share of the former German colony. Oral historians maintain that the regime in Accra failed to significantly develop the central Volta Region during the mandate period. They generally characterize the era as one of outright neglect by the British. During mandate rule, Klutse bluntly declares, "none of the white men came here."[63]

In contrast to their imperial predecessors, the British did not pursue a concerted agricultural policy in the central Volta Region. Except for attempts to encourage, without much success, the cultivation of cotton in the Kpandu area, the British focused their energies on the expansion of cocoa, the primary cash crop in the Gold Coast. Cocoa continued to spread considerably, particularly in the central Volta Region and the area immediately to its north. But, in general, the mandate power neglected to invest in the area's agricultural potential. As a result, Agbodeka argues "... the people of southern Togoland thought very little of the Government's agricultural policy."[64] Klutse argues the British merely were interested in the area as a source of manufactured and other goods. Discussing the mandate period, he explains:

> We had perfected many things before the whiteman came—the weaving of cloth, the use of tobacco, and the smelting of iron. As a result, we did not really need European-

made goods in those days the way the Gold Coast needed them. They rather came into Togo[land] to buy the things they could not find in their area, for example, cloth.[65]

The British also failed to continue to any significant degree the construction of roads and railways in the area. Communities raised the funds and organized the labor themselves to build roads in the central Volta Region and other parts of Southern Togoland, although Agbodeka argues communal labor was discouraged by the British since it would undermine the tax system.[66] The British regime provided only minimal resources for the improvement and expansion of communication networks. The development of these was limited to the inauguration of weekly motor vehicle service between Accra and the central Volta Region, the opening of about a dozen post offices in the area, and the extension of telephone service to a few towns.[67]

Despite the lackluster economic development of the area by the British administration,[68] agricultural output did continue to grow considerably, partly resulting in the enlargement of several towns in the central Volta Region, particularly Ho and Hohoe. Both became centers of trade and distribution points for agricultural products.[69] Akpafu grew, as well, not as a result of its commercial position, but because of the expansion of farming to surrounding areas of the town. A group of residents established a new settlement called Akpafu Mempeasem at the base of the hill, and the original town thus became known as Akpafu Todzi, which translates roughly as Akpafu "on the hill."[70]

The reception to British social policies in the central Volta Region was mixed. In terms of judicial affairs, the British proved to be less brutal than the Germans in the penalties they imposed. The arbitrary and excessive punishments characteristic of the German period for the most part were not perpetuated. "The British came and stopped all of these things and introduced the court system," explains Klutse,[71] but Adu maintains that "bribery and corruption … [were] practiced at their law courts."[72] While Gikunu asserts lashing did persist,[73] Adu states that corporal punishment was ended by the British. Adu explains that the British would simply "… lock you up for a day or two" if you violated their laws.[74] And, again, the British discontinued the legal requirement that all adult males perform forced labor.[75]

The British regime did not significantly extend access to western medicine in southern British Togoland. According to Agbodeka, by 1927, the only medical establishments in the area were a clinic for leprosy at Ho, a Catholic children's welfare center at Kpandu, and town dispensaries, which occasionally were visited by a traveling doctor and nurse.[76] Several years later, by 1935, hospitals were opened by the British in Ho and Hohoe and several other medical facilities were operated by Catholic and Presbyterian missionaries.[77] But, generally, western medical care remained out of reach for most of the people of the central Volta Region.

Opportunities to acquire western education did continue to grow, largely through the efforts of the Ewe Presbyterian Church. Although European missionaries, namely some Germans as well as the Scots who were selected to replace them during the First World War, proselytized during the mandate occupation, the supervision and expansion of Christian education in the central Volta Region largely was in the hands of Africans. The British contribution toward the extension of the religion is recognized by oral historians, however, as evidenced by Agbewu's assertion that "the English came to continue that [missionary] work."[78] Over the roughly two decades of mandate occupation, there was a considerable increase in the number of children enrolled in mission schools, according to the annual reports the British were required to submit to the Permanent Mandates Commission.[79]

It was in the political arena that the British encountered the strongest resistance to their policies in the central Volta Region. As explained above, beginning in the late 1920s, British Togoland increasingly was incorporated into the administrative structure of the Gold Coast and indirect rule was introduced in the mandate. While the Germans implemented a similar method of governance through chiefs, the British system granted greater authority to these local rulers. As a result, powerful chiefs emerged during the mandate period who were in a position to expand the area under their authority, especially through their control of cocoa farming. The chiefs of larger towns, such as Ho, thus benefited enormously from amalgamation with the Gold Coast and could be relied upon by the British regime to support this policy. In return, the British, who sought to minimize the number of states in Togoland in order to simplify administration of the region, encouraged the expansion of local polities.[80] As Nugent explains, "[t]he aim was, therefore, to rationalize the native authority system by amalgamating 68 small divisions into a number of more compact states."[81]

Even though some chiefs approved of the British regime's policy in Togoland, most of the people of the central Volta Region actively were opposed to the prospect of incorporation into the Gold Coast. Agbodeka points out that those chiefs who failed to take advantage of the "profitable proposition" of amalgamation emerged as critics of British rule, particularly of the Native Administration Ordinance, which granted ultimate power over chiefs to the governor of the Gold Coast. This policy, again, was a breach of the mandate agreement passed by the League of Nations. Chiefs often resisted British authority by refusing to organize the collection of taxes and the creation of treasuries in their communities. It was not until 1935, for example, that the Avatime area, which includes Amedzofe, carried out these orders.[82]

Oral historians explain that the British tended to be more "democratic" than the Germans before them, but they argue that the end result—that is, colonial control of political affairs—was identical. A chief of Waya, Togbe Lavlo V, elaborates this point when comparing the Germans with the British:

> The British ... taught us democracy, which was mixed up with our traditional chieftaincy affairs. Though democracy is good in itself, one realizes there are certain pitfalls in it. The British used cunning ways to gain dominion over the Gold Coast at the time. They virtually took power from the traditional rulers and mixed it up with British rule.[83]

Based on this interpretation, therefore, indirect rule may have been touted as a method of governance in which "traditional" authority remained somewhat intact, but it nonetheless resulted in the seizure of power from local chiefs. Another chief in Waya, Togbe Kuleke, supports this argument when he states: "The Germans used iron hands to administer our people while the British used free will to do the same."[84]

The "honesty," "order," and "discipline" which so characterized the German occupation disappeared during the British period, according to many oral historians. Asase argues that "the British were rather lax as far as discipline" and explains that they were inconsistent in their expectations of the people they ruled. He continues:

> The British also taught us some good things, but they were not strict on us ... The British gave you the option to obey them or not. It was only when the British wanted something from you that they insisted on you obeying.[85]

Adinyra paints a harsher picture of the British when he suggests "they were not strong, discipline-wise ... The English brought greed and deceit,"[86] an argument supported by Adu, who asserts that "it was during the British era that we knew of the terms 'bribery' and 'corruption.'"[87] Alluding to his criticism of the administration of British Togoland, Togbe Kuleke concludes: "... because the British allowed for free will, there later developed indiscipline."[88]

The disappointment with mandate rule in British Togoland was widespread, especially in the central Volta Region, where the residents felt greatly neglected by the British regime in Accra and, at the same time, opposed the administration's amalgamation policies. "Although people had apparently come to accept the Mandates System and the tri-partite division [of the Ewe]," Amenumey suggests, "resentment continued."[89] In a study of Have, a town in the central Volta Region, Ken Kwaku details local grievances against the British, particularly during the long reign of the aforementioned Captain Lilley, who served as District Commissioner from 1926 to 1938. Foremost was British interference in chieftaincy affairs, which undermined the position of sub-chiefs to the benefit of newly appointed paramount chiefs. This placed the chief of Have under the jurisdiction of chief of Kpandu, now the Paramount Chief of the Akpini State. Second, the local economy "suffered a drastic deterioration" as the profitable cash crops of the German period "were not actively promoted by the British" forcing local farmers to migrate to other areas for work. Lastly, Kwaku claims there was a rise in social problems as the "strict German discipline" was replaced with "liberal" British policies. In short, the oral historians who he consulted echo those quoted above in depicting a period of political, economic, and social decline.[90]

Resistance to the mandate occupation was limited to nonviolent actions like the refusal to pay taxes. Public forums for the vocalization of opposition, such as the African press in the Gold Coast[91] and the Permanent Mandates Commission, perhaps were not fully exploited, largely because a unified, well-organized movement failed to emerge during this period. The dissolution of the League of Nations in 1939 was a disappointment to the peoples of British Togoland since the British no longer were required to answer to an international body and could proceed apace with the integration of the mandate with the Gold Coast colony. But, a second world war, once again initiated and mostly fought in Europe, provided another opportunity for those favoring Ewe unification or Togoland reunification to press their demands, as the future of the Togolands once again was the subject of international debate.

Trust Territory

Unlike the previous world war, no military battles between the Allies and the Germans were fought in the Togolands during the Second World War. The French administration in Lomé briefly allied itself with the pro-Nazi Vichy regime, but this action did not result in any military campaigns.[92] Across the border, the people and resources of British Togoland were mustered in aid of the Allied effort, a further infringement of Article 22 of the League of Nations Covenant, the document that specified how the mandated territories were to be administered. The British ignored the provision of neutrality, but since the League of Nations no longer existed, the regime was not held accountable for this violation. In fact, Daketsey argues, during the war "British sovereignty became more pronounced" in British Togoland.[93]

War between European imperialists again affected the lives of the people of the central Volta Region. In a repeat of the First World War, German missionaries were arrested by the British and expelled from the central Volta Region,[94] but the schools continued to function since most of the teachers were either Togolanders or Scots. The greatest inconvenience was the interruption of the flow of human and commercial traffic across the British-French Togolands border, particularly after the regime in Lomé fell under Vichy France. The Allied blockade of the latter extended to West Africa and, as a result, the people across the border from the central Volta Region experienced a shortage of goods, including salt, which was traded north from Keta in the Gold Coast. Additionally, compulsory labor was demanded by the Vichy administration in French Togoland, causing thousands to cross the border into British territory.[95] The situation improved somewhat when French Togoland rejoined the Allies, but the populations in both Togolands were required to contribute their share of raw materials, including palm oil and rubber, to the war effort.[96]

In another development reminiscent of the First World War, a resurgence of Ewe nationalism as well as agitation for the reunification of the Togolands occurred during this period. The latter was especially strong in French Togoland, where the population resented the requirements imposed on them by the French regime in aid of the war in Europe and elsewhere. The German-educated civil servants associated with the Togobund, formed in Accra in the 1920s, also revived their demands for the reunification of the two Togolands during the war.[97] Support for the unification of the Ewe, through the dismantling of the Togolands boundary, was voiced by all the Paramount Chiefs of British Togoland in September 1940, but they also stated they would be satisfied with the removal of customs restrictions at the border.[98] Once again, it was among the Anlo Ewe where calls for the unification of the Ewe were most resolutely enunciated. All these requests, in some instances, and demands, in others, were made in the form of petitions to the colonial regimes in Lomé and Accra. Both movements—the one for Ewe unification and the other for Togoland reunification—received boosts at the end of the Second World War with the creation of the United Nations and the subsequent emergence of political parties and organizations campaigning for either position.

In December 1946, the former British Togoland mandate officially became a United Nations Trust Territory when the United Nations General Assembly approved a British-French agreement on the Togolands. The United Nations was established the previous year in San Francisco and inherited the problem of the mandated territories. The international body designated "Administrating Authorities" responsible for the governance of the trust territories. British Togoland thus became a trust territory governed by Great Britain, its administrating authority. Beyond the change in terminology, Coleman points out the main distinction was that while the mandated powers were ordered simply to assure the "just treatment" of the peoples in their territories, under the trusteeship agreement, the administrating authorities were charged with guaranteeing "progressive development toward self-government or independence."[99] George Thullen further elaborates this point within the larger global context of the late 1940s:

> ... international trusteeship came to mean actual international supervision of colonial administration and was institutionalized as such in the United Nations trusteeship system. By the end of the war, Europe had lost its dominant position and its colonial empires were crumbling in the face of strong nationalist movements and militant ideologies. In this setting the newly-created trusteeship system was to provide a means for peaceful and orderly attainment of independence by dependent territories through evolutionary rather than revolutionary methods.[100]

The general anticolonial climate Thullen refers to shaped the constitution and activities of the Trusteeship Council as well as the related Declaration Regarding Non-Self-Governing Territories incorporated into the United Nations charter. While the Permanent Mandates Commission was composed entirely of mandated powers and, moreover, the League of Nations itself was comprised largely of imperialist nations, the United Nations included states from the developing world, although only three independent African nations—that is, Egypt, Ethiopia, Liberia—were members.[101] More significantly, the Trusteeship Council itself was divided equally between administrating authorities and nonadministrating countries, including UN members from South America and Asia, many of which recently regained independence and pursued an anticolonial politics.[102]

The Trusteeship Council sent visiting missions to the trust territories,[103] but it could only make recommendations to the Administrating Authorities, so its powers of enforcement were limited.[104] Since imperialist nations at this time still dominated the United Nations, the administrating authorities were assured of support of their continued occupation of the trusteeships. Nevertheless, the Trusteeship Council, even more so than the Permanent Mandates Commission, provided the Togolanders an international forum through which to present their grievances and demands. Indeed, the Ewe question commanded the attention of representatives at the first meeting of the Trusteeship Council in April 1947. The chairman of the council received a telegram from Accra which stated:

> All Ewe Conference comprising Ewe of French Togoland, British Togoland, Gold Coast, greetings. We deplore and protest against partition of Eweland. Request unification of Eweland under single administration to be chosen by people themselves by plebiscite.[105]

During the Second World War and in the years immediately following the victory of the Allies, several institutions espousing Ewe unification emerged on both sides of the Togolands border, largely as a result of what Amenumey terms an Ewe "cultural renaissance,"[106] led by a "cadre of Ewe teachers, clerks and businessmen."[107] Several important Ewe newspapers were established, including the *Ewe Newsletter*, published in Accra, and *Le Guide de Togo*, *L'Unité Togolaise*, *Le Togoland*, and *Negreta*, produced in Lomé.[108] These publications promoted the Ewe unification cause and sought to encourage an Ewe ethnic identity. Concurrently, several organizations were established, such as the Ewe Unionist Association, to campaign for the unification of all the Ewe under a single colonial administration.[109] As was the case with the earlier generation, these newspapers and organizations largely were led by Anlo Ewe and proposed the reunification of the two Togolands simply as a vehicle for the more immediate goal of Ewe unification. Yet, the earlier tactics of sending petitions to the colonial regime and international supervisory organizations as well as publishing articles in the local African press gradually were replaced by a more direct, better organized strategy for agitation through the founding of several Ewe political parties.

Political Parties

The postwar period witnessed the advent of nationalist parties throughout the African continent demanding the return to independence. One of the most dynamic and successful of these was the Convention People's Party (CPP), which served as the vanguard in Ghana's movement toward independence in 1957. Led by Kwame Nkrumah, the party played an important role in tipping the balance in favor of the integration of British Togoland with the Gold Coast. When the CPP was founded in Accra in 1949, several Ewe parties already were established both in the Gold Coast and in French Togoland.

The Comité de 'Unité Togolaise (CUT) was the leading nationalist party in French Togoland for approximately two decades after its founding in 1941.[110] Although initially broadly-based like the Gold Coast's CPP, the CUT's agenda was largely geared toward the Ewe unification cause after the Second World War and thus transformed into a mostly Ewe party. The founding of the CUT signified the first organized effort by Ewe unificationists to actively and directly engage the colonial establishment, in this case, the French regime in Lomé.

The entire movement proceeded to coordinate its efforts more efficiently on both sides of the Togolands border with the establishment in 1946 of the aforementioned All Ewe Conference (AEC), which was to function as an umbrella organization for all the Ewe nationalist groups emerging throughout Eweland. Based in Accra, the AEC affiliated itself with the CUT and agitated for a united Eweland, comprising the Ewe populations of the two Togolands and the Gold Coast, through nonviolent, "constitutional" means.

In spite of its name, shortly after its founding it appeared obvious that the AEC did not enjoy the support of the entire Ewe population. The Ewe unification movement continued to be dominated by Anlo Ewe, the majority of whom resided in the Gold Coast, just as they had led the efforts of the earlier generation of Ewe unificationists. This left the Ewe of British Togoland, particularly the Northern Ewe, once again opposed to the goals of the Anlo Ewe. The Northern Ewe followed the lead of the CUT and the AEC and, in 1943,[111] established the Togoland Union, a party based in Hohoe, which espoused "Togoland for the Togolanders." The Togoland reunificationists' primary goals were to unite the Ewe, escape from the domination of the Gold Coast, and prevent the incorporation of French Togoland into the French Union.[112]

The Togoland Union's support overwhelmingly was found in the central Volta Region, which became the primary field of competition between the opposed groups in southern British Togoland, that is, the Anlo Ewe-led AEC and the Northern Ewe-dominated Togoland Union. Dennis Austin succinctly summarizes the two strategies, confusing and often overlapping, presented by these groups in their quest to resolve the Ewe Question:

> Ewe unity could either be promoted by the integration of the British trust territory with the Gold Coast (thus confirming the existing administrative union between the two) but only at the expense of the Ewe under French rule. Or it may be promoted (through agitation at the United Nations) by the unification of the two halves of the trust territory, but only at the expense of the large number of Ewe who lived in the south of the Gold Coast. The difficulty was to how to decide which of these policies was the most likely to achieve the ultimate union of all sections of this energetic and able people—and under whose auspices.[113]

It must be emphasized, however, that while Ewe unification was the exclusive goal of the AEC, the primary goal of the Togoland Union was the reunification of the former German colony.

The conflicting stances of the Anlo Ewe and the Northern Ewe partly were attributable to the positions that the two groups held within their respective colonial territory. On the eve of the Second World War, for example, the Anlo Ewe elite began to construct an Ewe identity which transcended historic animosities. Greene presents the following argument:

This expansion in the way in which some Anlo began to view themselves as a people who shared important bonds with all other Ewe-speaking peoples, rather than with just the specific Ewe and Akan peoples with whom they had religious, economic, military, and family ties—developed in the mid-1930s.[114]

She concludes that the impetus for this development was the fear amongst the Anlo Ewe that their minority status within the larger Gold Coast, which had a majority Akan-speaking population, would be detrimental to the long-term development of their communities. Therefore, Greene explains, the Anlo Ewe

... also began to advocate the idea that the Anlo must begin to see themselves as one with the Ewes of British Togoland, and that all Ewes, wherever they resided, had to look to themselves if they were to develop the capability of managing their own affairs within the modern world-system.[115]

This interpretation is supported by Amenumey's assertion that the Anlo Ewe area of the Gold Coast was administered as a "hinterland" by the British regime.[116] Therefore, in the context of the increasing popularity of the CPP and its demands for independence, and with a wariness about their future in a non-Ewe dominated Gold Coast, the Anlo Ewe looked to their newfound brethren across the border as the key to their long-term prosperity. Significantly, the rhetoric of Ewe nationalism was put into practice by the Anlo Ewe, who delivered financial assistance to the Ewe of the two Togolands.[117]

It could be argued that the Northern Ewe elite resented the success of their Anlo Ewe counterparts. This attitude was grounded in the fact that the British regime posted educated Anlo men to prominent administrative positions in southern British Togoland, bypassing the local Northern Ewe elite. Additionally, the Gold Coast Ewe dominated the hierarchy of the Ewe Evangelical Church and attained influential positions in the fast-growing CPP. Writing during this general period, Coleman suggested that "The Anlo [Ewe] are feared and disliked by many Togoland Ewe ... because of their greater sophistication and educational attainments and their prominence in the leadership of the CPP."[118] As Amenumey puts it, the leadership of the Togoland Union thus "successfully exploited the latent anti–Gold-Coast-Ewe feelings in British Togoland."[119]

This animosity had historic precedents, of course, since the Anlo Ewe had formed alliances with the Asante against the Northern Ewe and other groups in the nineteenth century, as discussed in Chapter 2. Coleman argues the Anlo Ewe were resented "... because of their past connection with the slave trade and the memory of their part in bringing the Ashanti armies to Eweland."[120] Amenumey, however, is reluctant to completely accept this historical rationale and emphasizes it is more likely that the Northern Ewe resented the Anlo Ewe since "… their long association with the British and their superior knowledge of English" allowed them to occupy most of the key positions in the British Togoland administration."[121]

Another prevailing sentiment in the Northern Ewe area was that British Togoland was being exploited economically for the benefit of the Gold Coast.[122] The Togoland Union was therefore able to secure the support of the Northern Ewe as well as many speakers of the Central-Togo languages, particularly Buem, in their appeals to all "true Togolanders" to campaign for the re-unification of the two trust territories. Fearing domination by the Anlo Ewe, the Togoland Union appealed to these non-Ewe groups by emphasizing Togoland reunification, rather than Ewe unification.

The two opposed movements, one espousing Ewe unification and the other campaigning for the reunification of the Togolands, formed a brief alliance in 1951 when each agreed partly to alter their respective agendas in an effort to strengthen the Ewe position in the face of British indifference and French hostility.[123] At a joint meeting held in Kpalimé between the AEC, representing the Gold Coast and the French Togoland Ewe nationalist parties,[124] and the newly formed Togoland Congress, which succeeded the Togoland Union in 1951,[125] it was agreed that the two organizations would demand self-government or independence for the Togoland trust territories and, after this was attained, then consider the issue of Ewe unification. As important, the meeting proposed the UN organize a plebiscite to "ascertain the real wishes and interests" of the inhabitants of the trust territories. Both movements, therefore, had to make significant concessions in order to present this united front. The Togoland Congress agreed to allow the Ewe question to be considered in future and the AEC dropped its opposition to independence.[126] The latter organization decided that since earlier efforts to resolve the Ewe Question failed, the Togoland reunification platform offered the possibility of at least partial unification of the Ewe.[127]

Gold Coast Politics

A historic change occurred in the Gold Coast during the same year. Bowing to the success of the CPP's "positive action" campaign initiated in January 1950 and its subsequent victory in the February 1951 legislative elections,[128] the British regime asked the CPP to form a new government in Accra, with Nkrumah selected for the position of Leader of Government Business. One year later, Nkrumah's title was changed to Prime Minister of the Gold Coast, the first African to head a colonial government. The leader of the CPP and champion of African independence and unity now was afforded a position through which he could significantly influence the outcomes of the Togoland issue and, by extension, the Ewe Question.

Before it assumed power, the CPP was indifferent to the problems of Togoland, partly because the trust territory fell outside the arena of party politics until the early 1950s. Following the elections, the CPP quickly developed a position on Togoland, one that was resolutely in favor of integration with the Gold Coast. Coleman argues the party's policy was "imperialistic," in that it envisioned the reunification of the two Togolands as tied with Togoland's subsequent integration with an independent Ghana.[129]

The new CPP-led government successfully frustrated the recently created alliance between the Ewe nationalists and the Togoland reunificationists by the establishment in 1952 of the Trans-Volta-Togoland Region, which united southern British Togoland with the Trans-Volta Region of the southeastern Gold Coast.[130] Coleman explains that the unification of the Ewe "was one of the explicit reasons given for the creation of the new region,"[131] which not only brought together the two Ewe populations but, in the process, further integrated the trust territory with the colony. Moreover, British Togoland now was fully incorporated into the political life of the Gold Coast as its residents were represented for the first time in the colonial legislature.[132]

It is clear the British colonial regime and the CPP administration were in complete agreement that British Togoland should be disassociated of its special status and formally incorporated into the Gold Coast. According to Coleman, "… spokesmen for the British government repeatedly stressed that when the Gold Coast attained self-government the Trust Territory should remain integrated with it and that the Trusteeship Agreement should be terminated."[133] The revelation in July 1953 of what was termed a "most secret document" attributed to the CPP laid to rest any doubts about the party's position in the debate, as far as the Togoland reunificationists were concerned. Titled "The Future of Togoland under United Kingdom "trusteeship," the unsigned document asserted that British Togoland should not emerge from its trusteeship status before the Gold Coast returned to independence. Once the latter was accomplished, the trusteeship status of the territory should end and British Togoland would integrate with the Gold Coast. The document clarified that this agenda would be pursued through the submission of petitions by Ewe CPP cadres to the United Nations, the disbursement of financial assistance to British Togoland, and the securement of local positions in the trust territory for members of the party. Although the CPP denied authorship of the position paper, it confirmed the fears of the Togoland Congress, which termed it a "vulgar and treacherous document."[134]

Several factors influenced the CPP's prointegrationist position. First was the obvious fact that amalgamation would significantly expand the Gold Coast's population and land area. Secondly, Nkrumah advocated a radical brand of Pan-Africanism, which envisioned the erasure of colonial borders throughout the continent in the hopes of creating a united, economically self-sufficient African state. The failure of the CPP to preside over the integration of British Togoland thus would deal a serious blow, at the most local level, to this grand vision. It was anticipated that an enlarged, united, and independent Ghana would be in a position to expand its boundaries and incorporate French Togoland.[135] In keeping with this position, Nkrumah, as the new Prime Minister, appeared sincere about his desire to rapidly develop British Togoland as part of his larger program to industrialize and diversify the economy of the Gold Coast.

A more pressing concern for the CPP revolved around the Volta River Project, adopted by the party in 1951 as part of its national program. This project called for damming the Volta River in order to provide the Gold Coast's electrical needs, with part of the supply directed toward a proposed aluminum plant. A National Commission was established in July 1953 by the Gold Coast legislature to begin planning the project. It therefore was crucial that British Togoland, particularly the southern half of the trust territory, integrate with the Gold Coast in order to guarantee full control of the river and the projected dam.[136] Despite the apparent urgency in securing integration, the administration in Accra provided another example of its failure to consult with the people of British Togoland in the development of the trust territory when the National Commission neglected to include a single Togolander among its members. After protests, a pro-CPP representative from British Togoland was appointed to the body.[137]

The creation of the new Trans-Volta-Togoland Region produced the result probably hoped for by the British and the CPP (as well as the French). A split emerged within the AEC between those willing to accept the partial union of the Ewe *vis-à-vis* the establishment of the Trans-Volta-Togoland Region and those who insisted on pressing for the unification of all the Ewe, including the population in French Togoland. The second group feared that with the further integration of British Togoland into the Gold Coast, the French would be free to incorporate their trust territory into the larger French West Africa colony. The divisions within the AEC resulted in the defection of many its members to the CPP, which launched a campaign against Togoland reunification, including sending petitions to the UN, as outlined in the "most secret document." The CPP successfully exploited the splits amongst the Ewe parties and witnessed its support in British Togoland rapidly grow.

As the AEC gradually deteriorated, the Togoland Congress, too, lost some of the support the Togoland Union had earlier enjoyed, particularly from the non-Ewe populations of southern British Togoland. Enthusiasm for the party waned as a result of the AEC-Togoland Congress compromise, since Ewe unification was now placed on the agenda alongside Togoland reunification and independence. Additionally, strong resistance to the Togoland Congress developed in northern British Togoland, where the party was viewed as Ewe-dominated. Indeed, the Togoland Congress continued to strengthen its links with the CUT and Juvento parties in French Togoland, all of which espoused Togoland reunification positions and almost entirely were comprised of Ewe members.[138] In British Togoland, support for the Togoland Congress amongst non-Ewe peoples therefore was hindered by its reputation as an Ewe party, while at the same time the Ewe of the area were divided between those who advocated Togoland reunification and others supporting the CPP's drive for integration with the Gold Coast.[139] Besides the concerns about ethnic hegemony, many residents of British Togoland simply had no inclination toward reuniting the two Togolands. As Austin comments, "it was not easy … to see why the frontiers of a former German colony should be regarded with such affection as a possible homeland."[140]

Meanwhile, the government in Accra steadfastly pursued its agenda for integration. The Gold Coast Order in Council of 1954, which served as the colony's new constitution, created seven electoral districts, which crossed the previous Gold Coast-British Togoland boundary, thus fully linking the trust territory with the colony's political system. The administration slowly dismantled the few institutions that existed in southern British Togoland until it was fully integrated administratively with the Gold Coast. When a Visiting Mission from the UN Trusteeship Council toured British Togoland in September 1952, representatives of the Togoland Congress complained that the territory was being ruled directly by Accra and that the British had no intention of allowing its separate development toward self-government. Amenumey sums up the Congress' arguments as follows:

> The territory did not possess even one institution of its own, and was becoming each day more and more closely integrated with the Gold Coast, and it lagged behind its larger neighbour in almost every aspect of development.[141]

The Ewe question came to dominate political—and in certain respects, economic—life in the central Volta Region over the next decade. British and CPP policies in the area largely were geared toward influencing the debate in support of those advocating integration with the Gold Coast. The administration allocated "vast sums of money," according to Amenumey, toward the infrastructural development of the Trans-Volta-Togoland Region during this period, primarily for community development and the expansion of educational facilities.[142] For instance, in July 1953, Nkrumah announced that a special grant of £1 million had been earmarked for the improvement of communications and transportation in the trusteeship, including the construction of a bridge over the Volta River at Senchi.[143]

Confident of its impending role as the ruling party of an independent Gold Coast, the CPP appropriated significant financial resources to the Trans-Volta-Togoland Region, facilitated by its position as the majority party in the legislature. The CPP pursued the strategy outlined in the "most secret document," by providing subsidies for agriculture and placing CPP sympathizers in the local administration.[144] As an example of the former tactic, the CPP assured the generous disbursement of loans by the Cocoa Purchasing Board to farmers in the trusteeship.[145] These strategies did result in the increased popularity of the CPP in southern British Togoland at the expense of the Togoland Congress. In the 1954 legislative elections, for example, the CPP won 29,951 of the votes in the area as compared to the Togoland Congress' 26,214 ballots. Amenumey correctly points out, however, that the Togoland Congress captured the majority of the vote in the trusteeship districts in which the Ewe dominated.[146]

The Togoland Congress, which formed an alliance at the national level with other parties opposed to the federal structure the CPP proposed for independence,[147] exploited the widespread feeling that the trust territory was neglected by the Accra government. It highlighted the British regime's failure to develop the infrastructure of the trusteeship and to provide social services to its residents and voiced the fear that the proposed Volta dam would flood large sections of British Togoland. Additionally, the party tapped into the resentment of Togolander farmers for being forced to sell their cocoa to the Gold Coast marketing board.[148] Nonetheless, the Togoland Congress' support remained limited to the Ewe-speaking areas of southern British Togoland, while the CPP dominated amongst the non-Ewe majority of the trusteeship in the 1954 polls.[149]

After the CPP's sweeping victory in the 1954 elections,[150] the movements for Gold Coast independence and the integration of British Togoland with the colony both gained strength. These parallel developments were not coincidental, but firmly linked, since the CPP feared that if the status of the trusteeship remained unresolved it would potentially delay the Gold Coast's return to independence.[151] Unbowed in its efforts to win over the residents of British Togoland, the CPP held its 1955 Delegates Conference in Kpandu, one of the centers of the Togoland Congress' support.[152] During the same year, a Trusteeship Council Visiting Mission toured British Togoland and subsequently recommended that a plebiscite be held in the trust territory to decide its fate. This marked a significant departure from the positions of the earlier Visiting Missions, which were inclined toward the reunification of the two Togolands, a stance shared by the UN General Assembly.[153] With the adoption of Resolution 944(X) in December 1955, the UN encouraged Great Britain to organize a plebiscite in which the residents of British Togoland would decide if either (1) they wished to unite with the Gold Coast or (2) remain a trust territory with its ultimate political status decided in future.[154]

United Nations Plebiscite

The political situation in British Togoland on the eve of the plebiscite was a complex maze of competing interests and groups. The northern part of the trust territory was staunchly supportive of integration with the Gold Coast since many of the area's ethnic groups, particularly the Dagomba, the Gonja, and the Mamprusi, endorsed the British-French Togoland partition of the First World War, which placed most of their peoples under the administration of the British. Separation from the Gold Coast and reunification of the two Togolands thus would reimpose an international boundary dividing the majority of each of these groups.[155] As a result, the bulk of the population of northern British Togoland favored integration, the position held by both the CPP and the Northern People's Party (NPP), the strongest parties in the area.

The circumstances in the southern part of the trust territory were not as straightforward. A significant segment of the Ewe population opposed integration, as they backed the Togoland Congress' campaign for the reunification of the Togolands. This position especially was popular in the larger towns in the central Volta Region, including Ho, Hohoe, and Kpandu. A growing but still smaller percentage of the Ewe, however, switched allegiances to the CPP and thus supported integration, a stand advocated by most of the non-Ewe minority of southern British Togoland, including speakers of the Central-Togo languages.

The three largest parties operating in the trust territory—namely, the Togoland Congress, the CPP, and the NPP—each waged intensive campaigns in support of their respective positions. According to Austin, "violent antagonism" existed between the ruling CPP and the Togoland Congress in particular.[156] Kwaku highlights the preponderance of what he terms "chief-subject" conflicts, situations in which the chief backed the CPP while most of his community opposed integration with the Gold Coast.[157] The Togoland Congress continued to crusade for the unification of the two Togolands, which proponents argued either could be a step toward an independent Togoland or result in incorporation into an eventual Gold Coast federation.[158] The party's strength remained almost exclusively in the southern part of the British trust territory,[159] where it warned that integration would result in "slavery for the people of British Togoland and loss of the territory's culture, identity, and personality."[160]

The pro-integrationist positions of the CPP and the NPP were strengthened somewhat by statements issued by British officials who, despite the appointment of Nkrumah and a CPP administration in Gold Coast, ultimately were responsible for the administration of the trust territory. For instance, when Charles N. Arden-Clark, Governor of the colony, toured the central Volta Region in 1955, he threatened that should the Ewe wish to remain a trusteeship they could not rely on Great Britain to continue its role as Administrating Authority.[161] The prointegrationists also profited from the efficacy of the CPP, which organized mass assemblies in the largest towns of British Togoland, including Ho, Hohoe, and Kpandu, strongholds of the Togoland Congress. The CPP appealed to the fears that should it elect not to join the Gold Coast, British Togoland would fail to develop on its own. Kate Skinner emphasizes the importance of competing rallies held by the CPP and the Togoland Congress in the Central Volta Region. She explains these events provided opportunities for local elites to educate ordinary Togolanders about the plebiscite and collect funds for their campaigns. Skinner argues, "They provided a forum for an eclectic and participatory political culture, and ensured a degree of mutuality and reciprocity in an otherwise unequal relationship between representatives and supporters."[162]

The minority of Northern Ewe whose primary goal was Ewe unification faced a difficult dilemma of whether they wished to unite with the Ewe groups of French Togoland or the Ewe of the Gold Coast (see Table 5.1). Again, Austin offers a concise summary of this predicament when he writes the Ewe were forced to choose between

> ... the bringing together of all the Ewes in an enlarged, ex-British state, in the form of a 'greater Ghana'; or in the reunification of (some of) the Ewes in a restored ex-German Togoland. The former solution meant the disappearance of Togo as a separate state; the latter, the detachment from Ghana of some at least of its Ewe-speaking districts.[163]

The official position of the CPP was that the unification of all these Ewe groups would be best facilitated by the integration of British Togoland into the Gold Coast, after which a campaign to amalgamate French Togoland would be pursued.

Table 5.1 Ewe populations in 1956[164]

Gold Coast	British Togoland	French Togoland
376,000	137,000	397,700[165]

On the eve of the plebiscite, the CPP government issued a "White Paper" detailing its intended policies in anticipation of independence. The document assumed British Togoland would be integrated with the Gold Coast and thus proposed the following: (1) the new nation would be named "Ghana"; (2) the Trans-Volta-Togoland Region would remain intact as one of the six regions of this new state; and (3) Ghana would be constituted as a unitary state with increased devolution of power to the regions.[166] The White Paper clearly revealed the CPP's confidence that the integrationists would prevail in the plebiscite.

Indeed, victory belonged to the integrationists on May 9, when 58% of those participating in the plebiscite voted for integration with the Gold Coast.[167] Voters were asked to choose between union with the Gold Coast or separation from the colony. Generally speaking, the northern part of the trust territory voted overwhelmingly in favor of union while the south voted largely for separation (see Table 5.2). Additionally, based on district results, most of the Ewe supported separation while the majority of non-Ewe voted for union. Only two of the six districts in the trust territory voted in favor of separation, namely Ho and Kpandu, together constituting the bulk of the central Volta Region population.[168] In fact, the area as a whole voted solidly in favor of separation.[169]

Table 5.2 Results of 1956 Plebiscite in British Togoland[170]

	Southern section	Northern section	Total
For union	42%	79%	58%
For separation	58%	21%	42%

Ghana's drive toward independence rapidly accelerated. Two months after the plebiscite, legislative elections were held in which the CPP once again emerged with a resounding majority of the votes.[171] Several weeks later, the UN decided to terminate British Togoland's trusteeship status once Ghana attained independence.[172] The Gold Coast Legislative Assembly voted in August to declare the independence of Ghana within the British Commonwealth.[173] Finally, one month later, the British Colonial Secretary announced Ghana would be granted independence on March 6, 1957.

And thus, at just after midnight on that very date, the flag of the new nation of Ghana was raised in front of the Legislative Assembly in Accra. At the Old Polo Ground, Nkrumah proclaimed Ghana "free forever" amid thousands of shouts of "freedom!" At that minute, the areas comprising Ghana, which the British had occupied for periods ranging from roughly forty to one hundred years—that is, the Gold Coast Colony, the Asante Protectorate, the Northern Territories, and the

British Togoland Trust Territory—ceased to exist, and Ghana became the eighth independent nation on the African continent.[174] Freed from decades of European colonial rule, the people of the central Volta Region were part of a new nation most of them had voted against joining less than a year earlier.

While a crowd of thousands in Accra celebrated the return to independence, discontented Togoland reunificationists protested the new nation's birth. As Gikunu recalls, "It was a tug of war when it was decided that part of Togo should become Ghana in the days before independence."[175] In Jasikan, a town north of Hohoe, the local Togoland Congress branch encouraged all "Togolanders" to boycott independence day events.[176] Several days before the historic event, protests erupted in Kpandu, where those opposed to integration attacked government offices displaying the flag of Ghana.[177] On independence day itself, a group of Togoland Congress members carried out what Austin characterizes as "a clumsy attempt at a local armed rebellion"[178] at Alavanyo, a town east of Ho near the border with French Togoland. According to Austin, these rebels "… had banded themselves together in camps, marched up and down in ragged military formation, and practiced with shotguns."[179] Simultaneously, throughout the central Volta Region, residents trashed government buildings, including the post office in Amedzofe, and destroyed Ghanaian flags.[180] The administration in Accra responded with force, dispatching troops and police to the area, resulting in at least three deaths in Kpandu[181] and between five and seven others amongst the Alavanyo rebels.[182] Furthermore, the possession of guns and ammunitions in the Kpandu and Alavanyo was prohibited by the Ghanaian government.[183] Later, S. G. Antor, one of the founders of the Togoland Congress, was arrested and charged with complicity in what has been since termed the "Alavanyo riots."[184]

Clearly, a great deal of hostility toward the integration of British Togoland into Ghana existed in the central Volta Region. This area had been the heartland of the Togoland Congress, which drew most of its support from the three largest towns (Ho, Hohoe, and Kpandu), in and around which the majority Ewe population resided. These towns mostly remained loyal to the Togoland Congress and its pursuit of Togoland reunification and opposed to the CPP's campaign to integrate the trusteeship into Ghana. Undermined by, among other factors, the array of resources available to the governing party, the numerical superiority of the non-Ewe population of British Togoland, and the reluctance of these same groups to support what appeared to be an Ewe cause, the Togoland reunificationists were forced to acknowledge defeat and accept the new order. Thereafter, the Togoland Congress virtually was shut out of the political process and the CPP assumed its place as the dominant party in the Volta Region.[185]

Notes

1. Apoh asserts, however: "Kpando oral accounts revealed that some Togoland chiefs and people, who the Germans armed to fight on behalf of Germany, buried their guns and turned them over to the British afterwards" (357).
2. E. D. K. Daketsey, *The Northern Ewe Under Mandatory Rule 1914–1946: Myth or Reality?*, Unpublished M.Phil thesis (Legon: University of Ghana, 1985), 56.
3. F. K. Buah, *A History of Ghana* (Accra: Ghana Universities Press, 1972), 163. Again, Eweland during this period stretched from the Gold Coast through German Togoland to Dahomey, but also included minority groups, such as speakers of Central-Togo, Guang, and Akan languages, especially in what is today the central Volta Region.
4. Amenumey, *Ewe Unification*, 9.
5. Paul Nugent, *Smugglers, Secessionists, and Loyal Citizens on the Ghana-Togo Frontier: The Lie of the Borderlands Since 1914* (Athens: Ohio University Press, 2002), 27.
6. Daketsey, 57. Under this agreement, negotiated in Lomé, the British assumed administration of the Lomé, Lomé-Land, Misahöhe, and Kete-Krachi districts, while the French controlled Anécho, Atakpamé, and Sokodé-Bassari. Mangu-Yendi was divided in two, with the regimes of the Gold Coast and Dahomey each responsible for the administration of one-half of the district. Additionally, the British supervised the colony's wharf at Lomé as well as its railway system (Amenumey, *Ewe Unification*, 10–11).
7. Daketsey, 59–60.
8. *Ibid.* For a summary of the removal of the German missionaries, see Debrunner, 144.
9. Oswald Kwame Klutse (oral historian in Ho), in discussion with the author, April 16, 1997.
10. Togbe Kuleke (oral historian in Waya), in discussion with the author, June 16, 1997.
11. Debrunner, 146. Interestingly, Debrunner argues that many of the mission communities in Togoland began to fracture even before the First World War. Ernst Bürgi, the President of the North German Missionary Society in Togoland at the time, stated that "a few of these settlements had become retrograde because of disputes and quarrels, and because of the strong ties of pagan [*sic*] family feeling" (*Ibid.*, 147). Bürgi was a Swiss national and therefore was not expelled from Togoland during the war. In response to the deterioration of the church's activities in the area due to the absence of the German missionaries, Bürgi embarked on an energetic campaign to ordain African pastors and transfer more responsibilities to them (*Ibid.*, 150).
12. *Ibid.*, 149.
13. *Ibid.* Debrunner explains that a Bremen-based company operating in Lomé at first provided assistance, but once German firms were seized by the British regime, this source of income also was obstructed. Additionally, American Lutherans, who were allied with the North German Missionary Society and supported its activities, provided financial assistance but, even together with help from Swedish Lutherans, it was insufficient to maintain the mission's operations in Togoland.
14. *Ibid.*, 146. The author states: "… even many Christians in times of crisis took refuge in the old faith."
15. *Ibid.*, 148.
16. Agbodeka, 90.

17. Seth Adu (oral historian in Ho), in discussion with the author, March 7, 1997.
18. For more on the politics of language in German Togoland, see Lawrance, "Most Obedient Servants." Despite efforts by the regime to mandate instruction in German in missionary and governmental schools, Lawrance shows how learning English was far more popular amongst Togolander students. He also explains how proficiency in a standardized Ewe spread amongst Ewe and non-Ewe due to its usage in missionary schools.
19. Debrunner, 148.
20. *Ibid.*, 153. Bürgi recognized the imminent cessation of German instruction and thus had earlier encouraged the teaching of English, despite the opposition of many German missionaries.
21. Mathias Yevu Tegbe (oral historian in Hohoe), in discussion with the author, June 17, 1997.
22. Mosis Kofi Asase (oral historian in Ho), in discussion with the author, April 15, 1997.
23. Debrunner, 154.
24. *Ibid.*
25. Greene, 142.
26. Debrunner, 154.
27. "Literate" here refers to those Anlo Ewe who were able to obtain western education and thus acquired fluency in written English (or other European languages). In using this term, I am accepting Amenumey's classification of the leadership of the Ewe unification movement as being the "literate class."
28. Amenumey, *Ewe Unification*, 9.
29. Buah, 163.
30. Claude E. Welch, *Dream of Unity: Pan-Africanism and Political Unification in West Africa* (Ithaca: Cornell University Press, 1966), 58.
31. Amenumey, *Ewe Unification*, 11. The Trans-Volta Region was one of the regions of the Gold Coast colony and bordered the southern part of Togoland occupied by the British.
32. As quoted in *Ibid.*,, 12.
33. Edward Kodzo Datsa (oral historian in Amedzofe), in discussion with the author, April 17, 1997.
34. Article 22 stated that the "tutelage" of the peoples residing in the mandates is "… entrusted to advanced nations." Although a member of the League of Nations, the Soviet Union refused to appoint a representative to the Permanent Mandates Commission largely in opposition to this article (R. F. Betts, "Methods and institutions of European dominance," Chapter 13 in *UNESCO General History of Africa*, VII, *Africa Under Colonial Domination 1880–1935*, ed. by A. Adu Boahen (Berkeley: University of California Press, 1985), 314.
35. The northern part of British Togoland constituted 18,638 square kilometers (7,196 square miles), while the southern area comprised 15,139 square kilometers (5,845 square miles) [David Owusu-Ansah, *Historical Dictionary of Ghana*, 3rd ed. (Lanham, Maryland: The Scarecrow Press, 2005), 240]. The neighboring British colony was divided into three administrative areas: the Northern Protectorates (or Northern Territories), Asante (in the center), and the Gold Coast Colony (in the south), which together constituted the Gold Coast Colony and Dependencies.
36. James S. Coleman, "Togoland," *International Conciliation*, 509 (September 1956): 8.

37. *Ibid.*, 15.
38. Nugent, *Smugglers*, 15.
39. Daketsey, viii.
40. Amenumey, *Ewe Unification*, 23.
41. Francis Agbewu (oral historian in Akpafu Todzi), in discussion with the author, June 17, 1997.
42. Daketsey, 67. Nugent challenges these claims in *Smugglers*, arguing the boundary drawn by European imperialists was not entirely arbitrary and that Africans on both sides of the border played roles shaping, maintaining, and benefiting from the border.
43. Ewe also was used in missionary education. North German missionaries and African Christians produced literature in Ewe, including the Bible, hymn books, and school texts during the German occupation (Debrunner, 164).
44. Agbodeka, 91; Amenumey, *Ewe Unification*, 28–9; and Debrunner, 164.
45. Edward Kodzo Datsa (oral historian in Amedzofe), in discussion with the author, April 17, 1997.
46. The church alternatively was known as the Ewe Church, the Ewe Presbyterian Church and the Ewe Evangelical Church but, in 1927, the latter name was officially adopted (Samuel Decalco, The Historical Dictionary of Togo (London: The Scarecrow Press, 1996), 120).
47. Debrunner, 162. While the North German stations on the British side of the border were supervised by the Scottish following the ejection of the German missionaries, the missions in French Togoland were not yet absorbed into an already-established society (*Ibid.*, 161). This was one of the factors leading to the formation of a (mostly) independent Ewe church.
48. To further emphasize the maintenance of this affiliation, the Ewe Evangelical Church's first leader, Andreas Aku, was confirmed by the Bremen mission (*Ibid.*, 163). The links with the North German Missionary Society were stronger in the British Togoland branch of the Ewe Evangelical Church. Beginning in 1929, the church in French Togoland became affiliated with the Société des Missions de Paris, which represented the Ewe Evangelical Church to the French regime and supervised instruction in its schools (Amenumey, *Ewe Unification*, 29).
49. Debrunner, 163.
50. *Ibid.*, 164.
51. Amenumey, *Ewe Unification*, 29.
52. *Ibid.*
53. *Ibid.*, 28.
54. *Ibid.*, 23.
55. *Ibid.*, 25.
56. *Ibid.*, 26. Nugent writes: "… as Lilley and his colleagues were fond of pointing out, the Ewe did not constitute a single 'tribe'" ("'A few lesser peoples'," 167).
57. Amenumey cites 1922 as the year of its founding (*Ewe Unification*, 27), Decalco mentions 1929 (75), and Lawrance, in a more recent and extensive study of the Togobund, identifies 1924 (Benjamin N. Lawrance, *Locality, Mobility, and "Nation": Periurban Colonialism in Togo's Eweland, 1900–1960* [Rochester: University of Rochester Press, 2007], 127).
58. Amenumey, *Ewe Unification*, 27.
59. As quoted in *Ibid.*
60. Lawrance, *Locality*, 129.

61. *Ibid.*, 139.
62. Coleman, 34. This assertion is supported by letters from Togolanders to Gruner during that decade.
63. Oswald Kwame Klutse (Oral historian in Ho), in discussion with the author, April 16, 1997. According to a Leagues of Nation publication, the total European population of British Togoland in 1921 was 20 while the figure rose to 43 in 1938. This compares with figures for the "non-native" population of French Togoland of 210 in 1921 and 529 in 1938 (League of Nations, *The Mandates System: Origin—Principles—Application* [Geneva: League of Nations, 1945], 93 and 95).
64. In a similarity with the Germans, the British were unsuccessful in their efforts to discourage shifting cultivation (Agbodeka, 88).
65. Oswald Kwame Klutse (oral historian in Ho), in discussion with the author, July 17, 1997.
66. Agbodeka, 89.
67. *Ibid.*, 88–9.
68. Infrastructural development in French Togoland was far more extensive and the peoples of the former German colony recognized the inconsistent development of the two mandated territories. As Amenumey argues, "It is true there had been some material development in the territories but it was not uniform, due largely to the different policies pursued by Britain and France" (Amenumey, *Ewe Unification*, 35).
69. Agbodeka, 90. Hohoe especially became important as a "clearing house" for cocoa, according to the author.
70. Julius Agbigbi (oral historian in Akpafu Todzi), in discussion with the author, June 17, 1997. Agbigbi elaborates on the reasons behind the founding of the new town: "As we increased in population, the space up here [in Akpafu Todzi] became inadequate. That was why they moved down. Also, others who had their farms at the foot of the mountain decided to live near their farms instead of moving down and climbing up everyday." The Akan Twi term "mempeasem" roughly translates as "do not look for trouble" or "I do not want trouble."
71. Oswald Kwame Klutse (oral historian in Ho), in discussion with the author, April 16, 1997.
72. Seth Adu (oral historian in Ho), in discussion with the author, March 7, 1997.
73. Hillarius Gikunu (oral historian in Waya), in discussion with the author, June 16, 1997.
74. Seth Adu (oral historian in Ho), in discussion with the author, June 15, 1997.
75. Agbodeka, 89.
76. *Ibid.*, 91.
77. *Ibid.*, 92.
78. Francis Agbewu (oral historian in Akpafu Todzi), in discussion with the author, June 17, 1997. Atakumah also states that "… the other imperial powers continued [the Germans'] teaching" (Jane Atakumah [oral historian in Kpandu], in discussion with the author, March 5, 1997).
79. These form the primary source material for Agbodeka's discussion of the mandate period. See Agbodeka, 85–92.
80. *Ibid.*, 86–7.
81. Nugent, "'A few lesser peoples,'" 167.
82. Agbodeka, 87.
83. Togbe Lavlo V (oral historian in Waya), in discussion with the author, February 19, 1997.

84. Togbe Kuleke (oral historian in Waya), in discussion with the author, June 16, 1997.
85. Moses Kofi Asase (oral historian in Ho), in discussion with the author, April 15, 1997.
86. Alfred Adinyra (oral historian in Amedzofe), in discussion with the author, April 17, 1997.
87. Seth Adu (oral historian in Ho), in discussion with the author, March 7, 1997.
88. Togbe Kuleke (oral historian in Waya), in discussion with the author, June 16, 1997.
89. Amenumey, *Ewe Unification*, 35.
90. Kwaku, 77–78.
91. *The Gold Coast Leader*, in particular, published letters and articles by residents of the two Togolands, especially those critical of the French regime in Lomé.
92. The colonial government of French West Africa, based in Dakar, supported the Vichy regime from June 1940, when the French metropolitan government fell to the Nazis, until the Allied occupation of North Africa in June 1943. After the latter development, Dakar allied itself with Charles de Gaulle's Committee of National Liberation, headquartered in Congo-Brazzaville.
93. Daketsey, ix.
94. Edward Kodzo Datsa (oral historian in Amedzofe), in discussion with the author, April 17, 1997.
95. Amenumey, *Ewe Unification*, 36.
96. *Ibid.*, 37.
97. Coleman, 34.
98. Amenumey, *Ewe Unification*, 37.
99. Coleman, 3.
100. George Thullen, *Problems of the Trusteeship System: A Study of Political Behavior in the United Nations* (Geneva: Libraire Droz, 1964), 12.
101. South Africa constituted a fourth "African" state, but was governed by a white minority regime, which mimicked the situation in the European-occupied colonies on the rest of the African continent.
102. Amenumey, *Ewe Unification*, 187–8.
103. The Trusteeship Council sent a total of three visiting missions to the Togoland trust territories, one each in 1949, 1952, and 1955 (Coleman, 43).
104. In addition to the visiting missions, the Trusteeship Council also considered petitions from the populations of the trust territories, reviewed annual reports prepared by the administrating authorities, and issued updates to the General Assembly on the status of the trusteeships (*Ibid.*, 52).
105. Quoted by Edmond Kwam Kouassi, "Africa and the United Nations since 1945," Chapter 29 in *UNESCO General History of Africa*, VIII, *Africa Since 1935*, ed. by Ali A. Mazrui (Berkeley: University of California Press, 1993), 873.
106. Amenumey, *Ewe Unification*, 35.
107. *Ibid.*, 37.
108. *Ibid.*, 39.
109. *Ibid.*, 42.
110. The CUT's origins, however, extended back to 1939, when the French regime created an organization to counter the increasingly vocal demands by Nazi Germany for the restitution of Togoland. When the CUT was founded as a political party in 1941, its official

affiliation with the French government ended. The leaders of the CUT, including Augustino de Souza and Sylvanus Olympio, emerged as the principal figures in French Togoland in its efforts toward independence in 1960 (Dennis Austin, *Politics in Ghana, 1946–1960* [Oxford: Oxford University Press, 1964], 192n and Amenumey, *Ewe Unification*, 42).

111. Austin identifies this as the date of the party's founding, while Amenumey lists 1947.

112. Coleman, 31.

113. Austin, *Politics in Ghana*, 189–90.

114. Greene, 144.

115. *Ibid.*

116. Amenumey, *Ewe Unification*, 7.

117. Greene, 145. Austin offers the argument that the Anlo Ewe had a closer historic and economic link with the Ewe in the neighboring French Togoland rather than with the Northern Ewe of the British trusteeship (Austin, *Politics in Ghana*, 190).

118. Coleman, 35.

119. Amenumey, *Ewe Unification*, 119.

120. Coleman, 35.

121. Amenumey, *Ewe Unification*, 120. Along with the Anlo Ewe, the Peki Ewe, who mostly resided in the Gold Coast, also supported the Ewe unification movement and held top positions in British Togoland.

122. *Ibid.*, 122.

123. The two administrating authorities did create a "Joint Council for Togoland Affairs" in 1952 to work toward the concurrent development of the two trusteeships and to resolve border problems, but the body met only once and was boycotted by the unificationists, who protested the electoral process for delegates. In French Togoland, CUT refused to participate in these elections (Coleman, 64–6 and Kouassi, 875).

124. In addition to the CUT, a new Lomé-based Ewe nationalist party was founded in 1951 called the Mouvement de la Jeunesse Togolaise or simply "Juvento." Largely comprised of former members of the CUT youth wing, Juvento pushed a more radical agenda, such as independence for the trust territories (Amenumey, *Ewe Unification*, 133). Both the CUT and Juvento at time were labeled "communist" by the French and their members continuously harassed by the Lomé regime.

125. The headquarters of the Togoland Congress was in Borada but, according to Amenumey, its center of support remained Hohoe. The party also published *The Togoland Vanguard* (*Ibid.*, 139). The Togoland Congress was the result of the merging of the three organizations, namely the Togoland Union, the Togoland National Farmer's Union (founded in 1949), and the Togoland Youth Organization (1950) (Coleman, 35). Austin also lists the United Nations Association of Togoland as one of the groups comprising the Togoland Congress (Austin, *Politics in Ghana*, 190).

126. Amenumey, *Ewe Unification*, 124–5. In a continuation of the policy of the mandate-era unificationists, the AEC formerly envisioned a unified Ewe state under British colonial rule.

127. Coleman, 33.

128. The CPP won 38 out of 84 seats in the Legislative Assembly. The CPP's defeat of the mostly Akan-dominated United Gold Coast Convention (UGCC) in these elections led

to the dissolution of the latter. The remnants of the UGCC were to reorganize themselves over the following decade or so, under the leadership of K. A. Busia.

129. Coleman, 38.

130. The Trans-Volta-Togoland Region was comprised of 13 districts, each of which was partly situated in the Gold Coast and British Togoland (Austin, *Politics in Ghana*, 234).

131. Coleman, 18.

132. Previously, the trust territory, along with the Northern Territories, had no representation in the Gold Coast Legislative Assembly. The Ashanti Protectorate sent members to the legislature beginning in 1946 (*Ibid.*, 18).

133. *Ibid.*, 15–6.

134. Quoted in Austin, *Politics in Ghana*, 193. Also, see Amenumey, *Ewe Unification*, 136–7 and Coleman, 39.

135. Austin, *Politics in Ghana*, 192.

136. Amenumey, *Ewe Unification*, 171.

137. *Ibid.*, 145.

138. *Ibid.*, 140.

139. *Ibid.*, 144.

140. Austin, *Politics in Ghana*, 191.

141. Amenumey, *Ewe Unification*, 144.

142. *Ibid.*, 81.

143. *Ibid.*, 172 and Austin, *Politics in Ghana*, 234.

144. Amenumey, *Ewe Unification*, 172.

145. *Ibid.*, 174.

146. *Ibid.* The AEC refused to participate in these elections. The Ewe strongholds were the electoral constituencies of Ho East, Ho West, and Kpandu North, of which the latter included Hohoe (Austin, *Politics in Ghana*, 235n). The administrative and electoral ordering of the area was quite confusing. While British Togoland's official status remained that of a UN trust territory, the northern part was administratively integrated with the Northern Territories protectorate, while the southern area was united with the southeastern Gold Coast colony as the Trans-Volta-Togoland Region. Some of the electoral districts in the southern part of British Togoland crossed the border and included areas of the Gold Coast, while a few were situated exclusively within the trusteeship.

147. These included the Northern People's Party (NPP), the Moslem Association Party (MAP), and the Gold Coast Party (GCP). Founded in April 1952 and led by S. D. Dombo Duori-Na and Mumuni Bawumia, the NPP's base of support was amongst the populations of the Northern Territories and northern British Togoland. It was staunchly opposed to the CPP's drive for a federal system. The NPP's 1954 Election Manifesto argued in favor of northern British Togoland's integration with the Gold Coast while the southern part of the trusteeship should be allowed to decide its own fate. The MAP was created in 1953 and drew its support largely from the Muslim neighborhoods (or "Zongos") in the towns and cities throughout the Gold Coast. The GCP descended from the earlier UGCC, and was led by Busia. Founded in May 1952, it was a party with support generally limited to the Asante and surrounding Akan areas (*Ibid.*, xii–xiii, 181, 230, and 233).

148. *Ibid.*, 233–4. Austin adds that cocoa prices in French Togoland were significantly higher at this time. The Cocoa Marketing Board set fixed prices each season.

149. Three Togoland Congress legislators were elected, one each from the Ho East, Ho West, and Kpandu North districts. The CPP captured eight of the 13 seats allocated to the Trans-Volta-Togoland Region, while the remaining two seats went to independents in the Anlo Ewe area (*Ibid.*, 241).

150. Colony-wide, the CPP won 72 out of the 104 seats in the Legislative Council, while the NPP emerged as the second strongest party with 15 positions. In terms of actual votes, the CPP captured 55.4 percent. All the members of the Nkrumah's new cabinet were CPP members (*Ibid.*, 347).

151. Coleman, 40.

152. Austin, *Politics in Ghana*, 300.

153. Coleman, 50 and Austin, *Politics in Ghana*, 201. In November 1953, the Trusteeship Council decided that integration of British Togoland into the Gold Coast should not take place until *after* the two Togoland trust territories had achieved self-government or independence. The Council reversed this decision in 1954.

154. Amenumey, *Ewe Unification*, 259.

155. In addition to the Ewe, however, the British Togoland-French Togoland border also separated the Chakosi, the Konkomba, the Kotokoli, and the B'Moba in the northern parts of the trusteeships (Austin, *Politics in Ghana*, 191).

156. *Ibid.*, 312. While the NPP remained opposed to the CPP's drive towards a unitary state, it was allied with Nkrumah's party in the plebiscite campaign in the trusteeship.

157. Kwaku, 81.

158. Coleman, 28.

159. Coleman argues the following groups supported the reunification of the two Togolands: cocoa farmers opposed to the Cocoa Marketing Board; market women frustrated by the border; chiefs whose polities were divided by the British-French boundary; minority ethnic groups weary of domination by larger groups in the Gold Coast; and individuals opposed to a centralized government in Accra (*Ibid.*, 36).

160. Amenumey, *Ewe Unification*, 264.

161. *Ibid.*, 263.

162. Kate Skinner, "Reading, Writing and Rallies: The Politics of 'Freedom' in Southern British Togoland, 1953–1956," *Journal of African History*, 48/1 (March 2006): 145.

163. Dennis Austin, "The Uncertain Frontier," *The Journal of Modern African Studies*, 1:2 (June 1963): 140.

164. *Ibid.*, 141. Austin published his study in 1963 and thus uses the terms "Former Gold Coast," "Former British Togoland," and "Togo," instead of the colonial-era names of these territories listed here. Austin's figures, however, were based on Coleman's 1956 study of Togoland (Coleman, 13).

165. Austin combined the figures of several groups Coleman had listed separately but which Austin assumed were part of the larger Ewe ethnicity. These ethnic groups are the Ana, Adja-Ouatchi, Fon, and Mina, which Coleman dismissively states the "more nationalist-minded Ewe" claimed were assimilated with the Ewe (*Ibid.*). The Ana and the Mina are

indeed part of the larger Ewe grouping, but the Adja-Ouatchi and the Fon, although closely related linguistically and culturally to the Ewe, are recognized as distinct ethnicities.

166. *Ibid.,* 41.

167. Turnout was 82%, that is, 160,587 out of 194,230 registered voters participated in the
plebiscite (Amenumey, *Ewe Unification,* 266).

168. The UN earlier considered whether to separate the trusteeship so that if a group of neighboring districts voted one way and the remaining districts the other, the preferences of either would be respected and the trusteeship permanently divided, with one area integrating
with the Gold Coast and the other remaining a UN trust territory. This idea was rejected
in July 1956, that is, after the plebiscite had been held, when the Trusteeship Council
recommended to the General Assembly that the wishes of the majority of the voters of
the trusteeship be recognized and that British Togoland in its entirety be integrated with
the Gold Coast at independence (Coleman, 77–80). Coleman explains the UN concluded
that "With its cultural divisions, small population, and poverty in resources (*except for a
small central area*), British Togoland could not be made a viable, independent political unit"
(*Ibid.,* 16; my emphasis). Besides Ho and Kpandu, the other districts were (from north to
south) Mamprusi, Dagomba, Gonja, and Buem Krachi (Austin, *Politics in Ghana,* 310).

169. Only one local council each in the Ho and Kpandu districts voted in favor of integration.
The local districts, which include the sites in which I conducted my research, all supported
separation (Coleman, 73).

170. Based on Amenumey, *Ewe Unification,* 266 and Austin, *Politics in Ghana,* 310. One local
council each in the Mamprusi and Dagomba districts in the north voted for separation
(Coleman, 72). For the numbers of votes cast, see Austin, "The Uncertain Frontier," 142.

171. The party won 71 of the 104 seats in the Legislative Assembly. In the Trans-Volta-Togoland
Region, the Togoland Congress surprisingly won two seats, while eight went to the CPP,
two to the Federated Youth Organization, an Anlo Ewe party, and one to an independent.
Colony-wide, the NPP once again emerged as the second-strongest party with 15 seats,
while the newest party, the National Liberation Movement (NLM), picked up twelve.
Formed in September 1954, the NLM was led by Busia and Bafuor Akoto and found its
support almost exclusively among the Asante (Austin, *Politics in Ghana,* xii, 350, and 354).

172. This decision was made by the Trusteeship Council in late July (Coleman, 70).

173. The vote was 72 out of 104 in favor of this motion, the same ratio of CPP to non-CPP
members in the legislature.

174. Including Ghana, there were only eight independent African nations at this time, the others being Egypt, Ethiopia, Liberia, Libya, Morocco, the Sudan, and Tunisia. I reject any
characterization of apartheid South Africa as an independent African nation.

175. Hillarius Gikunu (oral historian in Waya), in discussion with the author, June 16, 1997.

176. Amenumey, *Ewe Unification,* 275 and Buah, 165.

177. Amenumey, *Ewe Unification,* 276.

178. Austin, *Politics in Ghana,* 37.

179. *Ibid.,* 372. Amenumey states that two military training camps were discovered by Ghanaian
officials in the vicinity of Alavanyo (Amenumey, *Ewe Unification,* 276).

180. *Ibid.*

181. Austin, *Politics in Ghana,* 372.

182. Amenumey, *Ewe Unification*, 276.

183. *Ibid.*

184. Austin, *Politics in Ghana*, 372. Antor had earlier warned the then—Gold Coast government that the people of British Togoland might resort to force to prevent the integration of the trusteeship into the colony. The Togoland reunificationists realized after the UN motion supporting integration, however, that they had lost the battle. A February 1957 petition, signed by Antor and the chief of Ho, among others, demanded that British Togoland be constituted as a separate region of Ghana rather than incorporated into the new Volta Region, as planned. Antor appealed to Togoland Congress supporters to refrain from violence after the disturbances in the central Volta Region detailed above. Although Antor and Kojo Ayeke, another founding member of the Togoland Congress, were sentenced to prison for plotting an "insurrection against the incorporation of Togoland into Ghana," these sentences were dropped on appeal. Both men were members of the Legislative Assembly (Amenumey, *Ewe Unification*, 275–6).

185. The losing parties in the 1956 legislative elections, namely the NPP, NLM, MAP, and the Togoland Congress, along with the Anlo Youth Organization and the Ga Shifimo Kpree (the latter party drew its support among the Ga, the ethnic group indigenous to the Accra area), formed the "United Party" in November 1957, headed by Busia. These parties were all mostly ethnically-based and thus hoped to improve their prospects by uniting against the multiethnic CPP. In fact, the impetus for the creation of this party was a law passed by the Ghanaian Parliament soon after independence banning all political parties based only upon "tribal" or regional support (Austin, *Politics in Ghana*, 384 and Kevin Shillington, *Ghana and the Rawlings Factor* [New York: St. Martin's Press, 1992], 10).

CHAPTER SIX

German Scholars, Performance, and Sites of Memory

In the euphoria which generally greets almost any transfer of authority anywhere in the world at any period in history, most of the people of Togoland welcomed the British as "liberators" during the First World War and cursed the Germans who had occupied their lands and imposed their will on them. When the reality of how the changes resulting from the imposition of a new colonial order would affect their lives, however, many of these same Togolanders, particularly in the central Volta Region, began to recall what they considered to be the positive aspects of German rule and compared these unfavorably with British occupation. In other words, memories of the German occupation began to be formulated immediately after that experience had come to an end. Togolanders ordered and articulated the ways in which they recollected the roughly thirty-year period of German rule and the longer German missionary presence in the area. This process evolved within the context of continuing colonial occupation, now by the British, who had defeated the Germans. Additionally, this construction of memory occurred against the backdrop of German "remains" and "reminders," including physical structures like mission buildings, landmarks such as the hill named after a German district commissioner, or even individual German missionaries still working in the area. All these factors, the existence of which attested to the many decades of a German presence in the central Volta Region, helped shape how people remembered the immediate "German" past. These remains and reminders were testaments to the

German "contributions" to the area, including Christianity, western education, and infrastructural development. Still, what explains the nostalgia of oral historians in more recent decades?

In order to analyze the "production of history," it is essential to understand the environment in which those shaping our understanding of the past operate. In terms of the oral history of the German occupation of the central Volta Region of Ghana, examining the impact of the following four factors is crucial:

(1) the historical context;
(2) the backgrounds, agendas, and biases of the oral historians;
(3) the performance of oral history; and
(4) the continuing German presence.

Historical Context

The long-term historical context was detailed in the preceding chapters on the German and British periods leading up to the return to independence. It is informative to briefly summarize the main themes of both of these eras and present a sweeping overview of more recent Ghanaian history in order to situate this historical context.

As explained in Chapter 4, oral historians generally do not distinguish between the era of formal German colonial occupation and the period of German missionary activity, which both preceded and antedated the existence of the German Togoland colony. Consequently, the German presence in the central Volta Region is remembered by oral historians primarily for the introduction of Christianity and western education and only secondarily for any economic developments in the area.

The first of these three German associations, that is, the introduction of Christianity, is of utmost importance to oral historians, since it was the Germans who "brought the word of God," according to Badasu.[1] Gikunu argues that Christianity was the "main thing" the Germans provided the people of the central Volta Region, although they also "… brought education and higher learning to the land."[2] These assertions by oral historians are obviously supported by the written history, which identifies the North German missionaries as the first to spread the Christian faith and establish western schools in the area. As a result, both these introductions are directly related to the Germans by residents of the central Volta Region at present.

Simultaneous with these associations is the belief of oral historians that the Germans were hardworking colonialists who oversaw the development of the area's infrastructure and agriculture. This notion is clearly evident in the oral history, which includes extensive details on the plant and crop introductions, road (or path) construction, and building of structures attributed to the Germans. Despite the fact that oral historians acknowledge most of this development was the result of the forced, unpaid labor of Togolanders, they present the era as one of progress, both economic and social, particularly in comparison with the decades that followed.

Indeed, in stark contrast to the German period, the central Volta Region was seemingly neglected by the British, who occupied the area first as a "mandate power" and later as an "administrating authority" of the trusteeship. This negligence is consistently recollected by oral historians, who generally volunteered comparisons between the German and British periods, but were sometimes directly solicited for this feedback, during the course of our interviews. Oral historians recognize that the special status of Togoland, that is, first as a mandate and later as a trusteeship, contributed at least partly to the disregard of the area. For example, Klutse summarizes the British occupation as follows: "No European came to Togoland per se to rule us, so the whole of Togoland did not benefit so much. We were taken as a 'cared-for' country."[3] His latter statement is clearly in reference to Togoland's conditions as a mandate and a trusteeship.

Since the British initially viewed themselves only as "temporary stewards" of Togoland, they failed to significantly invest in the area's infrastructural and agricultural improvement.[4] As a result, the residents of the central Volta Region judged the British unfavorably in comparison with the Germans. This assertion is based not only on my analysis of the oral history, but is an argument presented in the written history of the period, as well. For instance, Crowder suggests the following:

> As far as the African inhabitants of the former German colonies were concerned, their lot was not noticeably improved by the change of masters. Indeed some Africans compared their former masters favourably with their new ones, and in Cameroon and Togo, a certain nostalgia for the earlier regime grew as the French introduced their forced labour and the British proved less energetic than their Teutonic cousins in developing their territories.[5]

This nostalgia for the German period was also recognized by Coleman who, in a study of the Togolands published on the eve of the 1956 UN plebiscite, observes:

> The very name "Togoland," notwithstanding its origin, provided a useful symbol for the idealized community—to which latter-day nationalists in the southern areas of both halves of Togoland could relate all things desirable as against the unattractive realities of existing or prospective territorial arrangement.[6]

It is therefore discernible from both the written and oral histories that the people in those areas strongly opposed to the British occupation, particularly the central Volta Region, formed a positive appraisal of the German period and expressed dissatisfaction with British rule. Consequently, Agbodeka concludes that "... Southern Togoland did not, on the whole, receive British rule favourably."[7]

Despite the longstanding and widespread opposition in the central Volta Region to integration with Ghana, it was inevitable after the plebiscite in British Togoland, and it became a reality at independence in 1957.[8] Ignoring the random acts of sabotage perpetuated by some disgruntled Togoland Congress activists, the CPP continued the campaign to broaden its appeal in the newly created Volta Region. More importantly, Nkrumah's government attempted to rectify the historic underdevelopment of those areas that had comprised the former British Togoland and were now part of the Volta Region by investing heavily in infrastructural development.[9] This activity was a continuation of the CPP's more limited policies, due to the constraints of the colonial economy, during the short period of "self-government" in the years leading up to the return to independence. Ghana's first government was responsible for an ambitious program of nation-wide industrial expansion, including the opening of the Volta Dam, the construction of the harbor at Tema, and the building of major roads. After the February 1966 coup that overthrew Nkrumah, however, Ghanaians experienced gradual economic decline, pervasive corruption in the public and private sectors, and a heightened sense of ethnically-based politics under successive military and civilian regimes that governed Ghana until 1983.[10]

In the central Volta Region, a perception of domination by the Akan, particularly the Asante, and the neglect of the non-Akan areas of the nation, marked this era. The fear expressed by the Anlo Ewe elites earlier in the century, that is, that they would face Akan supremacy in an independent Gold Coast in which the Ewe would constitute a minority, became a reality, despite the brief sense of relief that resulted from the incorporation of the Ewe population of the former British Togoland.

While countless generations before them had failed to unite, the Northern Ewe, Anlo Ewe and other Ewe groups increasingly embraced the notion of a common Ewe ethnicity after the return to independence. This process was facilitated by numerous factors, including that the Ewe shared a "standard Ewe"[11] and worshipped in the same church.[12] A popular oral tradition was gradually accepted throughout Eweland, one that emphasizes the collective experiences of the various Ewe groups, rather than the history of divisions and conflicts. Central to that history, which includes the tradition of long ago migrations from Notsé and the more recent invasions and enslavement by Asante armies, is the experience of peripheral colonialism. As argued in the previous chapter, the Anlo Ewe areas were regarded as a "hinterland" of the Gold Coast whilst the Northern Ewe region existed outside the colony as first a mandate and later a trusteeship.

Both groups, however, experienced decades of contacts with Germans, mostly through the work of missionaries. This historic German presence in most of the Volta Region, including the Anlo Ewe areas of the south, is one of the experiences accentuated by the Ewe in highlighting their common past and, as importantly, their distinctiveness from the non-Ewe majority of Ghana. The "success" of Ewe nationalism, after centuries of division and decades of opposition to the concept of a larger Ewe identity, plays an important role in contemporary Ghanaian politics as well as in the Ewes' perceptions of their past, including the German occupation.

In fact, the influence of Germans, particularly missionaries, is one of the many factors which shape Ewe conceptualizations of their identity. The characteristics that make an Ewe an Ewe, according to oral historians, are rooted to varying degrees in the experience of Ewe-German interactions. Gikunu, for example, explains the relationship between the two groups during the German occupation as follows: "The Germans loved the Ewe very well because the Ewe have the three main attributes, hardworking, truthfulness, and ability to understand other languages" which the Germans themselves possessed.[13] And, in a reminder that the Togoland reunification movement was based in Hohoe, Tegbe, an oral historian in that town, asserts: "We the people of Hohoe are Togolese [i.e., Togolanders]. Our people persevered, got their education. Anything they did, they did thoroughly and truthfully."[14]

The recent development of Ewe nationalism is strongly tied with continued feelings of nostalgia for the German occupation. Both influence the other. The Ewe claim exceptionalism within Ghana because they alone (among the larger ethnic groups) benefited from what they perceive to be the positive aspects of decades of the German presence in the Volta Region, and that perception in turn reinforces the favorable portrayal of that historical experience in the oral narratives.

A related Volta (or Togoland) nationalism operates in non-Ewe areas of the Volta Region, as well. While the significant population of non-Ewes in the region maintain their linguistic and cultural distinctiveness to varying degrees,[15] they share with the Ewe the historic experiences of German missionary activity and colonial occupation. These groups largely opposed Togoland reunification during the British period and subsequently supported integration with the Gold Coast in the 1956 plebiscite, but the more recent perception of neglect within an Akan-dominated Ghana has served to accentuate their shared knowledge with the Ewe of historic contacts with the Germans. This is evidenced by the fact that even those oral historians in towns comprised mostly of speakers of the Central-

Togo languages, such as Amedzofe (where Avatime is spoken) and Akpafu Todzi (Siwu), present interpretations of the German occupation that hardly differ from the oral history articulated in the Ewe towns.

Thus, the German occupation is not regarded as a far-off historical episode unrelated to the contemporary world, but shapes people's perceptions of their own identities. The recent history of the central Volta Region, stretching back over one hundred years to the arrival of the first German missionaries and extending to the immediate past of military and civilian Ghanaian regimes, serves as one of the contexts in which the oral history of the German occupation is presently constructed. Yet, it was within the political context of the end of the twentieth century, not in the distant past, in which the oral history examined in this book was formulated.

A gradual and remarkable reconstruction of Ghanaian society occurred after the 31st December Revolution in 1981. It is no exaggeration to assert that this revolution ushered in a new era in the history of Ghana, one that resulted in the current and longest lasting period of multiparty democracy.[16] Under the leadership of Fl. Lt. Jerry John Rawlings, the Provisional National Defence Council (PNDC), the body that governed the nation during the 1980s, instituted a program of infrastructural development across Ghana, notably in historically peripheral areas.

During the revolution, the people of the central Volta Region and, indeed, all of the Volta Region, witnessed the first concerted effort since the Nkrumah era to develop the area's economy. For example, electrical power from the Akosombo Dam, which straddles the border of the Volta Region, only reached the towns of the central Volta Region in 1983, two years after the revolution and nearly 20 years after the inauguration of the dam.[17] This example of neglect is especially glaring, but is illustrative of the inattention paid to the Volta Region by the successive regimes which followed Nkrumah. As during the British occupation, these regimes based in Accra benefited from the agricultural surpluses produced in the Volta Region and the power generated by the river, which forms most of its border with the rest of Ghana, but failed to invest to any significant degree in the development of its existing or potential resources.

Like the CPP, the PNDC recognized the historic roots of the Volta Region's underdevelopment. At an economic development seminar held shortly after the electrification of the area, for instance, then PNDC Regional Secretary, Austin Asamoah-Tutu, proclaimed that the Volta Region "… is one of the less economically developed regions of the country. The reason for this undeniable fact is not obscure. It stems from the Region's political history." Asamoah-Tutu chronicled the history of the region in his address, beginning with the German occupation, through the years of rule by the British, who he states had a "lackadaisical attitude" toward development, and including the period since independence, when the Volta Region failed to reap the benefits of minimal development extended to the neighboring areas in Ghana.[18] This comprehension of the area's history, simultaneous with the will to rectify decades of underdevelopment, served to solidify backing for the PNDC in the Volta Region. This translates at present into near unanimous support for the opposition National Democratic Congress, the political party founded by Rawlings in the early 1990s.

At the time of my research, the experience of over 40 years of independence only deepened feelings of neglect amongst the people of the central Volta Region, a factor which not only affected the way in which people operated within the democratic system in Ghana, but also how they remembered the German occupation. Oral historians looked back with nostalgia on the German period in a continuation and elaboration of the popular memory which evolved during the British era. Tegbe argues with conviction that "after the Germans, no government has ever come to surpass what the Germans did for us. I can assure you of that."[19] Within the larger historical and the more recent political contexts, therefore, the German occupation was presented by oral historians as a golden age.

Oral Historians

As I explained in the first chapter, most oral historians interviewed during our research were recommended to us by residents of their communities since they were regarded as particularly knowledgeable about the German period. When we explained to any group of people that our interest was learning about the German occupation, a number of individuals were usually identified who would be able to tell us the oral history of that historical episode. Not all of these oral historians were elderly and most of them did not have long-term, direct relationships with Germans. Yet, the majority of these oral historians did have one or more "German connections" which enhanced their reputation as experts on the German period.

These connections could be direct and/or indirect and historic and/or contemporary, but without exception, they informed presentations of the German occupation by the oral historians. The connections could include one or more of the following, a sample list of several which were volunteered by some of the oral historians:[20]

(1) parent(s) worked with German missionaries;[21]
(2) father employed by the German colonial regime;[22]
(3) parent(s) educated by German missionaries;[23]
(4) sibling(s) held position(s) in Ewe church;[24] and
(5) oral historian worked for and/or was educated by German missionaries.[25]

All of these connections affected the way the German occupation was described since they predetermined to a significant degree the arsenal of examples and anecdotes the oral historians shared with us. If the oral historian her/himself had worked closely with Germans, they would most likely seek to emphasize the positive attributes of the German presence by offering their own experiences as evidence. Those oral historians whose connections were indirect, for example, one of their parents had been educated by the Germans, would relay the stories and impressions they received from the person with the direct connection, again accentuating the favorable aspects of the German period.

It is among the group of oral historians who possess direct connections that the "German Scholars" of the central Volta Region are found. A term widely employed in the communities of the area, especially among elderly residents, the German Scholars are men (never women) recognized as experts on the German period. Most of them acquired their western education from German or German-speaking Swiss missionaries after the German occupation and were actively involved in the Evangelical Presbyterian Church (EPC), the successor to the Ewe church. Some of these men can still speak basic German and most can sing Christian songs in German. The term dates back to the colonial era, as evidenced by Kwaku in a study of Have. He characterizes the German Scholars as collaborators who were resented by those who were not western educated:

> To maintain the living style befitting their new status—European footwear, dress, and rather curiously, spectacles—the village scholars often collaborated with the German merchants to cheat the local peasants by short-weighing their produce or short-changing them on their payments.[26]

The oral historian Nyavor, a German Scholar himself, offers the following definition of the term: "It refers to all those who went to German schools and all those who served under the Germans."[27]

Seth Adu was the epitome of a German Scholar. Aged 102 when we interviewed him, Adu was a retired shopkeeper who was educated by German missionaries at Ho. He was attending college in Lomé when the First World War began. Forced to end his schooling, but nearly fluent in German, Adu found work at Swiss-owned shops around the central Volta Region and beyond. Throughout, he remained active in the EPC and maintained contacts with some of the missionaries who had returned to Germany and Switzerland. Over the years, Adu sang German songs on local radio programs, during which he also discussed the German period. During the course of our interviews, he occasionally spoke German. Even in a very large town such as Ho, Adu is recognized as a German Scholar. Indeed, when he passed away in 1999 at the age of 104, the funeral program asserted:

"Togbe Seth was one of the few German Scholars in the Volta Region who could speak, read, and write the German Language with perfection."[28]

Many of the other oral historians we interviewed were identified as German Scholars and they clearly had the most direct German connections. Yet, nearly every one of the oral historians possessed a German association of one sort or another which both influenced the way in which they presented the German occupation and, furthermore, determined the very fact that they were even identified by their communities as individuals able to recount the oral history. Many oral historians emphasized their German connections during our interviews, as evidenced by the following comments by Mosis Kofi Asase:

> My parents were trained by the Germans so we have the German spirit in us. By the German spirit, I mean honesty, humility, and godliness. These are the virtues that the Germans imparted on our parents and they in turn imparted on us ... Even though I wasn't trained by the Germans, I have their spirit and I like their kind of training.[29]

While some oral historians were identified as German Scholars and others possessed secondary connections to the Germans, still other oral historians emerged as experts on the German period for more peripheral reasons. Eugenia Kodzo Yawa, a 101-year-old woman in Ho and the mother of the Reverend Mensah of Hohoe, proclaimed the following at the onset of our first interview with her: "I have become very important, as far as German history is concerned!"[30] Yawa's statement is based on her assertion that she heard the first shots of the First World War in Togoland as she was selling goods in Ho. This story, which she detailed for us, positioned Yawa as someone with a connection to the German past and, by extension, an oral historian of the period. Adding to her reputation as an authority on the German occupation is another story about her uncle, who was repeatedly imprisoned by the German authorities.[31] Additionally, the fact that Yawa's son was a minister in the EPC solidified her public association with the Germans. Although not a "German Scholar," a category reserved for men, she was regarded as an oral historian of the German occupation.

The backgrounds of the oral historians thus shaped the agendas and biases, which emerged in the oral history presented to us. Every one of the oral historians possessed these agendas and biases, which were formed by the relationships they maintained during their lives and by their understanding of the historic and contemporary contexts in which they operated. It is not a coincidence, for example, that the oral historians most sympathetic to the Germans were found in Ho, Hohoe, and Kpandu. These three towns, which witnessed the most noticeable economic development during the German occupation, emerged as the centers of support for the anti-integration Togoland Congress, and at present are strongholds of the opposition NDC. Conversely, the oral historians of Akpafu Todzi and Waya were less enthusiastic (yet still generally sympathetic) in their appraisals of the German period and included more negative examples of German policies in their recollections. These towns, much smaller and peripheral within the region, experienced the more devastating aspects of German rule, such as the forced agricultural policies (in Waya) and the destruction of the local iron industry (Akpafu). Additionally, Akpafu Todzi is located within the area of the former southern British Togoland which was less supportive of separation from the Gold Coast. All these historic and contemporary realities produced agendas and biases which, combined with the oral historians' individual backgrounds, shaped the oral history of the German occupation.

Performance

Almost all of these oral historians presented their narratives with several or more bystanders present. As explained in Chapter 1, the interview settings ranged from semiprivate spaces, including the sitting rooms of oral historians, to public venues, such as town meeting places. With only a very few exceptions, each of the interviews was a "public spectacle" by the fact that, in addition to the oral historian(s) and the researchers, a larger audience—consisting of family members, friends, neighbors, and/or children—was always present. The presentation of the oral history in each of these cases became a "performance" of sorts, and the oral historians, I argue, were constrained by community views of the "accepted" oral history of the German occupation.

Divergence from this accepted oral history would often be carefully controlled and successfully undermined by oral historians, especially the German Scholars. Dissent was often not even possible, especially at group interviews. My co-researchers and I interviewed Gilbet Joel Nyavor, an oral historian in Kpandu, on three separate occasions. He was recognized as a German Scholar and, as significantly, held the position of court historian in Kpandu. Each of these interviews was conducted in the chief's palace with three other men seated alongside Nyavor in chairs opposite where my coresearchers and I were placed.[32] All four of these men held positions within the Kpandu court and agreed to be interviewed for our project. During each of these interviews, however, only Nyavor spoke. Undoubtedly, he was very knowledgeable about the German occupation as well as the overall history of the town. Nyavor was acknowledged in these interviewing settings as the expert and the other participants remained silent. My coresearchers and I thus failed to learn if any of the other men had conflicting opinions or complementary information.

In Waya, the air of authority was of an even more obvious and symbolic nature. In that farming community, our initial contacts were made through the chiefs, who subsequently organized an early morning town meeting during which we were permitted to interview the adults of the town. The women were seated under one tree and the men under another, while the chiefs, male elders, queen mothers, and my coresearchers and I faced the congregation of men and women by the trees. This group interview was launched by the head chief of the town, Togbe Lavlo V, who presented a lengthy and authoritative history of Waya, from its origins through to the German occupation and up to the British period. Within this context, it is hardly surprising that divergent interpretations of the German and the British occupations were not presented. In fact, most of the two hours we spent in Waya on that day were monopolized by two of the chiefs, who spent a considerable amount of the time contrasting the German and British periods. Roughly a half-dozen men volunteered information while only a single 96-year-old women raised her hand to make a contribution. This group interview in Waya is a profound example of the interview as public spectacle,[33] but serves as a convenient model from which to present other related arguments.

In the above two cases, a German Scholar (in Kpandu) and two chiefs (Waya) were not challenged as the undisputed experts on the German occupation and were exclusively responsible for presenting the oral history to us. Dissenting voices were not heard and, in fact, most participants in the interviews remained silent.[34] In each of these communities, it is the elders, whether German Scholars or chiefs or religious officials, and nearly always men, who control the interpretation of the past. Due to their age but, as importantly, their status within society, they are recognized as primary authorities on the histories of their communities. As a result, they are not only afforded recognition as oral historians, but are placed in positions in which they are able to manage the oral history.

With only a few exceptions, including a student[35] and a farmer in his mid-30s,[36] all of the oral historians we interviewed held such positions (to varying degrees) within their respective communities. Their neighbors deferred to them when they were asked about the German occupation. Their interpretation of this historical episode was almost always accepted and rarely contradicted. When asked about his impressions of German rule in comparison with the British, for example, Gikunu maintains: "What the elders have said shows that they like the Germans more than the British." This statement serves a dual purpose. On the one hand, Gikunu is supporting his observations by linking them with the opinions of the elders. At the same time, Gikunu is attempting to position himself in this category, as evidenced by the following assertion: "... those of us who have heard a lot and seen a little, feel that the Germans' stay here has been very beneficial to us."[37] The air of authority rests with the elders and they are acknowledged as the rightful inter-preters of the past.

The men and women of a Ghanaian community are expected to display verbal control in public discourse, as well, especially in front of the elders. This may also help explain why oral historians refrained from emphasizing the negative aspects of the German period. Yankah argues that:

> The verbal restraint traditional society exercises in front of elders ... implies a recip-rocal expectation that elders cultivate exemplary expressive habits, i.e. speech that observes the norms of decorum. The elder's speech is expected to be lofty, controlled and tempered with caution. Its emotive content is often carefully distilled to befit his dignity and bearing.[38]

In the setting of a public interview, therefore, it is likely that oral historians would attempt to avoid controversial discourse. My presence as an outsider, and obviously of European descent, may have also encouraged oral historians to avoid excessively negative portrayals of the German occupation.

Despite the social constraints placed on speech, and though the number of female oral historians we interviewed was disproportionately small, it is discern-ible that women regularly offered a more critical assessment of the German oc-cupation than their male counterparts.[39] Theresa Nyagbe of Hohoe (Figure 6.1), for instance, disputed the assertion that the Germans introduced any new crops to the local agriculture or that residents of the Central Volta Region desired or even needed the road construction attributed to the German regime. There is little in the oral history they presented to suggest a basis for this gender discrepancy, although at least two of the women had German connections which were hardly positive.[40]

It is obvious that on several occasions, the dissenting opinions of women were not tolerated by German Scholars and other men recognized as experts on the German period. In Waya, for instance, the aforementioned woman who partici-pated in the group interview, Catherina Ama Kwadzo Kugbleadzor, was repeated-ly interrupted by her male counterparts sitting under the opposite tree. This may be indicative of the restraints placed on women in such public settings, particularly in the presence of chiefs and elders. According to Yankah,

> In parts of Africa, women are generally perceived as repositories of wisdom and knowledge; yet the channelling of this knowledge is subject to social constraints. The chief's palace, the most common ground for rhetoric and formal argument, is not al-ways open to women.[41]

In a more glaring example, Nyagbe, a woman who we had to virtually insist on being allowed to interview, was silenced by Mathias Yevu Tegbe, a German Scholar (Figure 6.2), as evidenced by the following excerpt from their joint interview:

> Nyagbe: In the early days, the females were not allowed access to education because it was feared that they might get pregnant along the way ...

> Tegbe (abruptly interrupting): I remember that when the Germans came, they acquired land from my great grandparents to build a church.[42]

The above exchange occurred after Tegbe, who had attempted to prevent us from interviewing Nyagbe, finally relented but decided to remain present as we interviewed her. This case in point illustrates how the dynamics of the interview as public spectacle shape the oral history we collected.

The historical and the contemporary political contexts described above function as larger organizing principles in the articulation of the oral history, while the performance of it, within the context of the public spectacle, adds another, more immediate influence.

German Presence

I have explained how an audience, especially if it includes elders such as chiefs or German Scholars, serves to reinforce the maintenance of the accepted oral history of the German occupation. These public spectacles, moreover, occur within the public spaces of the central Volta Region, many of which are replete with evidence of the German past.

It is nearly impossible to escape reminders of the German presence in any of the towns of the area, both large and small. In Ho, there is the hill named after Galenkui, the eyeglass-wearing district officer who lived atop it, as well as another hill on the opposite side of town where the Bremen mission station was located, and many of the original buildings still stand today.[43] In the midst of these structures, now being used by a secondary school, is a large bell, commemorating the historic relationship between the EPC and the North German Missionary Society. Although Ho is a small city in which such landmarks could easily be unnoticed within the maze of streets and buildings, they stand prominently as constant reminders of the German presence, and are recognized by the community-at-large. Indeed, any visitor to Ho on a tour will be taken to the Bremen mission site to see the German structures.

Figure 6.1 Theresa Nyagbe, an oral historian in Hohoe. (Photo by Dennis Laumann)

In a much smaller town like Waya, the reminders are even more apparent. According to one of the chiefs, Togbe Kuleke, these landmarks serve to remind the younger generations of the German presence in the town. He explains:

Those who are a bit old know [about the German period], but those who are not can not know. However, we do tell them that the Germans came to live here and they themselves saw certain things that showed that the Germans were here. For example, the chapel that has collapsed, the children know it as a building put up by the Germans.

Figure 6.2 Mathias Yevu Tegbe, an oral historian in Hohoe. (Photo by Dennis Laumann)

Besides the chapel, the evidence of the German past in Waya includes the town's nursery school building, a structure built during the German period; a mango tree located in the center of the town, planted during the occupation; and the gravestones marking the burials of German missionaries at the cemetery. In fact, several of our interviews were conducted in a building labeled, in large painted letters, the "Bremen House." According to Togbe Kuleke, this structure, on the site where a building constructed during the German period had previously stood, was named in honor of the Bremen missionaries "… so that anybody who comes here can easily deduce that they were actually here."[44] All these landmarks—the buildings, the gravestones, and the mango tree—serve as daily reminders, decades after the last German missionaries left the central Volta Region, that the Germans resided and worked in Waya. Indeed, Badasu offers, as an example, that he "... grew up to learn that [the Germans] built houses or put up buildings where we now have the secondary school."[45]

These landmarks are not limited to Ho and Waya. Each one of the sites in which we conducted interviews boasts one or more of these types of remains and reminders, the most common and widespread being churches and schools built during the period of missionary activity by the Germans and tree-lined roads constructed during the German occupation. Missionary gravesites are located at Akpafu Todzi and Amedzofe, too, and much older physical structures, dating to the period of German colonial rule, are also found, such as the cotton ginnery factory at Kpandu. The significance of these remains, that is, as constant reminders of the German presence, is acknowledged by oral historians. Adinyra states: "We also took care of the things [the Germans] left behind, so that [if] any of them comes back [they] can see that the things they left behind were taken care of."[46]

In addition to these physical landmarks, knowledge of the German presence is reinforced at relevant public events. Often, the German Scholars play a leading role in local ceremonies. In a great coincidence, my co-researchers and I arrived at Akpafu Mempeasem to interview a group of retired pastors, who were recommended to us by oral historians in Hohoe, just as they were meeting to organize the centennial commemoration of Bremen missionary activity in Akpafu planned for the following year. It is common for Germany's historic role in the area to be acknowledged at bilateral functions, too. During our fieldwork, for example, a meeting between a visiting team from the German Young Men's Christian Association and the then-Volta Regional Minister, Modestus Ahiable, served as an opportunity to recall "Ghana-German Co-operation in the region," according to a newspaper article on the event.[47]

The publications of the EPC also shape how the Germans are remembered. The church organizations in many of the towns of the central Volta Region, including Amedzofe and Waya, publish brief histories of the EPC, which emphasize the leading roles of German and German-speaking Swiss missionaries to the development of the religion in their communities.[48] These publications regularly include contributions from the German Scholars, some of whom hold positions in the EPC, and certainly influence the recollections of others who have read them. While the potential audience for these church histories is limited, they certainly inform the group of men largely responsible for the oral history of the German period.

These texts, along with the remains and reminders scattered throughout the central Volta Region, some dilapidated and abandoned and others preserved and still in use, provide yet another contextual layer in the formulation and articulation of the oral history of the German period. It is nearly impossible to forget the German presence and, moreover, easy to recognize the contributions of the Germans to each of the communities of the area. The continuing German presence and commemorations of German connections thus serve to reinforce the accepted oral history.

Notes

1. Atafe Badasu (oral historian in Waya), in discussion with the author, June 16, 1997.
2. Hillarius Gikunu (oral historian in Waya), in discussion with the author, June 16, 1997.
3. Oswald Kwame Klutse (oral historian in Ho), in discussion with the author, July 17, 1997.
4. This term is used by Crowder in reference to the mandate period. Michael Crowder, "The First World War and its consequences," Chapter 12 in *UNESCO General History of Africa*, VII, *Africa Under Colonial Domination 1880–1935*, ed. by A. Adu Boahen (Berkeley: University of California Press, 1985), 309.
5. *Ibid.*, 309.
6. Coleman, 5.
7. Agbodeka, 87.
8. On the other side of the former British-French Togolands border, independence came a little over three years later. After the two-year period as an "Autonomous Republic" headed by Nicholas Grunitzky ended in 1958, Olympio's CUT emerged victorious in a UN-supervised vote in French Togoland. The former trusteeship became independent in April 1960. Olympio's regime was marked by fiscal conservatism as well as border conflicts with Ghana and ended with his murder by Gnassingbé Eyadéma in a January 1963 coup, the first in West Africa.
9. Nkrumah's government pursued a similar policy in northern Ghana, which as the Northern Territories had also been largely neglected by the British, who were preoccupied with the cocoa-producing southern areas of the Asante Protectorate and the Gold Coast Colony.
10. Nkrumah was overthrown by members of the military and police whilst on a visit to Vietnam, in a February 1966 coup widely believed to have been aided by the United States Central Intelligence Agency. For the remainder of his life, Nkrumah served as Co-President, with Sekou Touré, of Guinea. The following regimes ruled Ghana from the overthrow of Nkrumah until the December 31 Revolution in 1981:

    (1) National Liberation Council (NLC) (from February 1966 to September 1969): headed by Major-General Joseph A. Ankrah and, after April 1969, Brigadier Akwasi Amankwaa Afrifa, the NLC was marked by stronger economic and political ties with the capitalist world and the cessation of Nkrumah's more progressive domestic programs and foreign policy. Although several Ewes participated in the

coup, they were pushed out of the ruling regime. Busia was put in charge of a Political Committee to supervise the transition to civilian rule, arguably ensuring that his largely ethnically-based Progress Party would emerge victorious against token opposition in the August 1969 elections;

(2) Second Republic (from September 1969 to January 1972): some in Ghana characterize this short-lived regime headed by Busia as "democratic," but it curtailed political activities by the opposition. For example, Busia banned the Nkrumahist People's Popular Party, censored all public displays of Nkrumah's image, and in August 1971, outlawed all "direct or indirect" mention of Nkrumah. The Pan-Africanist orientation of the Nkrumah years was reversed by Busia, as evidenced by diplomatic overtures to the apartheid regime in South Africa and the forced deportation of one million non-Ghanaians as a result of the Aliens Compliance Order. The current ruling party of Ghana, the National Patriotic Party (NPP), traces its lineage to the Progress Party and upholds Busia as one of its ideological founding fathers. Moreover, Edward Akufo-Addo, the father of current Ghanaian President Nana Akufo-Addo, served as a ceremonial president of the Second Republic. Busia was overthrown in January 1971 whilst in London for surgery;

(3) National Redemption Council (NRC) (from January 1972 to October 1975): initially dedicated to the eradication of corruption and mismanagement, this regime headed by Lieutenant Colonel (later promoted to General) Ignatius Kutu Acheampong became characterized by these same shortcomings fairly soon after assuming power. In recent years, however, scholars have begun to more positively assess the Acheampong years, highlighting a number of innovative programs such as "Operation Feed Yourself," implemented by the NRC in 1973 and designed to encourage the expansion of agriculture. In July 1972, the NRC repatriated Nkrumah's body from Guinea, where he had been briefly buried after his death in April 1972. Acheampong served as a near-dictator during this period, reserving for himself the posts of minister of finance, defense, and sports;

(4) Supreme Military Council (from October 1975 to June 1979): comprised of commanders of the Army, Air Force, Navy, Border Guards, and Police, this regime, also headed by Acheampong, further consolidated the military's control of the administration of Ghana. Acheampong served as the SMC's executive enjoying extensive power. Resistance to military rule grew, however, and the SMC responded by arresting opposition leaders and harassing their supporters. Acheampong was overthrown in a "palace coup" in July 1978 by Lieutenant General Frederick W. K. Akuffo, who served as Head of State under the SMC;

(5) Armed Forces Revolutionary Council (AFRC) (from June to September 1979): led by a group of radical junior officers, this three-month transitory government headed by Rawlings conducted trials of former government officials on charges of corruption and crimes against the state and assured the transition to democratic, civilian rule. Acheampong, Afrifa, and Akuffo, along with several other military leaders, were executed over the course of several weeks following the coup. Later that month, elections were held in which the Nkrumahist People's National Party (PNP) defeated the mostly Akan-based Popular Front Party headed by Victor

Owusu. Hilla Limann of the PNP was elected president in runoff elections in July and was inaugurated in late September;

(6) Third Republic (from September 1979 to December 1981): Ghana's return to civilian rule was a disappointment to many Ghanaians, as the country experienced an economic crisis and large and small-scale corruption pervaded society. Opposition to the government became more pronounced during the summer of 1980 and the leaders of the former AFRC were persecuted by Limann's government, which became increasingly ineffective and unpopular, culminating in the Revolution of 1981. For popular, radical histories of Ghana, see Kofi Nyidevu Awoonor, *Ghana: A Political History* (Accra: Sedco Publishing, 1990) and Shillington.

11. The dialect of Anlo Ewe promoted by missionaries earlier in the century as a standard Ewe continues to retain that distinction, although it has not obliterated regional dialects, including those among the Northern Ewe, as people's primary tongues.

12. Most Ewe belong to the Evangelical Presbyterian Church (EPC) or to the Roman Catholic Church. In 1959, the Ewe Evangelical Church, discussed in the previous chapter, changed its name to the EPC in order to recognize its minority of non-Ewe congregants, such as speakers of the Central-Togo languages. As Johnson Agblemafle explains, the church's name was altered because "people in other parts of the Volta Region argued that it was not only the Ewe who form the church so if it was called 'Ewe Mission' then only the Ewe should join or belong to it. By this time, the name 'E.P.' had already been registered, so they wanted a name, which could maintain the initials. This was how 'evangelical' came into being" (Johnson Agblemafle [oral historian in Amedzofe], in discussion with the author, April 17, 1997).

13. Hillarius Gikunu (oral historian in Waya), in discussion with the author, June 16, 1997.

14. Mathias Yevu Tegbe (oral historian in Hohoe), in discussion with the author, June 17, 1997.

15. The Central-Togo languages, for instance, are still spoken throughout the Volta Region, but Ewe has definitely emerged as the lingua franca of the southern half of the region. Most oral historians in Amedzofe and Akpafu Todzi, two of the towns in which Central-Togo languages are spoken, selected Ewe as the language to be used in their interviews.

16. Following the brief return to civilian rule, the Revolution erupted on December 31, 1981. Rawlings emerged as Head of State of the Provisional National Defence Council (PNDC), which at first pursued a radical agenda to eradicate corruption, stabilize the economy, and promote agriculture. After a decade-long period of military-civilian rule, the resumption of multiparty democracy occurred with the November 1992 elections, in which Rawlings, as the candidate of the National Democratic Congress (NDC), defeated his rivals with 58.3% of the vote. A. Adu Boahen, the noted historian of Africa, came in second with 30.4%, as head of the NPP, while the former president of the Third Republic, Limann, captured 6.7% as the candidate of the Nkrumahist People's National Convention (PNC). The current Fourth Republic was inaugurated in January 1993.

17. N. D. Sodzi (ed.), *The Volta Region: Plans, Projects, and Prospects*, Proceedings of the Seminar on Economic Development of the Volta Region, December 5–9, 1983 (Accra: Nsamankow Press, 1986), iii. This followed the creation of Volta Region Development Association (VORDA) by the PNDC. The Volta River Project at Akosombo was officially

inaugurated in January 1966, one month before the military coup against Nkrumah and its implementation of reactionary policies.

18. Austin Asamoah-Tutu, "Opening Speech" in Sodzi, 1–2. For an elaboration on this theme in the Ghanaian state media, during the period of fieldwork, see "VR—A chequered political history," *Daily Graphic* (March 7, 1997): 16.

19. Mathias Yevu Tegbe (oral historian in Hohoe), in discussion with the author, June 17, 1997.

20. Oral historians were asked to provide brief biographies, as explained in Chapter 1, but most of the German connections listed here emerged unsolicited during the course of interviews.

21. Kwami Asamani (oral historian in Akpafu Todzi).

22. Nicholas Asamani (oral historian in Kpandu).

23. Mosis Kofi Asase (oral historian in Ho), Hillarius Gikunu (oral historian in Waya), and Oswald Kwame Klutse (oral historian in Ho).

24. Abra Janet Kumordzi (oral historian in Akpafu Todzi).

25. E. K. Addae (oral historian in Akpafu Mempeasem), Ehrenfried Adiku (oral historian in Hohoe), Seth Adu (oral historian in Ho), N. K. Dzobo (oral historian in Ho), Samuel Mensah (oral historian in Hohoe), E. T. Obro (oral historian in Akpafu Mempeasem), H. B. Obro (oral historian in Akpafu Mempeasem), and H. B. Ogbetey (oral historian in Akpafu Mempeasem).

26. Kawku, 76.

27. Gilbert Joel Nyavor (oral historian in Kpandu), in discussion with the author, March 5, 1997.

28. "Burial, Memorial and Thanks Giving Service for the Late Presbyter Seth Kwasi Adu."

29. Mosis Kofi Asase (oral historian in Ho), in discussion with the author, April 15, 1997.

30. Eugenia Kodzo Yawa (oral historian in Ho), in discussion with the author, April 18, 1997.

31. See Chapter 4 for details.

32. The other men were Bennard Komla Agbetetie, Lawrence Komla Ati, and Gershon Kofi Tagboto.

33. My coresearchers and I returned to Waya on June 16, 1997, when we interviewed oral historians, including the woman mentioned above, in less public settings.

34. Yankah discusses the "culture of silence" among the Akan. He notes: "In certain situations, silence may constitute a strategic expression of indifference by an adult, implying that it is not every situation that requires verbal intervention ... This is often in situations where a verbal intervention by the elder is considered capable of disrupting social harmony" (Kwesi Yankah, *Free Speech in Traditional Society: The Cultural Foundations of Communication in Contemporary Ghana* (Accra: Ghana Universities Press, 1998), 19).

35. Julius Agbigbi (oral historian in Akpafu Todzi).

36. Simon Kugbleadzor (oral historian in Waya).

37. Hillarius Gikunu (oral historian in Waya), in discussion with the author, June 16, 1997.

38. Yankah, 41.

39. Only seven of the 45 oral historians were women. See Chapter 1 for elaboration.

40. Atakumah is the granddaughter of Dagadu III, the King of Kpandu exiled to the Cameroons by the Germans, and Yawa visited her uncle in a German jail at Ho, where he was

repeatedly imprisoned for overstaying his permits to the Gold Coast. For details of both, see Chapter 4.

41. Yankah, 17. As mentioned above, Catherina Ama Kwadzo Kugbleadzor was the only women to speak during our group interview in Waya. Yankah observes the phenomenon of "women's relative silence within the domain of mixed gender" in his work (*Ibid.*, 18).

42. Theresa Nyagbe (oral historian in Hohoe), in discussion with the author, June 17, 1997 and Mathias Yevu Tegbe (oral historian in Hohoe), in discussion with the author, June 17, 1997.

43. See Chapter 4 for discussion of both these sites.

44. Togbe Kuleke (oral historian in Waya), in discussion with the author, June 16, 1997.

45. Atafe Badasu (oral historian in Waya), in discussion with the author, June 16, 1997.

46. Alfred Adinyra (oral historian in Amedzofe), in discussion with the author, April 17, 1997.

47. "Minister grateful to German Govt," *Daily Graphic* (January 1, 1997): 16.

48. See, for example, *Amedzofe E.P. Hame Nutinya: 1889–1989* (Amedzofe: n.d.). This text includes a brief history in English and historical photographs. Besides the locally produced literature, other publications from abroad with an emphasis on the Volta Region are available in Ho, where an EPC bookshop is located. These texts include a reprint of P. Wiegräbe, *Ewe Mission Nutinya: 1847–1936* (St. Louis: The Board of International Missions, n.d.). This brief history includes numerous colonial-era photographs and is printed in Ho.

Conclusion

Although a relatively brief and distant historical episode, the German occupation features prominently in the popular culture of the communities of the central Volta Region. This phenomenon is evidenced in various expressions, ranging from oral history to public commemorations and even literature. In the classic novel, *The Narrow Path*, for instance, Kofi, a student from Keta, narrates the following as he walks through Ho with friends from a Catholic secondary school:

> They took me to see the Ewe Presbyterian School—a place over three miles away—where our rivals, the Protestants, went to school. They showed me the old houses built by the Germans in the days when that part of the country was ruled from Berlin. They were big solidly-built houses, which were being used as the Presbyterian Middle School and their seminary ...[1]

These "solidly-built structures," remains from the German period, serve as reminders of the German presence in the area to Kofi, his friends at the Catholic school, and their "rivals" at the Presbyterian school. Earlier in the novel, Kofi is punished by his father, a school headmaster, with 25 strokes to the buttocks with a cane whip:

> As he brought the cane down for the last time, my father said "And one for the Kaiser." Was it our German rulers who taught our people such cruelty?[2]

The oral historians of the central Volta Region might answer "no," but probably acknowledge the Germans did flog Togolanders sometimes on orders from the German monarch.

As this book demonstrates, instead of focusing on the negative aspects of the German occupation—the forced labor, the excessive and arbitrary punishments, the financial burdens, and so forth—oral historians emphasize what they regard as the beneficial aspects of German rule and the positive legacies of the German presence. The German era clearly holds a special place in the memories of oral historians. "[The Germans] were very important people to us ...," Adu asserts. "They took good care of us. I can't deceive you."[3] During the German occupation, oral historians maintain, the principles of honesty, order, and discipline prevailed in the central Volta Region, and the Germans who resided in the area, in particular the missionaries, are recalled as diligent, admirable individuals who provided examples worth emulation.

Overall, the German period is recollected as a golden age of sorts, compared unfavorably with the British occupation beginning during the First World War as well as the current era since Ghana's return to independence in 1957. The honesty, order, and discipline, which predominated during the German era gradually disappeared after the departure of the Germans. The oral historians offer a mostly negative assessment of the British period, not only because of the failure of the British to continue the alleged infrastructural development of the Germans, but also since the British regime failed to maintain the perceived strengths of the German system. Revealingly, most oral historians, just as they often do not distinguish between the longer German missionary presence and the shorter German colonial occupation, equate the British era with the present. Datsa's comments are indicative of this tendency:

> As for the English time, we can see for ourselves, but [our grandparents] tell us some of the things that happen now could not have happened in Gruner's time ... they will tell you, "not in Gruner's time!"[4]

A statement by Togbe Kuleke, when asked about the British, exemplifies this inclination even more clearly: "From what I have seen today, I think the Germans are better."[5]

Of course, nostalgia—a longing for a romanticized past with which the present is negatively contrasted—plays a significant role in how the German era is characterized. Nyavor's following observation is indicative: "It is rather unfortunate [the virtues of the German period] are gone. People tend to deceive their fellow citizens. This was unheard of in the past."[6] It is clear oral historians formulate their recollections of the German period with an eye to the world in which they live. When Gikunu states "Today things are different" during the course of an interview, he is betraying the fact he is comparing the German occupation with the present.[7] Indeed, most oral historians, usually at the end of their interviews, would contrast specific aspects of the German period with contemporary practices and attitudes. "Corporal punishment has been banned in school," Tegbe observes. "That is why the children do whatever they want. In those days, you did whatever you were told to do ... Whatever rules existed were obeyed to the letter."[8] Yawa also bemoans the behavior of children in today's Ghana: "[The German period] was good because there was discipline, for any misbehavior was punishable. But, when children are playing in town like they are doing now, they are driven away, which we don't like."[9]

Our understanding of the past is shaped by numerous, conflicting, and complementary factors. At the most personal level, our individual backgrounds, biases, and agendas fundamentally determine the way in which we understand and articulate the past. In the case of the oral history of the German occupation, each one of the oral historians possessed one, several, or many connections to the Germans, both direct and indirect. In some cases, these connections were so immediate and extensive that oral historians were recognized by their communities as German Scholars. But, for the majority of oral historians, their membership in the EPC, the fact that their parents resided at a Bremen mission station, or their completion of primary school under the direction of German teachers, served to position them as experts on the German period. These were the individuals who were identified in the communities of the central Volta Region as the oral historians of the German occupation and it is they who communicate and control the accepted oral history of that historical episode. As Iwona Irwin-Zarecka argues, collective memory is "a socially articulated and socially maintained 'reality of the past.'"[10]

Control can be achieved through various measures. Sometimes, dissenting opinions are quickly silenced or contradicted, while at other times, oral historians monopolize an interview. But, generally, conformity is assured through the selection process itself. Due to their recognized expertise and positions within their communities, the men who control the oral history were the first, and very often, only oral historians recommended to us by their neighbors. Thus, the backgrounds of individuals determine whether they are recognized as experts and, once they have been afforded that authority, they assure that the accepted oral history they have helped formulate remains intact and undisputed.

Everyone operates within a larger historical and contemporary context, however, and processes and systems beyond our control shape the way in which we interpret the past. The oral history of the German occupation therefore cannot be understood without an appreciation of the events of this past century, during which the central Volta Region underwent a complete transformation from an area of independent, small Ewe polities operating within a regional economic system to a small Bezirk occupied by German imperialists in Lomé to part of a quasi-colony arguably neglected by its British landlords to a section of a much larger region administered by the Ghanaian government in Accra. During this entire period, ethnic, regional, and national identities were forged, contested, and altered, processes that were influenced by legacies of the German era and in turn influenced the ways in which memories of that era were constructed and articulated.

The oral history presented in this book constitutes a new historical source for the study of German Togoland and, as importantly, challenges the written historiography in many ways.[11] Moreover, as the testimony of Ghanaians in a limited geographic area who directly experienced German colonialism, or heard about it from their parents or other elders, it provides a localized, African history of the colony. It raises themes and issues that might be missing in colonial records and offers African perspectives on those that can be found in the archives. The oral history of the German presence in the central Volta Region of Ghana does not strictly conform to the anti-imperialist politics I had expected and that I embrace, nonetheless its collection, presentation, and analysis here contributes to our continuing efforts to offer African perspectives on European colonialism.

Notes

1. Francis Selormey, *The Narrow Path* (Portsmouth: Heinemann, 1996), 80.
2. *Ibid.*, 58.
3. Seth Adu (oral historian in Ho), in discussion with the author, March 7, 1997.
4. Edward Kodzo Datsa (oral historian in Amedzofe), in discussion with the author, April 17, 1997.
5. Togbe Kuleke (oral historian in Waya), in discussion with the author, June 16, 1997.
6. Gilbert Joel Nyavor (oral history in Kpandu), in discussion with the author, March 5, 1997.
7. Hillarius Gikunu (oral historian in Waya), in discussion with the author, June 16, 1997.
8. Matthias Yevu Tegbe (oral historian in Hohoe), in discussion with the author, June 17, 1997.
9. Eugenia Kodzo Yawa (oral historian in Ho), in discussion with the author, April 18, 1997.
10. Irwin-Zarecka, 54.
11. For a review of the literature, see Laumann, "A Historiography of German Togoland."

Index